IRON CURTAINS

T0373376

Studies in Urban and Social Change

IRON CURTAINS

GATES, SUBURBS AND PRIVATIZATION OF SPACE IN THE POST-SOCIALIST CITY

Sonia A. Hirt

WILEY-BLACKWELL

A John Wiley & Sons, Ltd., Publication

This edition first published 2012
© 2012 John Wiley & Sons, Ltd.

Wiley-Blackwell is an imprint of John Wiley & Sons, formed by the merger of Wiley's global
Scientific, Technical and Medical business with Blackwell Publishing.

Registered Office
John Wiley & Sons, Ltd, The Atrium, Southern Gate, Chichester, West Sussex, PO19 8SQ, UK

Editorial Offices
350 Main Street, Malden, MA 02148-5020, USA
9600 Garsington Road, Oxford, OX4 2DQ, UK
The Atrium, Southern Gate, Chichester, West Sussex, PO19 8SQ, UK

For details of our global editorial offices, for customer services, and for information about how
to apply for permission to reuse the copyright material in this book please see our website at
www.wiley.com/wiley-blackwell.

The right of Sonia A. Hirt to be identified as the author of this work has been asserted in
accordance with the UK Copyright, Designs and Patents Act 1988.

All rights reserved. No part of this publication may be reproduced, stored in a retrieval system,
or transmitted, in any form or by any means, electronic, mechanical, photocopying, recording
or otherwise, except as permitted by the UK Copyright, Designs and Patents Act 1988, without
the prior permission of the publisher.

Wiley also publishes its books in a variety of electronic formats. Some content that appears in
print may not be available in electronic books.

Designations used by companies to distinguish their products are often claimed as trademarks.
All brand names and product names used in this book are trade names, service marks, trademarks
or registered trademarks of their respective owners. The publisher is not associated with any
product or vendor mentioned in this book. This publication is designed to provide accurate and
authoritative information in regard to the subject matter covered. It is sold on the understanding
that the publisher is not engaged in rendering professional services. If professional advice or other
expert assistance is required, the services of a competent professional should be sought.

Library of Congress Cataloging-in-Publication Data

Hirt, Sonia.
  Iron curtains : gates, suburbs, and privatization of space in the post-socialist city / Sonia A. Hirt.
    p. cm.
  Includes bibliographical references and index.
  ISBN 978-1-4443-3827-0 (cloth) – ISBN 978-1-4443-3826-3 (pbk.)
1. City planning–Former communist countries. 2. City planning–Europe, Eastern.
3. Property–Former communist countries. 4. Property–Europe, Eastern. 5. Gated
communities–Former communist countries. 6. Gated communities–Europe, Eastern.
7. Europe, Eastern–Social conditions–21st century. 8. Equality–Europe, Eastern. I. Title.
  HT169.E82H57 2012
  307.1′21609171′7–dc23

                                                    2011043301

A catalogue record for this book is available from the British Library.

Set in 10.5/12pt Baskerville by SPi Publisher Services, Pondicherry, India

1 2012

To my parents who lived through iron curtains of various kinds.

Contents

List of Illustrations and Tables

Figures

Tables

Series Editors' Preface

The Wiley-Blackwell *Studies in Urban and Social Change* series is published in association with the *International Journal of Urban and Regional Research*. It aims to advance theoretical debates and empirical analyses stimulated by changes in the fortunes of cities and regions across the world. Among topics taken up in past volumes and welcomed for future submissions are:

- Connections between economic restructuring and urban change
- Urban divisions, difference, and diversity
- Convergence and divergence among regions of east and west, north and south
- Urban and environmental movements
- International migration and capital flows
- Trends in urban political economy
- Patterns of urban-based consumption

The series is explicitly interdisciplinary; the editors judge books by their contribution to intellectual solutions rather than according to disciplinary origin. Proposals may be submitted to members of the series Editorial Committee, and further information about the series can be found at www.suscbookseries.com:

Jenny Robinson
Neil Brenner
Matthew Gandy
Patrick Le Galès
Chris Pickvance
Ananya Roy

Acknowledgements

I could not have written this book alone. I am very grateful to the urban planning faculty of Virginia Tech, who supported my scholarly efforts throughout the last seven years. Several of the Virginia Tech faculty helped me with drafts of journal articles dealing with papers related to the topic which appeared in *Cities*, the *International Journal of Urban and Regional Research*, *International Planning Studies*, the *Journal of Planning History*, *Problems of Post-communism*, and *Urban Geography*. Paul Knox, Joseph Scarpaci, John Randolph, Gerard Kearns, Ted Koebel, Max Stephenson and Yang Zhang have been especially helpful. The same goes to Kiril Stanilov from University College London and Zorica Nedović-Budić from University College Dublin. My colleagues from Sofia, Emilia Chengelova and Iskra Dandolova, and from Belgrade, Zaklina Gligorijevic and Mina Petrovic, shared invaluable insights. Indeed, the book could not have been completed without their collaboration. The Institute of Sociology in Sofia collected some of the data. The project was funded by many organizations over the years, including the National Council for Eurasian and East European Research, the National Endowment for the Humanities, the American Council of Learned Societies, the American Councils for International Education, the International Research & Exchange Board, the Graham Foundation for Advanced Studies in the Fine Arts, the Woodrow Wilson International Center for Scholars, and Social Sciences and Humanities Research Council of Canada Virginia Tech's Institute for Society, Culture and the Environment. I also benefited from my contacts with the faculty and students of the Graduate School of Design at Harvard University, while I taught there as a visiting associate professor. My academic career would have been impossible without the kind support and mentorship of Jonathan Levine and Robert Fishman from the University of Michigan.

I am greatly indebted to Neil Brenner from Harvard University for his guidance through the book proposal stage and to Jennifer Robinson from University College London for her tireless intellectual leadership during the manuscript revisions. My gratitude also goes to the entire editorial board of *Studies in Urban and Social Change*, as well as to Wiley-Blackwell's Jacqueline Scott and Isobel Bainton. Julie Steiff from the University of Michigan edited the full draft. Many of the maps were prepared by my research assistants, including Anamaria Bukvic, Sandeep Gangaar, Lauren Kopishke, Sara Swenson, David Prichard, William Powell, Phillip Gabathuler and Guneet Kaur.

Above all, I am thankful to my family, my wonderful husband and daughters, for their love, patience and support through the years. Ultimately, I dedicate this book to my parents who not only lived through iron curtains of various kinds but also learned to thrive above them. I can only hope they taught me the same quality.

1

Introduction

[T]hus, when the universal sun has gone down, the moth seeks the lamplight of the private world.

Karl Marx

One of the most enduring images of the twentieth century was the dismantling of the Berlin Wall. Erected overnight in 1961 with barbed wire and later reconstructed with concrete and reinforced with guards and traps, the Wall was far more than an ugly physical barrier. It was – and for many of us, still is, even in its extinction – the iconic emblem of fear and division, the ultimate material symbol of "us" and "them" apart. The Wall was dismantled by ecstatic crowds on both sides of Berlin during several weeks in late 1989 and early 1990. The popular slogan "No more wars, no more walls, a united world" remained graffitied on its decrepit but still-standing blocks well through 1990.

Today, more than twenty years after the Wall's collapse, it is obvious that the united world, whatever the meaning of this elusive term may be, never materialized. Some walls fell, but many others were erected: some visible, like the US–Mexico border walls; and some less visible, like the new borders of the European Union, which now set apart a slightly expanded geographic version of the civilized West from its less deserving East European "others."

This book is about wall-making in Eastern Europe since the end of socialism. I believe that contrary to the expectations raised by the optimistic images of 1989, the last twenty years of East European history have been an exceptionally prolific period as far as wall-making goes. There are now all kinds of walls, material and immaterial, economic and political, legal and

Iron Curtains, First Edition. Sonia A. Hirt.
© 2012 John Wiley & Sons, Ltd. Published 2012 by John Wiley & Sons, Ltd.

social, which separate the newly rich from the newly poor, and the "right" from the "wrong" ethnicities. Some walls, of course, existed well before 1989 but have now become more solid. There also are many brand new walls in the form of state borders and partitioned cities.

Perhaps none of this new partitioning should be surprising. Spatial instability and border reconfiguration accompany most major societal overhauls, and the post-1989 systemic transformation – a time of radical "boundary instability" (Andrusz 1996) that brought an end to socialist multi-ethnic federalisms – has been a perfect illustration. The borders of what was once intended as a politically and economically homogeneous super-bloc stretching from the heart of Europe to the Far East corner of Asia – a super-bloc demarcated on its western side by the Berlin Wall – were dissolved. As globalization and the communications revolution undercut the ability of states to remain the primary scale on which socio-economic management is performed (Brenner et al. 2003; Brenner 2004a, 2004b), state borders caved in too; some vanished altogether, and new ones were created as new identities and alliances were formed. Still, what I find surprising is the raw dynamism with which a new border-building erupted after 1989 on a smaller, urban scale. The cities of Eastern Europe – sites of stark new social contrasts – were in a few short years invaded by a myriad of new ruptures and enclosures. In the process, their open, borderless, shared spaces were severely depreciated. Peculiarly then, the global "space of flows" that the Information Age (Castells 1989) brought to us all seems to be making its own anti-thesis: a local space of bounds.

This book tells the story of boundary-building, vanishing public space, and the rescaling of enclosure in the Bulgarian capital of Sofia. It is a personal book: I tell the story of my hometown even if I tell it through the lens of my experience as a scholar and professional who has spent the last eighteen years in the United States. My subject matter is the city, its form, its style, its planning. I analyze the changing urbanity of Sofia and show that the post-socialist period has been one of intensive corrosion of the collective urban realm and equally intensive construction of divided, explicitly private spaces, many of which are bounded by daunting physical barriers. The most obvious example is the new generation of fortressed homes – the local version of the "block-homes" that Steven Flusty (1997) described in Los Angeles. Such homes, which barely existed during socialism (only the top echelon of party apparatchiks had them), are individually fenced off, likely in response to the security concerns of a newly rich class surrounded by a sea of poverty. They began to spread around Sofia right after 1989 and attained the status of the new norm in residential architecture in the late 1990s. Their latest incarnation comes in the form of large, Western-style gated communities, many of which now "adorn" the city's sprawling outskirts. The phenomenon is not limited to

Sofia. There is a burgeoning literature on expensive gated housing in the post-socialist world, especially in wealthier cities like Moscow, Prague and Budapest (e.g., Bodnar 2001; Blinnikov et al. 2006; Cséfalvay 2009), where social contrasts are equally stark but global capital is more abundant. In fact if one combined all the iron, concrete, bricks and mortar that surround the new gated homes in East European cities (not to mention other types of enclosure), the sum would likely dwarf the volume of concrete used in the 150-kilometer-long, four-meter-tall Berlin Wall by a massive ratio. I do not mean to ignore the blatant contrasts between the Berlin Wall and its miniature successors: there is a principal difference between walls made to keep insiders in (e.g., the Berlin Wall and prison gates) and walls made to keep outsiders out (e.g., those around residential compounds; Marcuse 1997). Still, there is an intrinsic commonality: walls set borders; they part; they make an "us" and "them."

The example of upscale, walled housing in Sofia is but part of the story. A wider process of border-setting and fragmentation (and, since we are in the Balkans, shall we say *balkanization*?) of urban space is occurring. This process elevates the protection of private space, not only from crime but from any other perceived intrusions by "others," as a dominant cultural ideal at the expense of a perpetually shrinking public realm. I see it in dilapidated housing towers left over from socialism, where even urban residents of the most modest means have collected sufficient funds to install new locks and hire security guards to monitor the building entrance twenty-four hours a day. I see this in shiny supermarkets and glitzy business parks, often built by Western developers, which turn their backs to the city and are accessible only through a few controlled gates. I see this in vanishing playgrounds, quickly turned into paid parking, and in disappearing parkland transformed into private sports complexes, whose fences are installed before the local government could issue building permits. I see it in the exclusive far-flung new suburbs, where public infrastructure is so minimal that owning a Land Rover is a prerequisite to visiting them. And I see it in the new architecture – a generation of triumphantly individualistic buildings, whose stylistic purpose is to stand apart, shine alone, disconnect themselves from the street, or, in the words of one Bulgarian cultural critic, declare "war" on their neighbors (Dandolova 2002). I call it the architecture of disunity.

What drives this extraordinary process of urban partitioning, of shrinking urban publicness? To a great extent, its roots can be found in the changes in economic and political environment that ensued after 1989, especially the shift of power from the public to the private sector. The hypothesis this study explores, however, is that changes in the urban environment are not only dependent on post-socialist changes in politics and economics. Rather, to the extent to which space is a medium of culture,[1] the changing urbanity of Sofia is the story of the post-socialist cultural condition. The story follows from forty-five years of failed totalitarian attempts to sell a heroic philosophy dedicated to elevating the public good and defeating petty private interests – a time when the *private* home was the sole place of passive resistance against the state. The story continues for another twenty years, during which another heroic narrative – that of Western democracy – also grounded in some brave assumptions for a noble public realm, produced ambiguous results at best: results including the quick turnover of public resources to private parties, many of whom abused their public positions (e.g., the old *nomenklatura*) or rose to wealth by breaking the rules designed to keep a public realm alive (e.g., the new mafia). In this sense, I see the story of fragmenting public space in Sofia as a subset of a much broader condition. I call this condition *privatism*, privatism with a passion and a vengeance. Unlike privatization, which is an economic and political process of transferring material resources, privatism is a cultural condition which comes in reaction to the perceived gross failures of the socialist and post-socialist public realm. I believe it expresses itself in space much as it expresses itself in, say, corruption, law-breaking and tax-evasion – all common post-socialist social practices.[2] Privatism in my definition is the widespread disbelief in a benevolent public realm and the widespread sense that to appropriate the public may be the best way to thrive in private: To secede is to succeed.

I use the term *Iron Curtains*, which Winston Churchill coined fifteen years before the Berlin Wall was built, to express this process of urban secessionism and turning inward. It is a process of expanding the private, shrinking the public, and firming the border between them; it is a process of curtaining off, walling off and cutting off. Perhaps ironically, I find a metaphor that Karl Marx used in his dissertation to most vividly capture the swing from official socialist publicness to popular post-socialist privatism, in culture and in space. It is the metaphor of the nocturnal moth: when the universal sun goes down, Marx said, the moth seeks shelter in "the lamplight of the private world" (Marx and Engels 1975). Socialism – arguably the culmination of Western modernity (Bauman 1991; Havel 1992b, 1994) – promised to be that universal sun. Its demise ushered in, in Zygmunt Bauman's words, the ultimate "swarming time for nocturnal moths" (Bauman 1995).

Notes on Significance and Methodology

Through an in-depth case study,[3] the book contributes to the literatures on post-socialist social, spatial and cultural change, modernity and post-modernity, and globalization and urbanization. Even though empirical observations are derived nominally from a single city, their analysis is positioned within a global theoretical framework and is further enriched by perpetual references to processes of urban transformation that occur in other parts of the world – not only in other post-socialist contexts in Central and Eastern Europe, but also in Western Europe and the United States. Therefore, the study is an example of the implicitly comparative or quasi-comparative method (Bodnar 2001).

Countries like Bulgaria and cities like Sofia occupy a peripheral position in the literature (that is, Sofia's urbanism has never been the subject of an analytical English-language monograph, and Bulgaria is one of the most understudied East European nations; Ganev 2007). Sofia is neither a London nor a New York; it is not even a Moscow. It does not belong to the world of privileged "global cities" that seem to arouse an insatiable curiosity in urban scholars. Yet, in focusing on it, I second Robinson's (2006) call for studying "ordinary cities" (or, rather, her call for treating all cities as ordinary) – an approach that allows us to explore the complexity and uniqueness of urban places without perpetually forcing them into some hierarchical system and, consequently, neglecting all but the top tier.

So what exactly can one learn from a book on Sofia? Why should a scholar of post-socialist cultures or post-socialist urbanism read a case-based monograph? More broadly, why should a scholar of global urban transformations read about a particular post-socialist city?[4] My answer is as follows. The book is ultimately about privatization as a socio-economic process and privatism as a cultural condition, both of which are global in scope and integral to contemporary, post-modern capitalism. Post-socialist urbanity embodies privatization and privatism in such an unmediated, unrestrained form that it allows us to observe them with greater clarity than in Western settings, where their socio-spatial outcomes have been more gradual and subtle (Bodnar 2001; Humphrey 2002). Sofia, where predatory privatization and a dramatic decline of publicness have been the leitmotifs of the post-socialist period, provides an especially poignant example – one that comes very close to the extreme, exemplary case study that theorists of qualitative methodology describe (Yin 1984).

The study focuses on the privatization of space – one of the most important aspects of post-modern urban change, which has been thoroughly studied in Western cities (Sorkin 1992; Davis 1990; Ellin 1996, 1997; Dear 2000). It does so, however, in the under-analyzed post-socialist context. It makes the case that although privatization of urban space may be a global process, in post-socialist settings it has erupted with an astonishing virility not only because of the specific political and economic circumstances, but also because of the vigor of post-socialist privatism as a cultural condition.

In short, then, as the sole monograph on contemporary urbanism in a Southeast European capital, the book seeks to make a broader statement on issues of post-socialist urbanism in the tradition of several recent in-depth studies of East-Central European cities, such as Budapest (Bodnar 2001),

Berlin (Till 2005), and St. Petersburg (Axenov et al. 2006). What distinguishes the book from other contributions, however, is its unique focus on urbanism observed at the ground level as a means of telling the story of post-socialist cultural privatism. Because of its insights into post-socialist cultural change and post-modern urbanization, the book is intended for a wide audience of scholars in urban sociology, urban history, urban geography, cultural anthropology, urban planning, architecture and art history, as well as scholars who specialize in the study of Eastern Europe and the post-socialist world. Furthermore, as Ghodsee and Henry (2010) recently observed, in light of the intense debate about the proper role of the public sector in the economy and society that has spread in today's recession-struck Western societies, studies of East European-style privatizations may present an informative (and cautionary) tale for policy-makers, not only in post-socialist contexts, but in Western contexts as well.

The book takes an explicitly cultural approach without attempting to downplay the significance of political or economic forces as space-makers. As Eade and Mele point out, the task of "understanding the city" is not to establish a hierarchy of the three main factors that shape urban form (the social, the economic and the cultural), but rather to problematize their connections in particular cities and particular periods and continuously strive to develop ways to comprehend their intersections (2003: 3–4). Indeed, all of the aspects of spatial change discussed in the book, like all non-spatial social practices, can be viewed through an alternative, non-cultural lens. However, I have chosen to focus on culture, because it has remained surprisingly understudied as a causal factor in post-socialist urbanism. As I mention in Chapter 2, among the many books on the subject just a handful highlight culture. In ignoring it, scholars are neglecting a powerful variable that is not only shaped by the economic and institutional contexts but intersects with them and shapes them in return, a variable that affects space both directly (through people's views and ideals of space) and indirectly (by influencing economic and institutional behavior). Take, for example, the intense sub-urbanization process after 1989. The new spatial phenomenon is clearly influenced by the economic and institutional logic of post-socialism, as I reiterate in Chapter 6. The green and agricultural land that once surrounded the compact city was privatized, the regulations constraining the type of construction allowed at the urban edge were lifted, and building on the greenbelts became a profitable activity for the burgeoning private sector. The fact that construction intensified after economic stabilization around the year 2000, when the economy began to recover, affirms the link between economic growth and the pace of suburbanization in post-socialist cities, as others have shown (Timár and Váradi 2001). Still, can it all be explained without culture? Without it, how can we account for the views of many new suburban residents who express their intense desire to get out of Sofia and fulfill their dream of claiming their own space (i.e., suburban, private space) – the type of space they say they craved yet could not attain in socialist housing? How can we explain the proliferation of media and scholarly articles touting the virtues of the old (pre-socialist) Bulgarian family home? And how can we explain the facts that Sofia's new plans have portrayed suburbanization as a progressive, Western-style trend, and that Sofia's Mayor goes around proudly cutting ribbons at the opening ceremonies of new gated suburban communities? Aren't suburbs more than the spatial outcome of economic and political forces; aren't they also an ideal?

Because the study takes a cultural approach, the main method of investigation is qualitative and the main source of data is the semi-structured in-depth interview. I have conducted nearly one hundred formal and informal in-depth interviews over several months-long trips to Sofia. Of these interviews, thirty-six were conducted with "experts": actors who have actively participated in or influenced the production of urban forms in recent years or actors who have special knowledge of it.[5] The remainder of the interviews targeted residents and users of the new spaces of Sofia, especially in gated and suburban environments. In Chapters 6 and 7, I rely partially on quantitative data obtained from a standardized survey of a random sample of residents in the affluent southern outskirts of the city (this survey was conducted by the Institute of Sociology at the Bulgarian Academy of Sciences). Subjects for follow-up, in-depth interviews were selected from the survey respondents. For Chapter 8, I interviewed a selection of residents of six new gated communities.[6] In the interviews, residents were invited to share their views on the city (including its public spaces), their neighborhoods, their neighbors and their homes. Subjects responded to specific questions about where and how they lived before the end of socialism (assuming they were old enough to recall), how their lives and residential environment changed after 1989, how the city and their views of the city have changed since then, and what their ideal residential environment would be. They were also asked about their views of public institutions and their views of their neighbors and people generally,[7] as well as about their willingness to engage in voluntary civic activities. The overall goal of the interviews was to "measure" in qualitative terms people's ideals and preferences when it comes to common (urban) and residential (private) spaces, as well as their views on the state of the civic realm in Bulgaria. Whenever possible, I have used existing nationwide surveys on cultural preferences as well (especially in Chapter 2). Additional information on both ideals and preferences and on the restructuring of urban forms came from a review of the local academic literature, policy documents (e.g., master plans), newspapers, magazines, architectural journals and archives, and advertising materials. Because examining changes in the balance between the city's public and private spaces is a primary purpose of the study, I obtained information on the topic from a variety of additional pertinent sources, including municipal statistical and mapping data and data created and maintained by some professional, academic and non-profit organizations. Finally, since some of the discussion (e.g., on architectural styles) required visual illustration, I conducted an extensive photographic survey.[8]

Book Structure

I have selected what I believe are some of the most prominent aspects of privatization of space in post-socialist Sofia, including the outright loss of public spaces (e.g., public greenery) and the construction of explicitly private spaces. The latter I understand broadly to include: far-flung wealthy suburban areas that are generally inaccessible to the larger public; gated homes, compounds and even business parks; and structures like malls and hypermarkets that for architectural and/or financial reasons can be considered partially closed off to large segments of the population. Other examples of spatial privatization include various glitzy buildings and ensembles, which often usurp public space without public planning approval and, in their functional organization and architectural style, show little connection to their surroundings. I present a typology of privatizations (which I term *spatial secessions*) later in the book.

The book has ten chapters. Following this Introduction, Chapter 2 makes a case for a cultural interpretation of post-socialist spatiality, specifically for linking post-socialist privatism and post-socialist urbanism. I define two concepts which play a key role in my analysis, the concepts of the public and the private, in their social and spatial connotations. I discuss how views of the public and the private differ in capitalist, socialist and post-socialist settings. I outline the relationship between the public realm and public space, and the private realm and private space, and introduce my main thesis that new urban spaces in post-socialist cities like Sofia both reflect and reinforce privatism as a cultural condition. In this chapter, I also discuss data on current cultural values[9] in Bulgaria obtained from national and international studies. In Chapter 3, I review the basic differences between capitalist and socialist urbanism, and discuss the rich literature on the impact of the post-socialist transition on urban form. As I have already noted, much of this literature has focused on economic and political transformations as leading forces of urban change. Whereas I do not disagree with this approach, I add a complementary interpretation that stresses the importance of culture as an explanatory factor. I also outline the key spatial manifestations of privatism in the post-socialist city: these are the *spatial secessions* mentioned earlier. In Chapter 4, I present a thesis complementary to the one in the previous chapter. I engage with theories of modern and post-modern urbanization in a global context and argue that rather than being interpreted as unique phenomena, the socialist and post-socialist cities may be analyzed as variants of modern and post-modern urbanism. Post-modernism makes sense here because in many ways the demise of socialism can be interpreted as the demise of Western modernity, and the post-socialist city exhibits a number of spatial features that can be deemed archetypically post-modern. The decline of monolithic public spaces and their substitution with a mosaic of fragmented private spaces may be the most prominent of these features. Thus, I argue that if one is to investigate post-modern urbanism, few places are as good as post-socialist Eastern Europe.

In the remaining chapters, I focus on the case study. In Chapter 5, I present a brief history of Sofia, with an emphasis on the central elements of its urbanity during socialism, and discuss the new, post-socialist spatial phenomena mostly as outcomes of economic and institutional change. I show how Sofia fit into the classic model of the socialist city as conceptualized by French and Hamilton (1979) and others. I further show how the elements of socialist urban spatial structure gradually disintegrated after 1989 as a consequence of the processes of privatization and restitution of state resources: urban land, real estate and means of production. For example, I show how the city lost its once compact form and clear edge as the green fields and farmland that surrounded it during socialism were privatized. I discuss the intense process of commercialization in downtown Sofia, where residential and civic uses sharply declined. I review the shifting scale of residential buildings following state withdrawal from housing production. I also address the massive losses in parkland and other green spaces, which I already mentioned and which followed from the privatization of land and the weakening of planning regulation.

In Chapters 6, 7, 8 and 9, I present the bulk of evidence showing how people's views of their lives and their city, during and after socialism, are shaping the new spaces of Sofia (i.e., I make the case for privatism's influence on urban form). In the first three of these chapters, I take an in-depth look at the city's southern periphery, which has become the preferred residential location of the *nouveau riche*. The area includes some modest old villages which were developed further during socialism mostly with small summer cottages in the style of the Russian *dacha*. The influx of new residents leaving central Sofia after 1989 has transformed the social profile of the area, making it a place of stark contrasts, a place where post-socialist wealth and post-socialist poverty reside side by side, yet hardly intersect (for example, new residences are typically designed so that their owners do not have to set foot on a public street). My focus on these suburbs is premised on two observations. First, I believe they represent the landmark contribution of post-socialism to the city, much as the standardized housing districts from the 1960s and 1970s embody the essential socialist legacy of city-building; and second, their physical features – private streets framed by large single-family homes surrounded by two-meter-tall iron, stone or brick walls – make them the perfect spatial manifestation of post-socialist privatism.

Specifically, Chapter 6 first reviews the economic and legal forces that enabled the growth of post-socialist suburbia (I refer to suburbia as the "ninth ring" since, ostensibly, the socialist city comprised eight rings) and then focuses on the impact of cultural factors. The chapter also discusses the extent to which the suburbanization of Sofia is reminiscent of suburbanization in Western cities – a process Lewis Mumford once called the "collective effort to live a private life" (1938: 43). It further suggests some gender implications of the process. In Western settings, the suburban dream of quaint single-family living in green settings arose historically in part from a renegotiation of gender roles (that is, women became more removed from the city and assumed the role of guardians of domestic life; see, e.g., Fishman 1987). I explore how the gender underpinnings of suburbanization play out in the post-socialist context – in the context of societies in which women participated in the workforce at very high rates, in part because the public realm provided strong support systems such as child care and maternity benefits. I argue that to understand the appeal of post-socialist suburban living (and the seeming willingness with which some women accept the role of a suburban homemaker today), one must take into account the extent to which the private home was perceived as a refuge from the state during socialism. Furthermore, I point to the powerful renegotiation of the border between public and private roles which occurred after 1989. Specifically, what was once normally viewed as a public responsibility (e.g., child care, good child education) is now a private, family responsibility, and it is the women who have typically assumed that obligation (Hirt 2008b).

In Chapters 7 and 8, I explore the new suburban gated and heavily guarded residences, many of which are largely hidden from the public eye. I re-use the book title *Iron Curtains* as chapter titles because I believe these residences are the most paradigmatic manifestation of post-socialist privatism in the built environment. Chapter 7 examines residences that are individually walled from the street – the type that was more common during the 1990s. Chapter 8 discusses the large gated communities that have proliferated during the last five or ten years. I argue that the shift from individually gated homes to gated compounds reflects some economic realities: during the 1990s, the private real estate industry was so fragmented that it was not able to construct and market large-scale residential developments; this situation has recently changed, especially after the entry of foreign capital and foreign construction firms. However, the shift has also some cultural underpinnings. The 1990s seem to have been marked by some sort of "rugged individualism" and wealthy families tended to wall off individually.

During the second decade of the transition, however, many began to search for gated compounds where they could share space with people of a similar socio-economic status. I disagree with much of the literature on gated complexes, which claims that they represent an export of an American ideal and American development form to other parts of the world. On the contrary, I emphasize the extent to which gating in Sofia, especially during the 1990s, was a locally grounded phenomenon which not only reflects the vigor of the post-socialist culture of privatism but may even represent a return to pre-twentieth-century local building traditions – traditions of erecting gated family compounds, which were common during the difficult times when the Balkans were part of the Ottoman Empire.

In Chapter 9, I return to a city-wide focus. I take a journey through the new suburbs, but also through other parts of the city that have substantially changed since 1989 in order to tell the story of a brave new architecture. One could legitimately argue that this architecture, with its vibrant colors and diverse forms, is an improvement over the monotony imposed by the particularly severe version of modernism so beloved by socialist authorities in the 1960s and 1970s. Still, I argue that the new eclecticism, which includes various peculiar interpretations of the neo-Gothic and the neo-classical (I refer to the latter as *Mafia Baroque*; Hirt 2008b), leaves the old city scarred and injured, just as modernism did. I also identify several other architectural styles and discuss the general tendency of buildings and building ensembles to act as "islands" rather than as parts of a whole.

In the last chapter, I make a concluding argument for the significance of privatism as a cultural condition in understanding wall-making – in all its reincarnations – in today's Sofia. Finally, I reflect on the possibilities of reviving public space and rejuvenating the public realm in the twenty-first century.

Notes

1 Culture is of course a very complex term. Anthropologists have rightly argued (e.g., Humphrey 2002) that it is misleading to talk of culture in the singular: there is no single, monolithic national culture, let alone a single supra-national post-socialist culture, be it a culture of privatism or something else. My working definition of culture is a "mass belief system" (e.g., Inglehart 1997): a set of widely shared attitudes, norms and patterns of behavior in a given society at a point in time. As I hope to show in this book, attitudes and patterns of behaviors centered on deep skepticism toward the idea of the public realm are widespread in post-socialist Bulgaria; they have, I argue, affected the spaces of its capital city. Although similar skepticism has been attributed to contemporary capitalist cultures at large (I make this case in Chapter 2), I believe it has taken a much more radical form in post-socialist conditions.

2 These social practices can be explained in both political-economic and cultural terms. Let us take corruption. There is certainly a political economy to it. It may be seen as "rational behavior" which spreads under certain structural conditions: relatively poor societies with murky legal environments where underpaid public officials look for additional sources of income and private firms look for ways to make a profit by sidestepping laws, avoiding taxes, or gaining access to state resources and contracts (Rose-Ackerman 1996). Still, corruption takes people, both those directly involved in the act and those who tolerate them, at least to an extent, in society at large. Thus, it is partially a cultural phenomenon. As partial proof one can take "bribe games" experiments, in which researchers have found that if the same bribes and incentives are offered to people from a sampling of different countries, game participants coming from countries with high levels of corruption are less likely to view corruption as morally wrong and are more likely to engage in corrupt acts during the game. Findings like this suggest that corruption is linked to "social norms and preferences that have been internalized by the inhabitants of those [the highly corrupt] countries" (Barr and Serra 2006).

3 Like other in-depth case studies, the book strives to illustrate the critical relationship between the "theory and the case study, rather than between the case study and [some] universal population" (Syrett 1995, cited in Scott, J. W. 2009). It also strives to serve as a much-needed bridge between theory and real-life experience (Silverman 1993; Yin 1984).

4 The term "post-socialist city" is controversial. First, it presumes a "socialist city" and second, it raises the question of whether this "new" type of city is a stable construct distinguishable from the capitalist city. I have used the term for convenience throughout the book without siding with a particular theory. This subject is discussed in Chapter 3.

5 These experts were selected using the reputational method. They included architects, builders, urban planners and other urban policy-makers, members of the City Council, heads of municipal offices (e.g., one of Sofia's post-socialist mayors, the current and former Chief Architect of Sofia, the current and former head of the National Center for Housing Policy and Territorial Development), academicians (geographers, sociologists, cultural anthropologists, urban and architectural historians and theorists), heads of environmental and historic preservation non-profit groups, and real estate developers, agents and consultants. The purpose of these interviews was to elicit information on the most prominent processes of post-socialist urban and architectural restructuring, and their causes and consequences (as well as the personal views of the experts on these changes). The focus was on obtaining information regarding the processes that have to do with spatial privatization. Architects, builders and planners were also asked to explain the policy and regulatory environment in which planning and building processes occur in post-socialist Sofia.

6 More details on the survey methodology and the selection of subjects for further interviewing are included in Chapters 6, 7 and 8. All in-depth interviews were conducted in Bulgarian, translated into English, transcribed, and coded for common themes.

7 They were specifically asked about trust in government, trust in their neighbors, and trust in people generally, since trust is a basic building block of vibrant civic societies (see, e.g., Putnam 1993).

8 As in all research, especially interpretive research, I cannot claim that what I found was fully independent of how I found it (Emerson et al. 1995). My subjective bias is inevitably part of the story and, in some cases (e.g., in the chapter on architectural styles), may even *be* the story. At the same time, I have consistently striven to ensure the study's reliability and validity by using routine case-study techniques such as collecting multiple sources of evidence for data triangulation purposes (Yin 1984).

9 I have used the term "cultural values" here because it is commonly used by the surveys discussed in Chapter 2 (e.g., the World Values Survey). Some scholars, however, have argued that the term is problematic since it implies stability in the ends toward which people aspire. Swidler (1986), for instance, asserts that cultures are not made of values (understood as static ends toward which action is oriented) but rather people's repertoires for action (e.g., their habits, skills and styles of behavior that help them achieve desirable ends).

2

Public, Private, Privatism

"The act of saving the drowning is an act to be performed by the drowning themselves."

A popular saying in socialist Bulgaria coined by
the Russian/Soviet writers I. Ilf and E. Petrov

"We live in a state in which people wonder whether it exists."

Excerpt from an interview with a resident of Sofia, 2001

The terms "public" and "private" are some of the most familiar ordering categories in Western thought and in everyday life. The two make an easy dichotomy and appear to construct each other discursively: "the public is what the private is not" (Bailey 2002). Regardless of their seeming transparency, however, public and private are complex social constructs (Benn and Gaus 1983; Weintraub 1997; Kumar and Makarova 2008) and the boundaries between them have been the subject of a rich body of sociological literature.[1] The simple dichotomy "public" and "private" constitute is misleading for at least two reasons. First, the border between them is ambiguous (e.g., children's education is to an extent a private, family concern, yet in welfare states it is a free public good). And second, even if a border between the two could be defined, this definition would vary widely historically and culturally.[2]

For the purposes of this chapter, I use "public" and "private" in two main ways. The first has to do with the public and the private as social arenas. In this case, the public realm comprises the settings and mechanisms through which human interaction and decision-making with community-wide implications occur (Boggs 1997; Taylor 2004). This definition includes the formal institutions of power (e.g., the state) but could be expanded to

Iron Curtains, First Edition. Sonia A. Hirt.
© 2012 John Wiley & Sons, Ltd. Published 2012 by John Wiley & Sons, Ltd.

include a wide variety of politically engaged communities of citizens debating collective concerns in open forums outside the official state realm. The latter group constitutes the modern "public sphere" (Habermas 1989). It also constitutes the broad equivalent of civil society (Seligman 1992) – the realm of citizen networks and communities of interest and belief, whose existence is premised on high interpersonal and inter-group trust and who share an interest in advancing some aspect of community well-being (Putnam 1993). The private realm in this social definition includes the interactions and concerns that pertain to the more intimate worlds of individuals, families, and close circles of friends.

The second principal definition involves the public and the private as material arenas. In this sense, public spaces – parks, plazas, streets, playgrounds, etc. – are the physical loci open to everyone, at least in theory (in practice, some restrictions almost always apply; Lofland 1991). Such common spaces exist in opposition to explicitly private spaces, i.e., spaces used by small groups of people, spaces that are physically enclosed, or spaces to which access is limited via various material or non-material impediments. Walls – whether the walls of a residential home or the walls delineating political borders – may be the most obvious impediments, but others block access equally well, e.g., cul-de-sac streets that conjoin small numbers of individual homes (and thus "tell" strangers not to come near), and facilities that have high entrance fees and are inaccessible by mass transit.

Whether as social or spatial settings, the public and the private are integral to the human condition (Boggs 1997; Arendt 1958). Hardly anyone hopes to live in total seclusion, much as hardly anyone dreams of a total, Orwellian extinction of private life. Hardly anyone wishes to exterminate either all publicness or all privacy from city life; in fact, clearly demarcated public and private spaces comprise the essence of successful urbanity, as Jane Jacobs perhaps most eloquently argued (1961).

The public–private demarcation, however, obscures the extent to which some public is embedded in every private, and some private is embedded in every public (Scruton 1984). Take the public and private as material arenas. Any private dwelling, aside from a prison cell, permits a glimpse of the outside. Who wants to live without a window? Furthermore, the largest, most handsomely decorated quarter of almost any residence is the living room – the room where families gather and receive guests, the room that opens the private to the public. Likewise, common urban spaces do not obliterate the private; on the contrary, they guarantee it. To stroll through public spaces is an act of "uncontrolled play" (Lofland 1991); public spaces are scenes where one encounters "strangers" with no formal commitment aside from the most casual nod or glance, and where one expects to be free from overbearing scrutiny or intrusion (Goffman 1959). Where intense control and surveillance of private behavior occurs, public spaces lose their essential publicness. Because each public needs some private and each private needs some public, the border between public and private spaces is far from absolute. On the contrary, in architecture for example, a wide variety of artifacts enable a dialogue between fully public and fully private spaces, both visually and functionally: doors, front porches, balconies, front yards, interior courtyards, sidewalk cafés, ground-floor shops, etc. As Jacobs (1961) argued, this rich interim category of semi-public/semi-private layers is precisely what makes a city work. In inviting people to keep their "eyes on the street" – to view a "street ballet" of passers-by from the comfort of one's bedroom or walk into a street café while strolling through a plaza – these interim spaces provide a "balance between people's determination to have essential privacy and their simultaneous wishes for different degrees of contact, enjoyment, or help from the people around."[3] Borders, like rules, are made to be broken. A world where a rigid, impermeable border between the public and the private is erected is a world in which one fears the other, a world where both the public and the private are under siege (Scruton 1984).[4]

Interim categories are as essential to the successful existence of the public and private in the social world as they are in the spatial world. In fact, it does not take too much imagination to interpret the public realm defined by Habermas as an interim ground. The Habermasian public sphere is as autonomous from life in the private home and family as it is from formal public institutions; it occupies a mediating position between the state and larger society, thus allowing for democratic control of political life (Boggs 1997). The idea of a vital middle category of civic communities, needed to prevent both state tyranny and extreme societal fragmentation, can be traced in the writings of classic sociologists such as Emile Durkheim and Hannah Arendt. In fact, the relationship between the public and the private realms is probably best represented not by a dichotomy, but by a trichotomy that includes the all-important interim ground (Wolfe 1997).

In this chapter, I review how the notions of the public and the private as social realms differed in twentieth-century capitalist and socialist settings, and how they have changed in post-1989 Eastern Europe. Understanding these distinctions is essential to understanding the spatial changes of the post-socialist city, which are the subject of the rest of the book.

The Rise of the Private

In Western thought, the significance of the public realm as an ideal and a project dramatically expanded during the Enlightenment and modernity (Habermas 1989). This "rise of the public" was associated with both the increasing powers of the nation-state and the gradual broadening of the public sphere to include a wider circle of individuals, social groups and communities of interest, thus allowing them greater participation in political life. This powerful trend toward privileging the public, however, currently seems to be undergoing a process of negation: the contemporary era is in fact marked by the "rise of the private" (Bailey 2000: 395). There is some disagreement as to the historic origins of this reversal. Sennett (1977) traces it back to the nineteenth century, but most theorists see it as a more recent phenomenon. Boggs, for instance, argues that in Western, capitalist societies the "epochal shift" can be dated to the late 1970s; that is, it coincides with the dawn of the so-called late, post-industrial or post-modern capitalism (Boggs 1997). This view is echoed by a series of other prominent theorists, such as Jameson (1984), Harvey (1989a), Kumar (1997) and Giddens (2000).

The "rise of the private" and the parallel "fall of the public" comprise a complex set of interrelated trends. To begin with, there is a general decline of state powers. These powers are undermined by economic and political globalization, which have radically restricted the terrain of operation of nation-states. Other measures of decline include the reduction of state responsibilities as they are transferred to sub-state levels such as regions and cities, as well as to private corporations, and the profound shift toward entrepreneurial modes of urban governance (see, e.g., Scott 2009; Brenner 2003, 2004a, 2004b; Le Gallès 2000). De-regulation of industry, privatization of state assets, and weakening state commitment to social equity (e.g., through reducing state-provided unemployment and health-care benefits) complete the "rolling back of the charitable state" according to neo-liberal prescriptions (Wacquant 2009). Most importantly for my purposes, however, the "rise of the private" encompasses a process of cultural change at the level of mass beliefs and behavior (Boggs 1997). This change implies the shrinking of the public sphere understood in the Habermasian sense as the mediating ground between state powers and private interests, i.e., the shrinking of civil society (Bailey 2002). Measures of this trend include: popular skepticism of recipes for social progress, which are viewed as utopian; widespread distrust of public institutions as evidenced by low political participation (e.g., voting, party membership); and a declining capacity to form civic associations, captured perhaps most succinctly by Putnam's term "bowling alone" (Putnam 2000). The cultural shift is also loosely related to the rise of conservative, "family values" philosophies, which emphasize not only the virtues of individual autonomy and entrepreneurship but also those of traditional family structure, thus inevitably implying a more patriarchal view of the role of women both at home and in civic life (see, e.g., Pateman 1983; Ellin 1997: 124–53).

In summary, then, one may speak of late capitalism as an era marked by an ethos of *privatism*[5] – a culture that entails diminishing appreciation of broad-based collective narratives and actions, and a growing interest in issues centered on the personal and the domestic, the individual, the family and the narrowly defined interest group. In Krishan Kumar's words (1997), the ideals of privatization and individualization have become the "master themes of contemporary Western life." Katherine Verdery and Caroline Humphrey (2004: 10) refer to this as a culture of "enclosing the commons." This culture has propelled global transformations, resulting in limited access to and expanded private claims on a wide variety of formerly public resources, from public views to vital public resources like water. The common outcomes of these processes of privatization and propertization are social segregation and exclusion.

Public and Private during Socialism

During East European socialism, the notions of public and private as ordering concepts were so different from those in capitalist democracies that some scholars have questioned their utility altogether (Garcelon 1997; Kharkhordin 1997; Gerasimova 2002). In fact, "public" and "private" are difficult even to translate into the Slavic languages (Gerasimova 2002). For example, the straightforward Bulgarian translation of "private" is *chastno* (meaning also "partial"), but this word is usually attached to the word "property" (*chastna sobstvenost*). The word *lichno*, literally translated as "personal," is the adjective commonly used in phrases such as "private realm," "private sphere" and "private life." The broader use of "personal" as opposed to "private" may be partially premised on the fact that socialist doctrine regarded the personal as legitimate and carved out legal space for personal property (e.g., cars, dwellings and basic consumer goods) – the type of property that socialist citizens were allowed to possess. In contrast, private property meant extensive real estate or means of production, both of which were regarded as bourgeois and were thus legally prohibited. When socialism collapsed, the new regime lacked a term for the subsequent massive and unprecedented transfer of property from the state to private parties. Thus, instead of trying to create a new word derived from local linguistics, it modified the English word "privatization" into the Bulgarian *privatizaciya* and adopted the term wholesale.

The difficulties of translation are but a small reflection of the important ways in which public and private in socialist Bulgaria, and Eastern Europe more generally, deviate from Western notions. The most obvious difference is that the socialist public – understood as the resources, institutions and functions that constituted the state – was immeasurably larger than its Western counterpart. The state appropriated private property en masse at the onset of socialism (in Bulgaria, urban land and large private properties were nationalized by 1948). It also took on a number of responsibilities, such as providing jobs, housing and free education – goods that most people in the relatively poor pre-socialist, early-twentieth-century East European societies could have obtained only through private efforts. An augmented public sector logically translated into a shrunken private sector, in terms of resources and responsibilities as well as rights and spaces. The private as a cultural ideal entered hostile ideological territory in the early socialist years (Marx himself hoped for the total subordination of the private to the public; Walicki 1983). For example, the infamous Soviet *kommunalka* (an apartment shared by several families) not only offered cost-efficiency "benefits" but also served to reduce the autonomy of private life and subject it to public surveillance (Gerasimova 2002). The implicit social contract of early socialism was that the state would "take care" of its citizens' basic needs and overcome inequalities, while acquiring the right to put their private lives under a permanent public gaze[6] with the long-term goal of absorbing *res privata* into *res publica* (Crowley and Reid 2002).

The most remarkable thing about socialism's project to integrate the private into the public is the extent to which it failed. That Western observers of early Soviet life declared that "Bolshevism has abolished private life" (Walter Benjamin cited in Crowley and Reid 2002: 12)[7] only underscores the extent to which they failed to grasp the cultural outcomes of socialism. Regardless of Marx's grim view of the private, socialist regimes – perhaps realizing the impossibility of their ambitions – significantly weakened efforts to control and usurp the private between Kruschev's "thaw" and Gorbachev's *perestroika* (Crowley 2002; Gerasimova 2002). Contrary to popular belief, the private realm – albeit shrunken – carried on throughout socialism rather resiliently, especially west of the Soviet borders. In housing terms, for example, *kommunalka*-type apartments never spread in the East European countries. The Bulgarian state, in particular, sold most of the housing units it built from the 1960s to the 1980s to individual households. This gave socialist Bulgaria a homeownership rate of 84%, higher than that of the United States and Western Europe.

An even better testimony for a thriving private is the extent to which public scrutiny over the personal, the family and small circles of friends was cautiously but continuously lifted from the 1960s on. In the Bulgaria of the 1970s and 1980s, one could critique just about anything – even the state – as long as the damning words did not go beyond the four walls of the private dwelling. Once outside the home, one generally had to adopt a public persona that gladly accepted official socialist doctrines.[8] The home served as both a refuge from overbearing public scrutiny and a primary locus of opposition (passive though it may have been) against totalitarian rule. In this sense, the home and the household not only survived socialist efforts to subdue them to an almighty public sphere, but even acquired additional symbolic powers: What the private lost in size, it gained in sanctity.

Life under socialism, then, was marked less by the absence of the private
than by a divorce of the public and the private. Kharkhordin describes the
socialist individual as "dissimulated" – an individual who has learned that
what one says in private (at home, among friends) is and must invariably
remain the opposite of what one says in public (Kharkhordin 1995, 1997).
This clear separation between private and public not only permeated the
lives of "regular" citizens, but also defined the lifestyles of the elites. It was
common knowledge that while the socialist leaders graciously waved and
smiled at the masses during public parades, they liked to vacation in secluded,
super-securitized gated compounds along the sea coasts. And that the
younger family members of the Soviet Kruschevs, Brezhnevs and Gromykos,
as well as the Bulgarian Dimitrovs, Zhivkovs and Balevs,[9] spoke with passion
about socialism in public, but practiced Western consumerism with the
utmost dedication in private (see, e.g., Starr 1983, cited in Kharkhordin
1995). It is also well documented that subtly woven networks of personal,
private and even familial connections played a crucial role in the distribution of power and material resources throughout the socialist period (Harloe
1996). After 1989, these private networks proved to be remarkably resilient
(hence Stark describes the trajectory of early post-socialism as a movement
"from plan to clan"; Stark 1992).

There is another, perhaps even more important mechanism through
which a severe rupture between the public and the private became part of
everyday life. Although socialism failed to subdue the private, it succeeded
in usurping the interim category between public and private that exists in
Western democracies. In theory, socialist doctrine permitted citizens to form
associations to pursue their interests and beliefs. In practice, however, such
associations lacked autonomy from the intertwined organizational structures
of the state and the socialist party (although there were significant variations
within the Eastern bloc, with Central European citizens showing the greatest
capacity to form independent groups; see Pickvance, K. 1997). Most citizen
organizations did not form from the bottom up; rather, the party and the
state founded and sponsored them (Lovenduski and Woodall 1987). Their
chief function was to aid the state rather than challenge it. During the
1980s, of course, many indigenous groups with mostly pro-environmental
and housing agendas did form, such as Green Future and the Danube
Circle in Hungary, and the Socio-Ecological Union in the Soviet Union
(Pickvance, C. 1996; Pickvance, K. 1997). The Bulgarian version of these
social movements was Eco Glasnost, which started as a group of intellectuals
opposed to nuclear power plants (Eco Glasnost broadened its membership
and agenda widely in the early 1990s but has since become politically irrelevant). Aside from these developments during the 1980s, citizen associations
throughout the socialist era had little to do with the bottom-up networks
that prosper in democratic societies (Putnam 2000). Instead of serving as a

negotiating realm between state power and private interests, these organizations were part of the overall "dissimulation" scheme – in public, they claimed autonomy from state control; in practice, they were part of the intricate vertical network that the state had crafted to control its citizenry (see, e.g., Harloe 1996: 6–7).

How then can one describe the relationship between public and private during socialism? At the risk of oversimplifying, given the diversity of nations that made up the socialist bloc, we can extract three main points from the above discussion. First, the private – understood as the intimate world of self, family and friends – was subjected to state control far beyond what was common in the West. Still, it was never fully tamed and perhaps even gained in symbolic significance as a place of refuge. Second, the public – understood as the state – greatly expanded its powers and functions, becoming a Leviathan figure (Garcelon 1997) that spread its tentacles through all societal layers except the most intimate. Third, the Leviathan was wildly successful in usurping the middle terrain of citizen activism that forms the core of civil society.

The cultural outcomes of the socialist project can then be described as follows. Socialist citizens (aside from those who aspired to climb the ladder of power) perceived the public realm as something at best ignored and at worst feared, but generally to be avoided as it intends only to trouble them (Kharkhordin 1995). The word "public" (in Bulgarian *obstestveno*) carried a subtly negative connotation, evoking something hypocritical and not to be relied on for help. This attitude is well expressed in a popular joke from the 1980s that made a parody of pompous socialist slogans about the nobility of workers' sacrifice in building the new society: "The act of saving the drowning", the joke went, "is an act to be performed by the drowning themselves."[10] The private, in contrast, acquired the flavor of a forbidden fruit and thus gained legitimacy to the extent that advancing it at the expense of the public (say, by finding a creative way to bring goods home from work without being caught) came to be seen as a heroic act of beating the system. This point has been noted by a strikingly small circle of scholars, such as Shlapentokh (1989), Jowitt (1992) and Garcelon (1997), but it forms the very basis of post-1989 privatism as I define it. Finally, because the socialist regimes annexed the interim realm that balances state power with private interests, in most people's minds the public (with its negative connotations) included citizen activism of almost any sort. Thus, the public was equated with the state – an alien, unhelpful "official." Civic groups were included in this category. The public was defined in full opposition to the private, which, as the arena outside state control, was generally viewed in a positive way (Makarova 2006). Public and private thus formed a strict dichotomy; there was little benevolent ground in between.

Contrary to conventional wisdom, then, socialism did not obliterate the private; it obliterated the public – not as institutions, but as an *ideal*. It made the public into an alien "other" to the extent that a new public realm emerged after 1989 simply out of solidarity against the public per se. In so doing, socialism built its own Trojan horse that not only brought about its own demise but scarred the generations who lived through it with such skepticism toward ideologies preaching the public good that their ability to create a viable alternative, whether it be democracy or anything else, has been seriously compromised. Further, it propelled a full army, a powerful Fifth Column, of public nihilists and private enthusiasts into the post-1989 world, thus charting a course of path-dependence (Stark 1992) premised not on what it officially endorsed (collectivism) but on what it officially condemned (privatism). In inflating but debilitating the public, besieging the private, and erecting a firm, cruel border between them, socialism set the stage for a world in which the firm border persists, but it is the public that is now under siege.

Privatism Unhinged

The domino-like fall of socialist regimes in 1989 took both Western observers and East European citizens by surprise. Initial infatuation with the "velvet revolutions" and with the role of popular citizen unions like the Polish *Solidarnosc* led many to expect a golden age of West European-style democracies, renewed public realms and widespread civic engagement to unfold across Eastern Europe. History, however, had another surprise in store. Within a couple of years, East European citizens retreated from the public sphere en masse and rushed toward purely private concerns (Kumar 1997). Humphrey aptly describes this condition as a "culture of disillusionment" marked by a yawning "chasm of unbelief" (Humphrey 2002: xxii, 40). Bodnar (2001) refers to it as a decline in the significance of the idea of publicness in all its forms. The World Values Survey from the 1990s documented significantly lower levels of interpersonal trust and trust in public institutions in East European countries as compared to West European countries, as well as significantly lower rates of membership in citizen associations (Inglehart 1997). In general, voter turnout decreased throughout Eastern Europe during the 1990s, reaching levels lower than 50% in several states, including Armenia, Estonia, Macedonia and Poland (IIDEA 2002), suggesting continued disappointment with the post-socialist public realm. In some countries, of course, specifically the former Yugoslavia and the former Soviet nations, ethno-nationalism served as a powerful builder of collective identity and rose to fill the ideological vacuum that socialism left (von Beyme 1996). Bulgarians, however, flirted only briefly with ethno-nationalism in the form of anti-Turkish sentiment in the early 1990s; such feelings failed to lead to substantial collective mobilization (Volgyi 2007).[11] And whereas nationalism proved a fleeting trend in most countries, other types of ideologies such as patriarchalism seemed to be more powerful. The decline of public services, such as free child care, immediately placed an extra burden on women, and their participation in public life sharply decreased[12] – a fact which some political leaders in the early 1990s welcomed.[13]

Disillusionment with post-socialist society in general and post-socialist governments in particular settled in Bulgaria almost immediately after 1989, with surveys from the 1990s showing that three-quarters of the population saw the conflict between government and governed as the major contradiction of society (Gerasimov 1999). Multi-national surveys carried out around that time, which covered Bulgaria, also showed low trust in government, low interpersonal trust, and low civic and political participation rates, etc., compared to most other nations (e.g., see Inglehart and Catterberg 2002).[14] Interpersonal trust, a key building block for developing a strong civil society (Putnam 1993), has been declining in Bulgaria throughout the post-socialist period. According to the World Values Survey, in 1990 30.4% of Bulgarians believed that most people could be trusted. In 1999, the percentage declined to 26.9, and in 2006 it dropped further to 22.2 (World Values Survey, undated). Registered voter turnout too has been steadily declining since 1989,[15] and continued lack of trust in government is also readily apparent in the failure of any political party voted into power after 1989 to be re-elected. A representative survey conducted in Bulgaria in 2007 documented an astonishingly powerful "culture of disillusionment," to use Humphrey's (2002) term, and a strong nostalgia for the socialist past. Sixty percent of respondents believed that society was more humane just before 1989, and 62% believed that it was more just (Kolev et al. 2007).[16] The numbers were predictably much higher among subjects from the "socialist generation" (people who were over 60 years old at the time of the survey): 74% and 78%, respectively.[17] Yet they were remarkably high even among the youngest generation, those under 30 years old, the so-called "children of democracy." Among them, 33% believed that socialist society was more humane than the current alternative, and 37% viewed it as more just (only 15% thought post-socialist society was more humane and only 14% believed it was more just; the rest were undecided).[18] The survey showed that the respondents' skepticism had a particular direction – it was aimed at public institutions, at the state.[19] About two-thirds believed that the public sector is so corrupt that it is completely impossible for any Bulgarian to achieve prosperity with "honest work." The sociologists analyzing the survey offered the following observations. Most Bulgarians do not trust in the idea of a "good society" and see themselves as powerless to improve its current status. They have little interest in civic activities, and focus on personal and family betterment. The notion of a viable public realm is viewed as empty propaganda. Thus, the sociologists concluded, Bulgarians live in a state of radical "public nihilism"; they embrace a doctrine of deep disbelief and "perpetual dissatisfaction with the state, public institutions and public policies." Further, they embrace an ideology of "privatizing positives and publicizing negatives"; that is, they tend to attribute most positive developments in their lives and in the country as a whole to private, individual efforts and interpret negative developments as proofs of the structural inability of the public realm to deliver progress (Kolev et al. 2007: 6–7). It is precisely this widespread disbelief in the viability of the public realm that I call privatism.

Aside from the surveys quoted above, literature that comprehensively analyzes cultural norms and patterns of behavior centered on privatism in Bulgaria is scarce. However, work by Sorin Matei (2004) on Romania traces the general cultural trajectory that these two neighboring Balkan countries likely share. Matei, whose work is aptly subtitled "From Nationalism to Privatism," explains how Romanians, who once stunned the world with their determination to depose Ceausescu's regime, have become largely indifferent to most public endeavors. This indifference permeates everyday life in the most routine and seemingly benign ways (e.g., people dress up for private parties, but purposefully dress down for work or public events; they are often unsure of precisely what public holiday it is and celebrate it solely as a private day off; they perceive civic work as beneficial only if it leads to some tangible personal gain). Yet this indifference is important in that it perpetually diminishes the symbolic value of public activities and converts them, in people's minds, into private events. Matei's ethnographic observations lead to two conclusions. First, the "Romanian public spirit is dying" and there is a "deeper crisis in Romanian culture and society, a crisis of the spirit resulting from a resurgence of privatism and individualism that saps at the effort to find new forms of communal commitment." And second, this privatism is as much a reflection of mass disillusionment with the post-1989 state of affairs as it is rooted in the "socialist state's totalitarian effort to confiscate people's right to be autonomous social agents." This totalitarian effort ultimately caused the opposite of what it intended; it caused the turning inward of people's lives (Matei 2004: 40–2). Matei's conclusions mirror the ones advanced by Kharkordin on Russia. Kharkhordin (1995: 224) describes a vehemently "post-modern" Russian society, in which any ideological meta-narratives are steadily resisted by most Russians and in which values of "an almost unrestrained personalism and privatism" prevail to the extent that the only surviving collective meta-belief is "that there are no more beliefs capable of moving people."

The single and most illuminating in-depth study of Bulgaria published in English that touches upon the issue of privatism is the excellent monograph by Venelin Ganev, appropriately titled *Preying on the State* (2007). Ganev's work analyzes the massive privatization of state assets that was undertaken in Bulgaria during the 1990s and the dramatic shrinking of the public sector's resources and functions that accompanied it[20] – processes that led to the very stark social stratification of Bulgarian society in a few short years: in less than a decade, the wealthiest 8% of the Bulgarian population acquired spending powers exceeding those of the poorest 75% (Rajchev et al. 2000). Ganev's thesis is that the Bulgarian case counters the conventional wisdom of outside (i.e., Western) observers, who tend to attribute the failures of the 1990s to the eagerness with which East European reformers embraced neo-liberal doctrines for free markets and small government. On the contrary, the "reformers," many of whom were high-level socialist apparatchiks and their offspring busy converting their former political power into economic capital, took privatization far beyond what any neo-liberal doctrinaire could imagine. Massive state assets were appropriated by small elites not with the intention of advancing a free-market economy but for private gain. For them, a state with stable institutions was an obstacle to acquiring personal wealth. This is why they put such effort into state dismantling – an effort that succeeded largely because there was no strong civil society capable of stopping them. Ganev's study takes an institutionalist, elite-agency approach (it never mentions the term privatism), but nonetheless its findings can be viewed through a cultural lens. The findings suggest a condition of privatism defined not only by deep, inherent hostility toward the very idea of a public domain, but also a startling capacity to conceptualize it solely as an "object of extraction" – a condition of aggressive, predatory privatism that goes well beyond the passive withdrawal from public life that Matei describes.

Ganev focuses on elite behavior, but he also hints at popular reaction to the events of the 1990s. Perhaps surprisingly to Western observers, most Bulgarians lived through the fraud and corruption that defined the first post-socialist decade with a mixture of passive revulsion and resignation. Another Bulgarian scholar (L. Boyadjiev, cited in Kiosev 2005) took a more critical stand than even Ganev in saying that Bulgarians live in a state of "anarcho-pacifism"; i.e., they have come to accept chaos and public-sector corruption with quiet stoicism, without fighting back (this may be yet another definition of privatism).[21] The state of helplessness, of doubt that a public authority, a civic organization or anyone else will step in to defend what seems to be a collective interest over that of a private party, was well conveyed by a 60-year-old interviewee, Victor, a resident of one of Sofia's socialist-era complexes who used to be a full-time architectural technician but now works as a handyman to helps ends meet. Victor had recently observed his neighborhood's little playground being bulldozed by a private firm's construction equipment, perhaps illegally.

> I am no longer surprised. Honestly, it barely bothers me. We live in a state in which people wonder whether it exists. When lawlessnes becomes normal, it actually becomes "legal"; you know this. It's well . . . a lawful lawlessness, so I move on, take care of my business.

In making this observation, I do not mean to blame people like Victor for readily accepting victimhood, but to point out what some keen observers of socialism and post-socialism have noted: having been abused by a totalitarian system for decades, people accepted abuse as virtually inevitable (Sztompka 1991; also Stanilov 2007). Furthermore, for many, especially those who could benefit from the "lawful lawlessness," attempts to beat any "system" (e.g., by breaking laws or looting public property), be it socialist, post-socialist or capitalist, did not seem reprehensible. Conformity with the law is never "a hallmark of rapid change" (Marcuse 1996), but in post-socialist Bulgaria corrupt behavior gained an aura of normality to the extent that it became the *expected* conduct of anyone with power. (In fact, as Ganev mentions, since awards seemed to follow from breaking rather than abiding by the rules, some of the greatest rule-breakers of the 1990s attained celebrity status and even served as role models.) Unfortunately, corrupt behavior is not solely the province of political elites, but is also practiced by large segments of the middle- and lower-level government bureaucracy (Stoyanov 2008).

As in other East European nations, much has changed in Bulgaria over the last few years, especially since it entered the European Union in 2007. Arguably, the country has made noteworthy strides toward economic and institutional stability, and toward a more functional civil society than it had in the 1990s.[22] Given its large minorities, it is also often lauded as a successful multi-ethnic society (especially in contrast to neighboring Yugoslavia). Yet many of the problems from the 1990s, especially corruption,[23] still persist to the point that in mid-2008 the European Union suspended accession funds of 500 million Euros and revoked accreditation of the two government agencies that handled the financial transfers. Another grave issue yet to be resolved is the presence of organized crime – an issue that according to some observers has only worsened since 2007, as criminal networks now have greater incentives to interact with, influence and – when necessary – intimidate political elites in order to gain access to European Union funds (Petrunov 2006). A 2008 article in the *New York Times* (Carvajal and Castle 2008) cited a former Bulgarian intelligence chief who stated the problem succinctly: "Other countries have the mafia. In Bulgaria, the mafia has the country."

As I see it, many signs point to a deeply ingrained, unyielding culture of post-socialist privatism. One is the widespread persistence of subversive practices like rule-breaking[24] (at which Bulgaria seems to "excel," even relative to other nations from the former Eastern bloc). This culture not only shaped and was shaped by the massive privatization of property that was carried out in Bulgaria between 1993 and 1997, but also seems to have outlived it. In this sense, privatism as I defined it in the introduction – a widespread disbelief in a benevolent public realm and a widespread sense that to appropriate the public is to thrive in private – has been the true cultural hallmark of the last twenty years.

Post-socialist privatism is embedded but also deviates from the privatism that makes scholars like Sennet, Boggs or Kumar worry about a declining public realm in North America or Western Europe. Its broad markings – a weakened state, the mass transfer of assets and responsibilities from the public to the private sector, the declining appeal of collectivist narratives, a widespread political apathy – are similar to those that define the Western "rise of the private." But its dual origin, its rootedness in the dramatic failure of decades-long totalitarian attempts to subdue the private realm *and* the equally dramatic failure to establish a viable non-corrupt public realm after 1989, accounts for the virility with which it self-propels.[25] East European privatism is not a mere import of Western ideas (as influential as they may have been); it has its own, locally embedded dynamics. To put this informally, East European privatism is like Western privatism on steroids; it is privatism that has erupted with the intensity of the long-suppressed.

Unlike socialism or nationalism, privatism is not taught in school. It is not an official ideology glorified in textbooks. But privatism transmits well: it is observed and reproduced in everyday practices. It is a popular ideology driven by multiple intentions: sometimes to withdraw from the public realm, sometimes to appropriate parts of it, and sometimes to protest against it.

Here are a few small examples of how privatism is practiced, received and reinforced in Sofia. Asked about how his neighborhood had changed in recent years, and also why he built a solid fence around his family yard in the mid-1990s (even though his family had owned the lot, with no fence, for forty years), Ivan, a more or less successful middle-aged auto mechanic living in Sofia's suburbs, shared in a long interview:

> There is not much to see out there anyway, eh? I mean this not grandma's time, when you could see the greenery …. It's like a different place [now]. It's all new houses around and most of the new owners are not the friendliest lot …. And there are a lot of cars …. I tell you one thing I remember from a few years back. I am walking down to the store … and right behind me there is a whole entourage of black Mercedes, dark windows and all. And one of

these guys steps out of the car to ask me – politely, mind you – to step away because his boss is in a hurry. I mean he has the audacity to ask me, me to move from the public street to make room for the boss! Who is he? Is he Todor Zhivkov [Bulgaria's last socialist leader]? That for me was it [the tipping point] – the less I see of this, the better. I have four kids; what good does it do them to see that kind of stuff? It's my house, may not be much but it's what I got .... We have many friends, we see and welcome many people here, but I don't think I'm missing much by not peeking out every minute. I much prefer my yard; at least I keep it clean.

Another long-term suburban homeowner, an older woman named Anna, who once worked as secretary in a municipal office, spoke about how the place she lives in has changed over the last couple of decades in the following terms:

I tell you, these new people and the politicians who allow them to do what that is, whatever they want are shameless, shameless people. One of the best things here was that there was a lot of green space – I mean, it was not perfectly maintained as they show it now in the magazines, but it was here. See this on the right at the corner? There was a little piece of land here that I know was designated for a public park – I know this because I used to know the people who worked in the land registry back in the day. You see it's a house now. You know who built it? One of the former Chief State Prosecutors! He took it; that's what he did. I do not know how it even got privatized, if it was a park. I just saw the construction trucks when they came.... And then he didn't just build a house but fenced off almost the entire sidewalk in front of it so that his yard could be bigger. Now people can barely walk there to keep away from the cars.

Asked how family life has changed over the last two decades, Anna explained:

I think overall people became more closed up; families became more closed up. Like everyone became more suspicious and more afraid. Back when [I was very young] I lived in Sofia; I used to go to work by walking through the park. Of course you can't do this anymore .... It's hard for anyone, but for women it's even worse. My daughter-in-law was walking back from work one day, and it was just semi-dark, and some guys surrounded her. She threw her purse and ran, ran. Now my son has to wait for her and drives her back from work and she carries this spray thing that you can point to the [attackers'] eyes ... and then they put the alarm and build a tall fence just to be a bit safer.

The final example also comes from the interview with Ivan. Asked why he kept piling garbage in the overflowing small garbage can in front of his neatly fenced-off house, when it would take him just a few minutes to take it to the nearest municipal container, he replied:

Why should I make the effort? Make their [presumably the municipal workers'] job easier? The municipality doesn't care about people like us; if they did, they would clean up the roads and the sidewalks. Now they only do this in front of the "important" houses. You know how good the street looks in front of Kostov's house? [Ivan Kostov is a former Prime Minister] ....

So the municipality doesn't care, the state doesn't care. So why should I care?

Taking Privatism and Spatiality Seriously

The profound socio-spatial transformations of the East European city since 1989 have been explored by a vast literature including a number of excellent edited compilations such as Andrusz et al. (1996), Enyedi (1998), Ruble et al. (2001), Hamilton et al. (2005), Tsenkova and Nedovic-Budic (2006) and Stanilov (2007), and a smaller number of case-based monographs, mostly on the larger cities such as St. Petersburg (Axenov et al. 2006), Budapest (Bodnar 2001) and Warsaw (Tasan-Kok 2004). Such works have advanced a rich variety of theoretical perspectives and have used diverse empirical methods. Only a few, however, have attempted (typically in individual chapters) to make sense of post-socialist urban change in relation to culture. In fact, one often finds better examples of the cultural approach to analyzing urban forms in volumes written by cultural anthropologists, even though they rarely examine the built environment. Humphrey's (2002) thoughtful study of the villas of the "New Russians" and Boym's (2001a) excellent analysis of urban memory in Moscow are good examples here. The scarcity of cultural studies of the post-socialist city is a missed opportunity for anyone who believes, like Lewis Mumford, that urban environments represent changes in civilizational values "in legible script" (Mumford 1938: 403) or, like Kevin Lynch, that "city forms, their actual function, and the ideas and values that people attach to them make up a single phenomenon" (Lynch 1984: 36).

In recent years, there has been some increased scholarly interest in taking culture and post-socialist spatiality seriously. The best examples include Till's (2005) study of urban memory in Berlin, Goscilo and Norris's (2008) edited volume on historic preservation in St. Petersburg, Czaplicka et al.'s (2008) collection of essays on the making of national and European identity in Central European and Baltic cities, and Czepczynski's (2008) reading of select East European cities as "cultural landscapes." However, these otherwise excellent books seem to focus on how urban space represents and reinforces belief systems related to nation-building, ethnic identity, re-interpretation of the socialist and pre-socialist past, and cultural Europeanization. For the most part, such efforts are part of the elite-inspired, government-driven ideological projects that aimed to contribute to the legitimization of post-socialist regime change. Literature targeting the link between urban form and a widespread, popular set of cultural preferences – and I believe privatism fits this description very well – is much scarcer. Some notable exceptions include Ruble's (1995) study of housing privatization in Yaroslav, Bodnar's (2001) exemplary analysis of Budapest (however, neither Ruble nor Bodnar uses the term "privatism" or addresses it as a cultural phenomenon), and Makarova's (2006) illuminating study of the "interiorization" (i.e., the turning inward) of Moscow, which, however, is still in progress.

I can only speculate why the cultural approach to interpreting East European urban change has remained underrepresented in the literature, and why the influence of privatism has been barely mentioned. Perhaps most obviously, few scholars have noticed privatism as a cultural condition to begin with. Furthermore, since studying privatism involves observing many ordinary people going about their ordinary lives, it requires researchers to deal with a myriad of personal choices and preferences that tend to be less disciplined and coherent than those comprising most state ideologies. One cannot simply "read" privatism (or any other type of mass beliefs) in urban space as if space were a transparent medium of cultural expression (as Spiro Kostof once said, form is "lamely informative" of meaning, and one must understand cultures before grasping their spatial manifestation; 1991: 10). Thus, to study privatism intersected with urbanism, one needs to speak with and listen to the people who experience the new spaces in their daily lives. That is, one needs the tools of ethnography – a method that scholars of post-socialist cities have rarely used.

Speculation aside, however, there are two important reasons that privatism as both culture and urbanism must attract serious inquiry. First, privatism is a common denominator that helps us see a startling variety of post-socialist spatial trends – from loss of public space to bizarre architecture – not as mere fragments but as parts of a whole picture. This is not to say that the political economy cannot help us do the same, but that by using it as our only viewing lens, we miss parts of the equation.

Second, the culture–space relationship is reciprocal. Space is not a "passive physicality" (Bodnar 2001: 177), not just a blank canvas on which social (and cultural) phenomena proceed. Rather, it is one of the very "constructive dimensions" of social life (Brenner et al. 2003: 7). Thus, it is not only that privatism as culture shapes urban forms. Once these forms are erected – these daunting enclosures, these secluded suburbs and triumphantly individualistic architectural creations – they send messages that come to shape culture in return. This takes us precisely to where we started in this chapter – to the public and the private as social and spatial arenas. There is a long line of scholars who have noted the connection between a thriving public realm as a spatial arena and a thriving public realm as a democratic social ideal. Perhaps most brilliantly, Jane Jacobs (1961) argued that urban spaces marked by diversity – both spatial diversity in density, street type, uses, etc., and social diversity in income, class, race, etc. – are vital preconditions for developing a sense of "togetherness" between people without ties of kinship, friendship or class belonging. In her view, diverse urban places increase the level of comfort with "otherness" and inspire an interest in collective well-being based on the experience of sharing space. To push this theory further is to fall into physical determinism. Still, a link between the spatial and the social public (and private) realms undoubtedly exists. Spatial patterns tend to "materialize" the socially acceptable borders and relationships between the public and the private (Brian 1997), thus helping convert them into cultural norms. Furthermore, as the material setting for the "co-presence of those who would never otherwise encounter each other" (Lofland 1991: 198), urban public spaces help promote trust of strangers and tolerance of difference, rather than fear. They help teach skills of civility and urbanity (Rowe 1997) – "an essential precondition for building a public world" (Scruton 1984: 6). This is why the common Latin root of the words "city," "civic" and "citizenship" is more than a linguistic footnote,[26] why fenced-off compounds are more than a distasteful architectural artifact, and why theorists of spatial privatization and the "end of public space" (Sorkin 1992; Zukin 1995) fear a crisis of *publicness* in the broadest meaning of the term.

With these notes in mind, I now turn to the spatial characteristics and the borders between public and private in the socialist and post-socialist city.

Notes

1 Boundaries, as Wolfe (1997: 187) put it, are the prime "stuff of sociology."

2 For example, in ancient Greece the dichotomy implied an opposition between family life and a public sphere of collective debate, whereas in ancient Rome, the dichotomy implied an opposition between single individuals and the powerful state sovereignty (Arendt 1958; Bailey 2002).

3 In Marcuse's words: "Boundaries should invite their crossings; they should bring differences together at the same time as they support individual and group identities" (1997: 114).

4 Goffman (1959) appropriately referred to a world of total institutions and no individual freedoms in spatial terms as a "world without doors."

5 To clarify: privatism is not capitalism (not even just late capitalism), nor is it simply the cultural views associated with (late) capitalism. Privatism, as I define it, is a cultural mode entailing a weak appreciation of the public realm. As such, it can be associated with different types of societies: pre-capitalist, capitalist, socialist, post-socialist, etc. What the cited literature has shown, however, is that privatism has strengthened during late capitalism (in this sense, privatism is a global phenomenon). My argument is that in post-socialist nations like Bulgaria it has reached a much more radical form (in this sense, post-socialist privatism, or at least its intensity, is a locally grounded phenomenon).

6   In Bulgaria, surveillance was executed by the State Security agency (*Durzhavana Sigurnost*). Once employing hundreds of surveillance specialists, organized in seven departments (including Department 1, charged with monitoring the intelligentsia, artists and unions and Department 2, charged with monitoring the universities), this agency was disbanded in the early 1990s.

7   In Benjamin's defense, if he had visited Bulgaria in 1978 rather than Russia in 1928, he would have likely never made that statement.

8   Even this attitude changed during the 1980s, when it became acceptable to gently poke fun at the state while at work. The popular 1980s anecdote "The state cannot pay me as little as I work" (*Durzhavata ne moje da mi plati tolkova malko kolkoto rabotya*) well reflected a burgeoning culture of subtle anti-state sabotage at the workplace.

9   I refer to the families of the Bulgarian socialist leaders Gyorgy Dimitrov, Todor Zhivkov and Milko Balev.

10   In Bulgarian: *Deloto po spasiavane na daveshtite se e delo na samite daveshti se.*

11   There is a relatively new, radical nationalist party in Bulgaria appropriately named *Ataka* (meaning Attack). The party caused a great shock by getting voted into parliament a few years ago, but its support has now slightly eroded.

12   In Bulgaria, women made up only 10% of the 1991 National Parliament as compared to 21% in 1981. By now, however, they have regained the lost ground: the 2010 figure is 20.8%.

13   Mikhail Gorbachev, for example, spoke about the "true mission" of women as mothers and homemakers (cited by Corrin 1992). Vaclav Havel labeled feminism a refuge "for bored housewives and dissatisfied mistresses" (cited by Watson, P. 1993).

14   Unfortunately, comparable data for the socialist period is missing. The World Values Survey reports data on Bulgaria from 1990 on and the Eurobarometer reports from 2004 on.

15   The latest parliamentary elections drew 54% of registered voters, whereas the latest presidential poll drew 41%. Both figures are the lowest on record since 1989.

16   Such pessimism has only grown in recent years. In 2000, the first year during which the same sociological agency conducted this survey, the percentage of subjects who thought society was more humane under socialism was 54. The same percentage believed that society was also more just under socialism.

17   In fact, according to this survey, 63% of people over 60 years of age would like to have the socialist system restored.

18   In 2001, the New Europe Barometer found widespread disappointment with the post-socialist state of affairs and nostalgia for socialism across Eastern Europe, including among young people. The Bulgarians, however, were one of the most "disappointed" nations. A recent Pew survey confirmed these findings (see Ghodsee and Henry 2010).

19   A good example of this skepticism toward public institutions comes from another recent national representative survey, this time on the topic of "Public opinion of and tolerance toward the grey economy." The survey was conducted by the Institute of Sociology at the Bulgarian Academy of Sciences. According to the data, only 3.7% of the 1000 respondents believed that no government officials in Bulgaria are corrupt. Simultaneously, only 12% of respondents

claimed to always pay their taxes. The unpublished data was provided by Dr. Emilia Chengelova, Senior Researcher at the Institute of Sociology.

20 Ghodsee and Henry (2010: 5) describe post-1989 Bulgaria as a country dominated by an "unbridled, kleptocratic [type of] capitalism."

21 Perhaps the words of the Russian anarchist Peter Kropotkin make sense here. He once sarcastically described modern society as "Everyone for himself and the State for all" (cited by Putnam 1993: 165). In today's Bulgaria only the first part of the sentence seems to accurately apply.

22 In 2007, Freedom House gave Bulgaria scores of 2.5 in the civil society index and 2.89 in the overall democracy index (Freedom House's scores range from 1 to 7, highest to lowest). This puts Bulgaria in the middle range of the twenty-eight countries comprising Eastern Europe and the former Soviet Union (for example, the Czech Republic's scores are 1.5 and 2.15 respectively, whereas Georgia's scores are 3.5 and 4.68, respectively).

23 Transparency International gave Bulgaria a corruption score of 4.1 in 2006 (scores vary between 9.4 for Finland, Denmark and New Zealand as least corrupt, and 2 for Myanmar and Somalia as most corrupt). This makes Bulgaria one of the most corrupt nations in Europe, ahead only of a few other post-socialist countries.

24 I provide further examples of rule-breaking, especially as it relates to city-building, in the next chapter.

25 In this sense, privatism in Bulgaria is both old and new. It is old because by suppressing the possibility for a vibrant civic society the socialist regime seems to have produced widespread skepticism toward collectivist ideals and public institutions altogether. But it is new in the sense that it has only been augmented recently as a result of the failures of post-socialist society. Further, one could not as easily practice privatism during socialism (i.e., one could not easily appropriate public goods; only the top apparatchiks could). During post-socialism, the opportunities for practicing privatism (e.g., for abusing public resources for private profit) increased as well.

26 As James Holston and Arjun Appadurai (2003: 306) put it: "there is something irreducible and nontransferable, necessary but not quite sufficient, about the city's public street and square for the realization of a meaningfully democratic citizenship."

3

The Post-socialist City

Life in the towns and villages will have overcome the legacy of grayness, uniformity, anonymity, and ugliness inherited from the totalitarian era . . . . Every main street will have at least two bakeries, two sweet-shops, two pubs, and many other small shops, all privately owned and independent . . . . People will once more begin to experience the phenomenon of home . . . . Prefabricated high-rise apartment blocks and other gigantic public housing developments will no longer be built. Instead, there will be developments of family houses, villas, townhouses and low-rise apartment buildings.

Vaclav Havel, 1992a

The Socialist City

Did socialism make a "space of its own" (Lefebvre 1991: 54)? Is there a *socialist city*, a city whose spatial structure was sufficiently different from the structure of the twentieth-century capitalist Western city to warrant the very existence of the term? It is unlikely that this question, which French and Hamilton (1979) posed at the apogee of socialist statism, will ever be unequivocally answered.[1] Two main schools of thought can be distinguished, however, and their principal differences were well articulated by Gyorgi Enyedi and Ivan Szelényi in the pages of *Cities after Socialism* (Andrusz et al. 1996; also Sheppard 2000; Pickvance, C. 2003; Tsenkova and Nedović-Budić 2006: 3–20; Tosics 2005). The first school, which advanced the so-called ecological model (e.g., Van den Berg et al. 1982), argued that twentieth-century urbanization is inherently linked to modernity and industrialization. Since socialism and capitalism are modern,

Iron Curtains, First Edition. Sonia A. Hirt.
© 2012 John Wiley & Sons, Ltd. Published 2012 by John Wiley & Sons, Ltd.

industrial socio-economic orders, socialist cities were but a variant of the standard model of twentieth-century industry-led urbanity and followed evolutionary stages similar to those of Western capitalist cities, although with some delay. The second, so-called historical school emphasized the importance of the mode of production (the neo-Marxist approach) or the political order (the neo-Weberian approach) and claimed that the socialist political economy produced a distinct, autonomous urban model. The debate between the two is grounded in a deep-seated disagreement on two points: whether socialism was a unique societal model or a mere branch of Western modernity (a viewpoint I will attempt to bolster in the next chapter), and whether a specific socio-economic order – rather than some universal evolutionary forces – can produce a space of its own.

Despite this dispute, a broad agreement exists that cities during socialism exhibited at least some socio-spatial features that set them apart from cities farther west. Drawing on the work of Szelényi (1996), Häussermann (1996) and others, I review five main contrasts between the socialist and the capitalist city: (1) in overall spatial articulation; (2) in spatial scale; (3) in functional balance; (4) in social composition; and (5) in aesthetic character (Hirt 2006).[2]

The first difference was that socialist cities lacked the paradigmatic feature of twentieth-century capitalist metropolises – sprawling suburbs. In lieu of the low-density residential peripheries typical of Western (and especially American) cities, socialist cities had vast mass housing districts erected from pre-made panels in accordance with the tenets of modernist urban design. Even though such zones are common in many West European cities as well, socialist projects of this sort comprised a much greater share of the total urban area and dwelling stock. In many large East European cities today, over half of the urban population resides in such housing districts. These include Tallinn with 55% of the urban population, Warsaw with 56%, Bratislava with 77%, and Bucharest with 82%. The percentage for Sofia is about 60 (EAUE 2000; see also Hirt and Stanilov 2009). As a result, socialist cities were significantly denser and more compact than capitalist cities. They depended on mass transit, rather than private car travel, and had a clear edge framed by the last concrete towers of their housing districts (see, e.g., Sýkora 1999a, 1999b; Dingsdale 1999). The second difference was that, in socialist cities, there was less economizing with space. Public projects and places from parks to parade plazas, from housing estates to People's Palaces like those in central Berlin, Budapest, Belgrade and Bucharest (Figure 3.1) were characterized by a spatial grandeur that was hard to find in capitalist conditions (see also Banerjee 2004; Hirt 2008a). The third, functional distinction was that socialist cities were over-supplied with public and industrial functions[3] but under-supplied with retail. For example, in the early 1990s retail space per person was three

Figure 3.1 Socialist splendor – the People's Palace in Bucharest, the second-largest government building in the world after the Pentagon. The Palace is the jewel structure in a large complex of buildings erected in the 1980s after massive demolitions in the center of the Romanian capital.

times lower in Moscow than in Berlin (Tosics 2005) – a fact that should not be too surprising since in 1989, 243 of the 276 officially designated basic consumer goods were severely under-produced across the Soviet Union (Roberts and LaFollette 1990). Downtowns, in particular, were rich in public as well as residential uses, but they lacked the variety of commercial premises found in capitalist Central Business Districts (Bertaud and Renaud 1995). The fourth contrast was in social character. Socialist cities exhibited less social diversity, marginality and informality of people, places and behaviors than their capitalist counterparts. By all measures, they were safer and less socially segregated (e.g., Kovacs 1994, 1998; Węcławowicz 2002; Tulu 2003). The last difference, in aesthetics, was that socialist cities were much more dominated than capitalist cities by an especially spartan branch of modernism – the style of choice for most socialist governments since the 1960s. The visual result was an environment which was marked, as Havel depicted it in his *Summer Meditations* (1992a: 104), by such grayness,

Figure 3.2 This photo shows parts of Novi Beograd (New Belgrade)-the largest socialist-era in Serbia. The "Uniformity, anonymity and ugliness from the totalitarian era," which Havel among many others so eloquently described. The district houses 200,000 people. Photo by Town Planning Institute, Belgrade. Used by permission of Zaklina Gligorijevic on behalf of the Town Planning Institute of Belgrade.

uniformity and anonymity that it evoked outright boredom (Figure 3.2, Table 3.1). Socialist cities, then, lacked the diversity and spontaneity of spaces, styles and people that arguably make the soul of urbanity (Szelényi 1996). Instead, they projected an image of unity and orderliness that only a regime with extraordinary power to control space could produce.

The features of socialist urbanism described above were rooted in the nature of the socialist socio-economic order: a single-party state that owned most of the urban land, the large real estate and the means of production,[4] used centralized planning to control the economy, and produced and distributed the vast majority of housing (Szelényi 1983; Andrusz 1984; Ruble 1990). But socialist urbanism was as much an economic as an ideological product. Shaping space to shape a new society was *the business* of the socialist state to a far greater extent than in capitalist nations. Space itself was but a major socializing project whose goal was the conception of a new "socialist individual" uninterested in private gain and willing to contribute selflessly to society at large. Space was meant, then, to convey a clear ideological

Table 3.1 Spatial contrasts between the socialist and the post-socialist city

Spatial characteristics	Socialist city	Post-socialist city
Spatial articulation	Compact, high-density urban form and clearly articulated urban edge.	Intense residential (and, recently, commercial) suburbanization.
	Absence of sprawling suburbs. Metro-periphery comprises greenbelts, industrial zones, recreational zones and rural areas.	Sprawl, blurring of the urban edge. Loss of greenbelts and agricultural lands; conversion to low-density residential and commercial uses.
	Cities dependent on mass transit; no daily commuting from suburbs to center or between suburbs.	Start of commuting from suburbs to center and between suburbs; dependence on the private car.
Spatial scale	Less economizing in space. Vast scale of government buildings, ceremonial plazas, parks and other public spaces; vast public housing projects with large green common spaces and limited private spaces.	Decrease of spatial development scale (especially during the 1990s). Large civic spaces and housing projects no longer built (typically, only commercial projects are of vast spatial scale); proliferation of private spaces; spatial fragmentation.
Functional balance	Dominance of public and industrial uses, especially heavy industry; public uses especially dominant in city centers; industrial uses often located in prime urban locations; generous parks and green spaces.	Decline of public uses; massive de-industrialization; ceremonial plazas de-constructed for private uses (e.g., appropriated for commerce); public buildings converted to commercial use; public green spaces (gardens, parks, etc.) decrease dramatically.
	Scarcity of retail; absence of Central Business Districts.	Retail revolution; Re-emergence of Central Business Districts.
Social character	Mild socio-spatial stratification (although some stratification exists with social status declining from the city center toward its periphery). Less crime, informality and marginality.	Sharp socio-spatial stratification; re-emergence of ghettoes of wealth and ghettoes of poverty; status begins to rise in the suburban periphery. Re-emergence of marginality (e.g., homelessness, poverty, prostitution); radical informality, illegality, chaos.
Aesthetic character	Grayness, monotony, boredom; dominance of "socialist realism" (similar to neo-classicism) in the 1950s; dominance of modernism from the 1960s through the 1980s.	Rejection of modernism; pluralism and importation of Western styles; post-modernism and "Las-Vegas-ization" of the built environment.

message – that of a defeated private and a triumphant public (Crowley and Reid 2002: 1–22).

Each of the key features of urbanism described above was grounded as much in socialist economic mechanisms as in ideological doctrine. The striking monumentality of public places was possible because socialist authorities (unlike their colleagues in capitalist nations) could operate without much concern about land values or property disputes. But spatial grandeur was also heavily ideologically loaded – it was the indisputable proof of the victory of the public over the private (Banerjee 2004). Not only were the magnificent civic spaces built at a scale dwarfing that of similar projects from the pre-socialist era, but they stood in the place of the hundreds of private structures that had preceded them. The land-use specificity of the socialist city – the pre-eminence of industrial over other uses – was rooted in the efforts of socialist states to outdo their capitalist rivals in heavy industry. These efforts led to systematic under-production of consumer goods and a scarcity of commercial spaces (Sýkora 1998; Hirt 2006, 2008b). But restricting commerce was also an ideological project of urban "de-marketization" (see, e.g., Häussermann 1996; Carter 1979). Commercial uses had a bourgeois flavor; they smelled of private profit. Not only did they decrease in number, but, in Bulgaria for example, they languished even linguistically: "commercial" buildings ceased to be part of the architectural vocabulary.[5] The painfully bland persona of socialist housing estates had an economic explanation: standardization was dictated by the need for economies of scale, and the open spaces between buildings were often calculated and laid out to ensure that the large cranes lifting the panels could maneuver – a fact which along all the other restrictions stemming from using a small variety of pre-made panels seriously undermined the ability of architects and planners to actually *design* places in the true sense of the word (Lizon 1996; Hirt 2007a).[6] Yet the estates were the spatial hallmark of socialist ideology: they conveyed with greatest clarity what was dearest to the socialist heart: the ideal of a victorious public. Private space came in the form of tiny flats.[7] Its plebian status was underscored by the colossal proportions of the open green commons and the shared spaces of the large residential buildings, where a collectivist spirit was expected to thrive. Uniformity of design and construction prevented individuals from expressing difference or deviating from the norm, thus strengthening the overarching message of commonality and collectivism.

The emphasis on public space is not unique to socialist housing. It is a typical feature of modernist design, as Holston (1987) eloquently demonstrated in his analysis of Brasília – a point I reiterate in the next chapter. What distinguished socialist projects was not so much their fundamental spatial principles but the vigor with which they were applied. A sense of the public's primacy was transmitted not only by endowing it with gargantuan proportions but also by limiting transitional, semi-private spaces. Privacy could not be suppressed altogether – the four walls of the small apartment guaranteed it. But in-between spaces where small-group socializing occurs – balconies, porches, yards, cafés, shops – were few and far between.[8]

The spatial morphology of the socialist districts – large towers amidst a sea of overtly common spaces, with semi-private spaces generally scarce – forced urban life into one of two categories: an unavoidable but diminished private, and a dominant, uncompromising public. The possibility of reversing the ratio between the two and creating viable in-between spaces was frowned upon. This is why suburban-type private homes and yards were seen as "bourgeois-fascist" in, say, Bulgarian urban planning textbooks from the 1950s and 1960s (e.g., Neikov and Samodumov 1952; also Hirt 2007a). Not only did suburban living reflect capitalist-style social segregation; it provided *too much* private space. The link between the spatial and the social was, for socialist planners, unmistakable. In labeling the 1934 Master Plan of Sofia "bourgeois-fascist," Lyben Tonev, the chief author of Sofia's socialist Master Plan from 1945 – explained the link in plain terms. The old plan envisioned too many family homes with yards, Tonev said, and "it is the yard that makes the bourgeois" (Tonev 1987 [1945], cited in Tangurov 2000; also Hirt 2007a).

Regime Change

In 1989, Eastern Europe entered a period of systemic transformation[9] – "rapid institutional change within an environment of insecurity, instability and rapid socio-economic polarization" (Enyedi 1992: 6, cited in Scott 2009: 26). Instead of a quick pathway to prosperous capitalism, the transformation fulfilled Keynes's (1933: 245) grim prediction from sixty-five years ago: "a transition will involve so much pure destruction of wealth that the new state of affairs will be, at first, far worse than the old." In fact, the crisis of the 1990s turned out to be deeper than that of the Great Depression. In the early to mid-1990s, GDP decreased by about 30% in most countries. Unemployment rates rose sharply and in some nations reached a quarter of the population, inflation approached or entered the triple digits, and inequality indexes increased significantly (Andrusz 1996; Hamilton 1999; UNECE 2006, Dobrinsky et al. 2006; Verhoeven 2007; Hirt and Stanilov 2009; Tables 3.2, 3.3, 3.4 and 3.5). The economic downturn was severely aggravated by years-long ethnic strife, the breakup of multi-national federations, and other forms of political conflict.

Table 3.2 Real GDP/capita purchasing power parity (PPP) in selected East European countries during the transition

Country	Real GDP/capita PPP (US$)					
	1986	1991	1996	2001	2006	2007
Bulgaria	6.127	4.813	4.241	6.800	10.300	11.310
Serbia	–	–	–	6.157	9.089	10.019
Slovenia	–	9.878	11.248	16.100	25.437	27.900
Czech Republic	9.842	7.812	11.329	15.100	22.258	25.087
Slovakia	–	–	8.058	11.600	17.880	20.275
Hungary	7.468	6.080	7.035	12.400	18.244	18.956
Poland	5.090	4.500	5.991	9.600	14.890	16.322
Romania	5.629	3.500	4.646	6.200	10.467	11.455

Sources: Tosics (2005) and IMF (2009). Table prepared by Krista Hailey.

Table 3.3 Unemployment rates in selected East European countries during the transition

Country	Unemployment (%)			
	1992	1997	2002	2007
Bulgaria	15.2	14.4	18.0	9.6
Serbia	–	25.6	26.0	31.6
Slovenia	7.8	6.9	6.3	4.9
Czech Republic	2.6	4.8	7.3	5.3
Slovakia	11.3	11.9	18.6	11.0
Hungary	12.3	9.0	5.8	7.4
Poland	13.6	10.9	17.0	14.9
Romania	8.4	5.3	9.1	6.1

Sources: Andrusz (1996), UNECE (2006), US CIA (2009) and IMF (2009). Table by Krista Hailey.

Table 3.4 Inflation rates in selected East European states during the transition

Country	Average inflation (annual % change)				
	1991	1996	2001	2006	2007
Bulgaria	333.5	123.0	7.4	7.4	7.6
Serbia	–	–	91.8	12.7	6.5
Slovenia	–	9.9	8.4	2.5	3.6
Czech Republic	56.6	8.8	4.7	2.5	2.9
Slovakia	–	5.8	7.2	4.3	1.9
Hungary	34.2	23.6	9.2	3.9	7.9
Poland	70.3	19.9	5.5	1.0	2.5
Romania	161.1	38.8	34.5	6.6	4.8

Source: IMF (2009). Table prepared by Krista Hailey.

Table 3.5   Gini coefficients of inequality in selected East European states during the transition

Country	*Gini coefficients of per capita income (x100)*				
	1987/90	*1993/94*	*1996/98*	*2000/02*	*2007/08*
Bulgaria	23	38	41	37	29.2
Serbia	–	–	–	–	30 (2003)
Slovenia	22	25	30	28	28.4
Czech Republic	19	23	25	27	25.4
Slovakia	20	18	-	28	25.8
Hungary	21	23	25	28	26.9
Poland	28	28	33	35	34.5
Romania	23	29	30	32	31.0

Source: Verhoeven (2007), UNDP (2008) and US CIA (2009). Table prepared by Krista Hailey.

The current global economic downturn aside, however, the post-2000 period has been marked by solid GDP growth rates and a return to stability, especially in the new European Union members in Central Europe and the Baltic region (Table 3.2). Yet it is clear that some of the most archetypical and negative aspects of the 1990s, including high poverty and crime rates,[10] are here to stay. Stark socio-economic polarization – between countries, within countries, between cities and within cities – is another enduring aspect of the post-socialist transformation, leading some to view it as a bifurcated transition: one that leads to First World-style and Third World-style capitalisms simultaneously (Hirt and Stanilov 2009; Stanilov 2007).

Bleak predictions aside, what have been the chief parameters of change in the post-1989 period? At the risk of ignoring the great diversity in the extent and timing of post-socialist reforms across Eastern Europe, one can assert that the transformation entailed abolishing the definitional societal characteristics of the old, socialist order. To begin with, state control over the economy was terminated. State subsidies were withdrawn and prices liberalized, national economies were opened to global competition, and market forces became the chief mechanism of resource allocation. Vast amounts of land, property and means of production were restituted or privatized, and the private sector's share of GDP rose dramatically (in Bulgaria, for example, 75% of state property was sold by 2000, and the private sector share of GDP grew from 9% in 1990 to 75% in 2005; Yoveva et al. 2003). The single-party model was replaced by political pluralism.[11] Many of the technologically obsolete plants from the socialist era went bankrupt and were sold in pieces under various privatization schemes, thus reducing the dependency of East European economies on heavy manufacturing and contributing to the fast growth of the tertiary sector. Centralized economic planning was eliminated and most planning functions given to lower-level government tiers. The latter was part of a broader transfer of powers and functions (although not necessarily funding) from the state to a growing number of municipal and regional authorities,[12] as well as other sub-state actors (see, e.g., Andrusz et al. 1996; Tsenkova and Nedović-Budić 2006).

Although the above-listed parameters of social change could be classified as "internal" (i.e., they were nominally initiated by actors within the individual East European nations; Tosics 2005), they are embedded into and "mirror" the complex of transformations linked with globalization (Sýkora 1994): de-industrialization and post-Fordist economic restructuring (Amin 1994); post-Keynesian, post-welfare-state shrinkage of the public sector and concomitant sharpened social polarization (Bennet 1990; Fainstein et al. 1992; Marcuse and Van Kempen 2000, 2002); the growing influence of transnational capital and institutions, etc. It may be obvious, yet it is nonetheless important to reiterate that the collapse of the Eastern bloc was, after all, an exercise in the global spread of capitalism (Giddens 2006: 57); in fact, from the viewpoint of multinational capital, the Berlin Wall was but a barrier to trade and investment (Grabher 1997: 112, cited in Scott 2009: 64).

The Post-socialist City

The fundamental socio-economic and political transformation that followed the collapse of socialist regimes inevitably altered the chief mechanisms of city-building (Pickles and Smith 1998). The following features of the transformation were especially important for cities: the return of market mechanisms and the re-commoditization of space, change of ownership patterns, a shift of control from state to local levels, a sharp increase in the number of actors participating in city-building, and a fundamentally changed role for planning (e.g., Węcławowicz 2002). All of them entailed some reduction or scaling back of public-sector assets, powers, duties and responsibilities, and their shift to private parties. In Bodnar's words (2001:10), privatization was the leitmotif of the post-socialist period. It permeated all aspects of the urban realm, including housing, transport, and public space. Existing housing became the target of particularly vehement privatization in most countries (Clapham et al. 1996; in Bulgaria of course the percentage of privately owned apartments was already high,

84%, as noted in the previous chapter). Simultaneously, the public sector withdrew from the production and distribution of new housing. As a result, many East European states have private homeownership rates of about 90%[13] – a figure that dwarfs the meager 67% in the so-called "nation of homeowners," the United States. Disinvestment in public infrastructure (coupled with the East European public's newfound love of the automobile) brought about a sharp decrease in urban trips carried by mass transit, from 80–90% in the late 1980s to 50% in recent years; meanwhile, the number of private cars per person nearly tripled.[14] The legal environment also altered dramatically: new ownership patterns and laws were contradictory, especially in the 1990s, leading many of the new, private city-builders to simply ignore them (see, e.g., Nientied 1998; Hirt and Stanilov 2009). This behavior was aided by popular contempt toward public controls over urban space altogether – a condition termed the "legitimacy crisis" of public planning (Maier 1994, 1998; Nedović-Budić 2001; Hirt 2005a).

The cumulative spatial product of these forces has generally been referred to as the *transitional* or *post-socialist city*. Both terms are problematic and invite questions similar to those emerging from the debate on the socialist city. For example: what is post-socialism; is it a transition toward capitalism, or does it have its own logic (see, e.g., Stark 1996)? Is the term "transition" even meaningful (since it implies a known start and a known endpoint; Wu 2003; Tsenkova and Nedović-Budić 2006)?[15] And even if it is, are East European cities indeed "transitioning" into "standard" capitalist cities (see, e.g., Sýkora 1994)? Furthermore, given the vast disparities that have developed between East European countries since 1989, is there a single post-socialist city, or are there multiple sub-types (see, e.g., Tosics 2005)? Answers to these questions are ambiguous at best. Still, there is some scholarly consensus on the spatial evolution of the post-1989 East European city. I will review this evolution along the five aspects of urban structure discussed earlier (Table 3.1).

First, today's East European cities are neither compact nor defined by a clear edge. Low-density urban decentralization may have been the most notable process of post-socialist urban change (Stanilov and Sýkora forthcoming). Enabled by a complex set of legal, economic and cultural factors, suburbanization has been documented in many large cities (see, e.g., Ruoppila 1998 and Tammaru et al. 2007 on Tallinn; Kok and Kovacs 1999 and Dingsdale 1999 on Budapest; Sýkora 1999a, 1999b and Novak and Sýkora 2007 on Prague; Valkanov 2006 and Hirt 2007b, 2008b on Sofia; Nuissl and Rink 2005 on Leipzig; Rudolph and Brade 2005 on Moscow; Brade et al. 2009 on multiple cities in Eastern Europe). In fact, cities in many East European countries (e.g., Estonia, Latvia, Croatia, Slovakia, Poland,

Hungary and Bulgaria) are currently sprawling at rates far exceeding those in Western Europe (EEA 2006a, 2006b).

A second aspect of change was the dramatic decrease in the scale of civic developments. Although large-scale projects were erected, these were typically commercial mega-schemes, of which the Berlin's Potsdamer Platz is perhaps the most remarkable case. Few examples of large new public parks, squares and other civic spaces can be given. On the contrary, a typical feature of post-socialist development has been the aggressive appropriation of public plazas for private uses (see, e.g., Bodnar 2001 on Budapest's Moscow Square; also Stanilov 2007). Another feature is the sharp decrease of public green space – in small gardens and playgrounds in the old urban neighborhoods, in the open spaces in the socialist housing districts, and in once lush metropolitan parks and greenbelts. Moscow, for example, lost about 750 hectares of forests in its greenbelt between 1991 and 2001. During the same time period, forests in the metropolis declined by 15% and grass areas shrunk by 55%, whereas impervious surface increased by 26% (Boentje and Blinnikov 2007).

Simultaneously, the scale of housing development decreased as well, especially during the crisis-stricken 1990s. Not only did sheer housing output nosedive,[16] but the very character of new housing changed. As mass housing was no longer constructed, the popularity of the single-family home as a residential alternative sharply increased.[17] In addition, the re-emergence of land and real estate markets and the termination of government policies targeting housing egalitarianism, including the lifting of restrictions on residential mobility, led to the reintroduction of starker residential segregation into the urban fabric – the type of segregation that socialism had partially mitigated. The process has been well documented in several cities such as Budapest (Kovacs 1998; Dingsdale 1999), Prague (Sýkora 1999a, 1999b), and Tallinn (see, e.g., Ruoppila and Kährik 2003; Ruoppila 2005). To an extent, socio-spatial differentiation has followed historic, pre-socialist lines of division, but new enclaves of wealth and poverty have been emerging as well (e.g., *nouveau riche* areas in formerly green-field areas, and new concentrations of poverty in some of the socialist districts and in new informal peri-urban settlements).

The functional balance of East European cities evolved significantly as well. The decline in public and residential uses was accompanied by a much sharper reduction in industrial uses: vast chunks of old industrial enterprises in central urban areas became derelict.[18] Commercial uses, in contrast, skyrocketed. For instance, the number of retail spaces quadrupled, even in Belgrade, where economic growth has been lagging because of Serbia's wars, isolation and economic meltdown during the 1990s (Hirt 2008b). The scale of retail has, however, shifted over time: from small, informal spaces during the 1990s (e.g., kiosks, remodeled garages, and even apartments, entries and hallways converted to retail in old residential buildings; Figure 3.3) to much larger premises such as Western-style suburban malls and hypermarkets (e.g., Blau and Rupnik 2007 on Zagreb).[19] Along with poverty and marginality (e.g., homelessness and prostitution – the kind of behaviors that socialism suppressed), urban informality, spontaneity and illegality became the hallmarks of the transition. In the poorer nations of the Balkans, informality took the form not only of self-styled building additions, renovations and individual homes, but also of whole new neighborhoods. In Tirana, an estimated 25% of new dwellings were erected without building permits during the early to mid-1990s. In Belgrade, the figure reached 50% in 1997 thus making illegality the new norm (Nientied 1998; Vujović and Petrović 2007; Figures 3.4 and 3.5). The overwhelming feel of disorder often reported by visitors to East European cities was exacerbated by a wild mix of new decorations (signs, logos, graffiti; Figure 3.6) that appeared on existing buildings, and a "masked ball" of new (and revamped historic)

Figure 3.3 Kaleidoscopic mini-shops have moved into the entry halls and the ground-floor apartments of this concrete socialist-era residential tower in Belgrade, adding a new layer of color and spontaneity.

Figure 3.4 Private solutions: color and spontaneity become the new norm in Padina, a large neighborhood erected in Belgrade during the 1990s. The neighborhood buildings and infrastructure, which are known for their avowed eclecticism, have one common feature – they were all built illegally. The new Master Plan of Belgrade has proposed Padina's legalization, regardless of the many violations in building and planning codes throughout its built fabric.

architectural styles, many of them imported, that came to replace socialist-era monotony (Sármány-Parsons 1998: 222).

In short, the post-socialist urban change entailed the dissolution of the key features of socialist urbanism: (1) the end of compact spatial form; (2) a decrease in the scale of civic and residential spaces (including a shift toward individual dwellings); (3) a tilting of the land-use balance away from public (and industrial) and toward commercial uses; (4) an emergence of stark social contrasts, informality and marginality; and (5) the end of visual uniformity and the advent of a free mixing of styles. The overarching theme, however, is the stark increase in differences (social, functional and aesthetic) and the decline of commonality and publicness – public ownership, public uses, public services and public space. The post-socialist city is, then, in some sense a post-public city. It is a city in which publicness is perpetually undermined by new practices of private usurpation, withdrawal and partition or, as I call them, spatial secessions.

Figure 3.5 More color and spontaneity, this time Tirana style. This photograph shows the largest informal residential settlement on the outskirts of the Albanian capital. Photo by Sasha Tsenkova.

Figure 3.6 A Bucharest of billboards: a BUSINESS advertisement decorates this socialist-era residential building in the vicinity of the city center. Photo by Augustin Ioan.

Iron Curtains in the Post-socialist City:
A Typology of Spatial Secessions

Cities throughout history have always been divided (Marcuse 2002; Low 2003; Kostof 1991).[20] There are no "borderless cities," let alone "borderless worlds."[21] All cities have lines of disjuncture; only the types and causes of disjuncture vary. Like others, socialist cities had their own partitions – areas of relative wealth and relative poverty, which were separated by subtle and not-so-subtle borders (the gated and guarded government compounds being the most notorious example of rigid borders). The socialist partitions were, though, arguably fewer. Post-socialist cities have different and starker partitions than their predecessors; what are they? Answering this question might require writing several books, so I will stick to a particular form of partitioning that I term *spatial secession*.

Spatial secession is the willful act of disjoining, disassociating, or carving space for oneself from the urban commons.[22] Here is an incomplete list of mutually overlapping spatial secessions. All of them are customary in post-socialist cities, especially in Southeast Europe, and I will revisit them in various combinations in the later chapters of this study.

Spatial seizure

This is the act of appropriating public space for private uses as a result of the post-socialist re-commoditization of space. It can entail activities such as building permanent structures in formerly public spaces (greenfields, parks, forests, gardens, playgrounds, etc.), placing temporary structures (kiosks, booths, stands) in public squares or streets, and paving green space for private parking. The motive is generally private profit.[23] Spatial seizure can be done legally (land in the urban periphery is usually formally privatized prior to development) or illegally (building in parks is rarely permitted but it happens anyway, at least in the Balkans). Often, it is accompanied by the physical enclosure of the newly acquired land.

Spatial seclusion

This is the act of separating from the city through distance. The classic example is urban decentralization or suburbanization. The process has a rich history in the Western world: it originated in eighteenth-century England (Fishman 1987) but reached its climax in twentieth-century America (Jackson 1985). The roots of suburbanization are very complex.[24] Yet, there is little doubt that the aspirations of the upper classes (and, later, the middle classes) to escape urban density and chaos (as well as the urban poor and ethnic minorities) and settle in private green settings have historically been among the chief driving forces of suburbanization. The process seems to have found exceptionally fertile ground in contemporary Eastern Europe (EEA 2006a, 2006b; Stanilov and Sýkora forthcoming).

Spatial exclusion

Spatial seclusion and exclusion are deeply intertwined. Residential suburbs, which are beyond the reach of large segments of the population (because, for example, of their high housing values and the lack of mass transit options), are spaces of both seclusion and exclusion. A vast body of literature on class, ethnic and racial exclusion in the suburbs, especially in the American metropolis, has proven this point beyond doubt (e.g., Fishman 1987; Hayden 2004). Exclusion can also be enforced in non-residential spaces, both urban and suburban. For example, office complexes, private clubs, entertainment facilities and malls – all of which now exist in Eastern Europe – restrict public access via a variety of mechanisms: price, membership, security devices, etc.

Spatial enclosure

This is perhaps the most brutal way of seceding – by erecting formidable physical barriers and reinforcing them with multiple methods of restricting outsiders' access: video cameras, alarm systems, guards, etc. Enclosure is a step up in the hierarchy of simultaneous seclusion and exclusion (Low 2003). The paradigmatic examples of enclosure are gated communities, which have proliferated around the world (see, e.g., Webster et al. 2002; Glasze et al. 2006) including in Eastern Europe.[25] There are, however, many other examples. Malls – the contemporary alternative to the traditional main street – are also, ostensibly, walled off. They turn a blank façade to the outside, but have richly decorated interiors. They also enforce many rules that prohibit the free range of behaviors permissible on a public street or square (Ellin 1997; Figures 3.7 and 3.8). Gated office or entertainment complexes, as well as fenced-off streets and other open spaces, fit into the same category.

Statutory secession

This is the widespread process of violating public planning and building statutes following from the post-1989 "legitimacy crisis" of urban planning and regulation. It is part of the paradigmatic shift toward informality in East European city-building. Many acts of spatial seizure fit into this category, such as unauthorized physical or functional remodeling of existing buildings (even adding entire new floors), and construction of new structures or entire new communities either without a permit or in partial violation of

Figure 3.7 Belgrade's most famous downtown street, Knez Mihajlova (Prince Michael's). Full of crowds, shops, cafes, restaurants, offices, street vendors and street entertainers, Knez Mihajlova is easily one of the most vibrant and pedestrian-friendly traditional main streets in all of Europe.

a permit (exceeding density regulations, ignoring regulations for providing green space, etc.). Although these strategies are common in many parts of the world and are typically linked to urban poverty, in large Balkan cities such as Belgrade, Bucharest, Skopje, Sofia and Tirana they are practiced widely, even by urban elites, with the purpose of preying on public infrastructure and deriving private profit (Hirt and Stanilov 2009).

Stylistic secession

This is the "masked ball" of architectural styles that I mentioned earlier. Even though there is of course plenty of *good* architecture throughout Eastern Europe today, to say that post-socialist aesthetics has moved decisively toward the bizarre (or perhaps the *bazaar*) is not an overstatement. The colorful new cocktail of styles includes just about everything that fits under the post-modern umbrella in Western Europe and the United States and sometimes even goes beyond it. Some downtowns[26] and tourist districts[27] have applied the Las Vegas approach to architectural time-space compression (i.e., borrowing

Figure 3.8 Knez Mihajlova's alternative – the newest mall in Belgrade. This mega-structure, which turns a blank façade to the main street, is surrounded by enormous parking lots. Gregory Andrusz (2006) recently coined the post-socialist metamorphosis in the catchy metaphor "from wall to mall," perhaps neglecting the rather obvious point that the mall is a wall.

details from various periods and cultures, and thus retelling the world's architectural history in short). Affluent new suburban areas are especially keen on the aesthetic shock-and-awe effect. Writing about her hometown, Sármány-Parsons (1998: 221) described this trait bluntly as an architecture marked by a "particular disorientation of taste, which is not surprising to those familiar with the background of the Budapest *nouveaux riches.*" Aesthetic judgment aside, however, the goal of much new architecture seems to be precisely disjuncture, secession and partition, temporal (from socialist-era discipline) and spatial (from the public street).

Iron Curtains in the Post-socialist City: Some Reflections

If we accept that post-socialist cities are exhibiting increased levels of privatization and partitioning, the logical question is, of course, why? We need to consider this question in at least two ways. First, we must address it in global terms: if it is true that cities are always partitioned, why is partitioning more common, why are partitions more solid, and why is public space more aggressively privatized in certain historical and geographical contexts than in others? More importantly for my purposes, are contemporary cities particularly poignant examples of such privatization and partitioning; if so, why? Second, we must address the question in local or regional terms; that is, how do general explanations apply to post-socialist cities?

Stark devaluation of urban public spaces and aggressive partitioning seem to develop in societies undergoing major change, instability and upheaval. The transition from feudalism to capitalism, for example, was marked in spatial terms by a growth of enclosures (Bodnar 2001). Rapidly growing social stratification appears to be a major contributor to the phenomenon. As Low (2003) points out, during Europe's "long sixteenth century" (1450–1600), as poverty and polarization dramatically increased, so did elites' fears of social disorder; these trends led to various restrictions on public behavior and the hardening of barriers separating rich from poor. Early capitalism produced a myriad of spatial privatization and separation techniques, including the cul-de-sac, the suburb, and the bourgeois gated enclave, which served to protect its residents from the dreadful (and socially mixed) urbanism of industrial England, France and, later, America (Atkins 1993; Blakely and Snyder 1997; Low 2003). Of course, urban divisions may not have softened much through the nineteenth and twentieth centuries. Still, the commitment of the liberal bourgeois state (and later on, the socialist state) to advance some form of mass social welfare was reflected in various modernist ideals for cities rich in public space (I return to these in the next chapter). This in turn led to the unparalleled construction of explicitly public spaces (e.g., social housing, and public parks, boulevards, plazas and other places of collective consumption), where resources could be shared and diverse needs met, at least to some extent.

If this is the case, does the contemporary era reverse this modern trend? Is the new trend one of a decomposing "public city" (Watson, S. 2002), of an "implosion of modern public life" (Caldeira 2000: 297)? Evidence supporting this claim has been put forward from just about every world region. In Marcuse and Van Kempen's (2000, 2002) assessment, a "new spatial order" is emerging, an order that entails the perpetual devaluation of urban public spaces and produces urban forms in which "boundaries between divisions reflected in social and physical walls are increasing" and the "boundaries themselves are hardening" (2000: 3). From a macro-perspective, globalization is likely the major structural cause underlying increased divisions in cities (see, e.g., Fainstein et al. 1992). This is the case because globalization leads to a strengthened hand for capital and a diminished position for labor. It also reduces the state's ability (financial and otherwise) to provide public amenities, including space, thus leading to starker contrasts between the haves and the have-nots. Intensifying social polarization then leads elites to form heavily securitized or "militarized" spaces (Davis 1990, 1992), such as citadels and gated enclaves, ostensibly to protect themselves from crime and other "undesirable behaviors." At the same time, the poor are driven further into ghettoes.[28] While there is some agreement regarding the importance of globalization as meta-explanation, different scholars have put different emphases on the various factors that may underpin declining urban publicness.[29] For example, whereas some stress the primary role of economic restructuring (e.g., Fainstein et al. 1992), others argue that the neo-liberal state has been a dominant force in the creation and solidification of urban divisions (e.g., Marcuse and Van Kempen 2002). These debates are very visible in the literature on the global proliferation of gated communities – arguably, the modern-day culmination of urban partitioning and a main contributor to the erosion of public space in cities worldwide. Much of the literature on these communities, like the literature on other types of spatial privatization, is positioned within political economy theory. The role of capital (banks, firms, developers, etc.) has been discussed extensively, and the evidence clearly shows that gates tend to flourish precisely in contexts where severe social and economic contrasts exist, such as the United States, Latin America (see, e.g., Blakely and Snyder 1997; Caldeira 2000; Salcedo and Torres 2004; Manzi and Smith-Bowers 2005; Coy 2006; Webster and Glasze 2006; Sheinbaum 2008) and, recently, post-socialist Eurasia (see, e.g., Miao 2003).[30] State institutions have also proven complicit, for example by failing to provide security and services and by restricting funding for social housing. In some cases, governments have actively promoted gating to derive profit (see, e.g., Libertun De Duren 2006).

Cultural, behaviorally based explanations[31] of contemporary spatial privatization practices represent another branch of the literature. Regarding walled communities, anthropologists such as Caldeira (2000) and Low (2001, 2003) have suggested that gating is not necessarily a response to "objective" conditions, such as rising crime in socially polarized cities, and gates are not simply the result of people's desire for self-protection. Rather, gating may in fact intensify when crime decreases (i.e., when there is not simply crime, but "talk of crime," as a way of "ordering the world"; Caldeira 2000). In this sense, gated communities are essentially cultural, symbolic landscapes (Raposo 2006) serving to assert privilege and separation from urban commonality. In this interpretation, gating is the result of cultural impulses that ultimately affect the way in which people experience public spaces in everyday life (Caldeira 2000). These impulses are fed by various media and advertising "discourses of fear" that paint cities as inferior and dangerous places. Working in this tradition, urban design theorists such as Ellin (1996, 1997) define a broader condition of "urban escapism" or retreatism[32] – an umbrella cultural notion leading to a rich variety of contemporary urban and architectural trends whose collective outcome is the progressive depreciation of public space. Gated enclaves are just a part of this story; other parts include the ever-popular suburban ideal for a private home far from the city, the recent turn in architecture toward creating fantasy worlds devoid of local context (i.e., the architecture that "learns" from Las Vegas and Disneyland), and the recent trend in urban design toward building fancy new communities featuring an assortment of nearly perfect pseudo-historic *old-towne* charms: white picket fences, candy shops, town clocks, old-world bakeries, etc. (In the United States, these communities are known as New Urbanism, yet in my view they bear a strange similarity to Havel's romantic vision of a would-be Prague and its main streets, each with two bakeries, two sweet-shops, and two pubs, all of them private, plus the family houses, the villas, and of course the feeling of a private home.) Citing cultural theorists like Richard Sennett and Jerome Binde, Ellin points out that contemporary urbanism retreats from the larger community. It reflects a trend of inwardness and self-absorption, a newly sharpened focus on the individual, the family, the home, the small, the secure, and the interior, in opposition to a public world of uncertainty and failed ideals of collective progress. The concept is clearly a close relative of privatism as I define it, although, as I argued in the previous chapter, the post-socialist version may be starker.

How does this all apply to the post-socialist city and its spatial secessions? In my view, the post-socialist city offers a "perfect storm" of urban privatization prerequisites. Post-socialist societies are societies whose economic and institutional order collapsed abruptly under the powers of globalizing capitalism. Once relatively egalitarian, they have stratified very quickly, now comprising large impoverished masses and small classes of new capitalists (many, like the world-famous "New Russians" with rich connections to either the mafia or the public sector, or both). They are also marked by high levels of crime, instability and often outright lawlessness (with some exceptions, mostly in Central Europe). These societies are also characterized by an aggressive private sector, which acquired formerly public assets with record speed and is only minimally deterred by public regulation. The public sector, whose funds, powers and will to provide social services and safety nets have been dramatically reduced, has been dominated at best by ideologues deeply committed to its near-dissolution and at worst by "non-ideologues" who sought to use it as a source of private profit. Like other contemporary spatial privatizations, post-socialism's spatial secessions are doubtlessly embedded in capitalism's ongoing competition for and conquest of space as a profit-yielding commodity, as any good urban economist would tell us (e.g., Logan and Molotch 1987). Political conditions matter too: in post-socialism, this spatial conquest tends to appear in an especially raw form because it operates in an environment of limited state intervention (and often with state encouragement). I have little doubt that secessions would occur because of these economic and institutional conditions alone. But there is something more to them, I argue. The post-socialist spatial secessions are so condensed in time and so radical in consequence that they make urban privatizations in "normal" Western capitalist countries look a bit amateurish. Can one find a city anywhere in the Western world in which 30% of the public green space has vanished in fifteen years, as in Sofia? Does one commonly see entire large residential subdivisions being constructed in public parks in either Lisbon or Los Angeles? Is it routine to convert public playgrounds into paid parking in Paris? Does one find over there new neighborhoods in which about nine out of ten fancy homes are hidden behind tall walls? Does one see entire sidewalks taken over by such walls? Does one see vodka billboards covering the front façades of a nation's finest civic buildings, say the Louvre or the French Academy of Sciences? This type of radical urban unraveling may be happening in other parts of the world, but it is harder to find in the "established democracies" of Western Europe and North America – ostensibly the type of societies that the post-socialist "transition" was to lead toward. For this type of radical unraveling to occur, I think it takes a particular mass mindset, whether we call it retreatism, public nihilism, privatism or something else, a mindset that is deeply skeptical of publicness generally – public goals, public rights, public spaces. It is the mindset that pursues the perpetual decomposition of urban commonality not only with impunity but also without regrets ("Let's kill the playground, why not? Everyone does it"). And it takes also the conviction that Victor shared in the previous chapter: nothing can be done about it, so why bother? I think the most obvious of the spatial secessions in post-socialist Sofia would not have occurred if there had been a strong civil society, if many people thought that the public spaces could have or should have been defended. One way of reformulating the original thesis that privatism expresses itself in space is to say that the lack of a strong civic society (i.e., the shortage of social capital) has led in Sofia to the depletion of spatial capital – the city's collective spaces. Over time, spatial secessionist practices attained such an air of banality and ordinariness that they became the social norm, to the point that they endowed unregulated, ravaging post-socialist-type capitalism with the very legitimacy that allows it to go on.

Post-socialist urbanism looks fragmented, mosaic and chaotic – nothing like the disciplined whole that the old regimes could muster. It is perhaps much harder to make sense of because it is "produced by myriad individual decision-makers with contrasting interests and purposes in a multi-scalar renegotiation of places" (Dingsdale 2001: 176). But post-socialist urbanism is not unplanned (except in the most rudimentary sense; i.e., that it is not planned by state planners).[33] There is a clear logic to it that follows the rules of the game – economic, political and cultural – that seem to produce spaces with an exceptional proclivity toward appropriation, differentiation and bounding: curtains, not commons.

Notes

1 The issue becomes even more complicated if we consider the vast differences in the socialist political economy (and thus in spatial outcomes) across the Eastern bloc and the fact that socialism was not a monolithic period. The differences between Stalin's and Khrushchev's eras in the Soviet Union are an obvious example: not only did economic and political practices evolve but city-building processes, building technologies and even architectural styles changed as well (e.g., grand neo-classical public spaces were the hallmark of the Stalin's period, whereas Khrushchev focused predominately on standardized housing).

2 Under-urbanization (i.e., a relatively low proportion of residents living in cities) is also a typical feature of the socialist model, as the authors cited in the previous paragraphs have noted. Since I focus on the characteristics of urban structure (rather than those of the urban system), I do not discuss under-urbanization here.

3 E.g., St. Petersburg's industrial lands comprised 44% of its total area, Moscow's were 32% and Cracow's were 28% (as compared to about 5% in London and Paris).

4 In the more liberal socialist states like Poland and Yugoslavia, private ownership of means of production was allowed under certain restrictions.

5 Since commerce during socialism was conducted under state auspices, it was considered a public activity that was conducted in public buildings (*obshtestveni sgradi*). The old term "commercial buildings" (*turgovski sgradi*) was rarely used. Thus, the University of Architecture in Sofia had faculties specializing in the design of residential, public and industrial buildings, but none specializing in commercial buildings. The lack of formal recognition of commercial buildings has persisted until today, although recent discussions in magazines and among architectural faculty have introduced the topic for debate. As one architectural educator recently wondered: What is public about a commercial center?

6 The architecture of the socialist estates was clearly inspired by the creative advances of early-twentieth-century modernism, which were taught extensively in the architectural academies. In some of the more open countries (Yugoslavia comes to mind), this creative spirit arguably went on. In poorer and more orthodox socialist societies such as Bulgaria and Romania, however, the poor quality and limited variety of the industrialized panels severely restricted design possibilities until the 1980s, when some design experimentation began to gain speed.

7 In 1991, the average dwelling space in Sofia and in Bucharest was 14 sq m per person – much lower than in any West European country. Naturally, this had much to do with lower living standards. However, the figure even for Greece, which was not much wealthier at the time, was twice as great – 29 sq m per person (EUROSTAT, undated).

8   This applies to a lesser extent to countries governed by relatively liberal socialist regimes. For example, socialist housing districts in the Yugoslav capital of Belgrade were not only better supplied with commercial services, but also exhibited various experiments with semi-private yards and spaces in the 1980s (Hirt 2008a, 2009a).

9   Some East European countries, most notably Yugoslavia and Hungary, entered a period of transition to "market socialism" in the 1980s (e.g., Tosics 2005). Still, 1989 remains the threshold year for the region as a whole.

10 For example, Russia's murder rate increased from 9.4 per 100,000 persons in 1990 to 21.7 in 1995. It dipped slightly between 1996 and 1998, but began to rise again after 2000 and was estimated at between 18.9 and 29.7 per 100,000 persons in 2004. Today, Russia has one of highest murder rates in the world. Crime rates are also very high throughout most of the former Soviet Union. It is notable, though, that in most East European countries – unlike those in the former Soviet Union – crime rates have leveled off or slightly declined since about 2000. Still, they continue to significantly exceed those in Western Europe (United Nations Office on Drugs and Crime 2004; UN-HABITAT 2005).

11 It remains up for debate, however, how this pluralism functions in the context of strong traditions of top-down governance, corruption and other measures of a democratic deficit (see, e.g., Maier 1994, 1998; Pagonis and Thornley 2000; Bozoki 2003; Iyer 2003; Hirt 2005a; Tworzecki 2008).

12 In the 1990s, the number of municipal governments in the Czech Republic and Hungary doubled; in Slovenia and Bulgaria, it more than doubled (Tosics 2005).

13 Bulgaria's high percentage of private homeownership (84%) during socialism was an exception. Elsewhere, the percentage was significantly lower: 26% in Russia, 42% in Poland, 46% in the Czech lands, 56% in Slovakia, and 75% in Hungary (Clapham et al. 1996).

14 During the first fifteen years of the transition, the number of cars per 1,000 people rose from 119 to 314 in Bulgaria, from 200 to 373 in the Czech Republic, from 114 to 350 in Estonia, from 136 to 290 in Hungary, from 83 to 297 in Latvia, and from 99 to 314 in Poland (EUROSTAT, undated; also Hirt and Stanilov 2009).

15 Common wisdom has long resolved these complex teleological questions: one of the most popular jokes throughout Eastern Europe in the 1980s was that socialism is the longest way from capitalism to capitalism.

16 In Czechoslovakia, for instance, the average number of new dwelling units per year was 50,000 during the 1980s, but only 7,500 in 1993. By now, however, annual housing output in most Central European countries has rebounded to its pre-1989 levels (Stanilov 2007).

17 In Estonia, for example, the number of single-family dwelling units increased fivefold between 1990 and 2002 (Stanilov 2007: 184).

18 By 2000 or so, such dilapidated areas reached approximately 30% of the industrial land in Budapest and Warsaw and 40% in Bratislava (EAUE 2003; also Hirt and Stanilov 2009).

19 It is somewhat ironic that Havel's romantic vision that "every main street will have at least two bakeries, two sweet-shops, two pubs, and many other small

shops, all privately owned and independent" was overrun by malls and hyper-markets – all private, but none independent.

20 Marcuse (2002) offers a concise history of walling and other divisions in cities, which I will not repeat here.

21 My apologies here to Ohmae (1990).

22 To paraphrase Simmel, secession is "an interaction between two parties, one of which leaves" (Simmel and Wolff 1964: 119).

23 Building squatter settlements on public lands could also qualify as "seizure." However, since its purpose is not private profit but survival, I do not include it here.

24 Literature on the causes and origins of suburbanization is immense. I will address it in greater depth in Chapter 6.

25 There are specific theories explaining the current popularity of gated residential communities, which I will refer to in the following sections and chapters.

26 There is very significant variation across countries and within countries in this respect. Prague, for example, applies relatively strict design and planning standards for its acclaimed historic center; architectural abuses there have been relatively rare. Many Balkan cities including Sofia, however, do not have such standards.

27 This statement too should be applied with caution. Landmark tourist centers like Croatia's Dubrovnik have been relatively immune from rampant architectural abuse, again because of stricter planning and regulation. There are some historic cities and districts in Bulgaria too, which have been relatively well protected. What I refer to here, though, are the types of sights one finds in central Sofia: casinos decorated with Roman soldiers near Irish pubs adorned with plastic green leaves (see also Chapter 9). Other examples include Bulgarian villages, which now attract English "eco-tourists." Local authorities there have felt compelled to make the tourists feel at home by decorating buildings in the Tudor style.

28 Marcuse and Van Kempen (2000) refer to the following formations of socio-spatial division in globalizing cities: enclaves of the super-rich in expensive downtown locations, gentrified areas in older urban neighborhoods, middle-class suburbs, working-class tenement areas, ethnic enclaves, and excluded ghettoes (see also Marcuse 2006).

29 I cannot cover the complexity of this rich literature here. For a good summary of the various academic approaches (ecological, neo-Marxist, neo-Weberian, etc.), see Van Kempen and Özüekren (1998) and Van Kempen (2002).

30 This is a small sampling of the literature on gated communities. I will revisit it in greater depth in Chapter 8.

31 I discuss demand-side, behavioral explanations for the spread of gated communities in greater depth in Chapters 7 and 8.

32 Similar themes are discussed by several other authors writing on contemporary urban design (e.g., Loukaitou-Sideris and Banerjee 1998).

33 I agree here with Holston (1987: 125): "Like any other domain of cultural activity, architecture is not unplanned. There is no such thing, therefore, as the organic or spontaneous city. Those cities which do not result from planners' decisions are only in the narrowest sense unplanned. They are not unordered or even unthought."

4

Post-modern Urbanism Revisited

"Throughout its history, communism was modernity's most devout, vigorous and gallant champion – pious to the point of simplicity. It also claimed to be its only true champion ... it was under communist, not capitalist, auspices that the audacious dream of modernity, freed from obstacles by the merciless and omnipotent state, was pushed to its radical limits: grand designs, unlimited social engineering, huge and bulky technology, total transformation of nature."

Zygmunt Bauman, 1991

In this chapter, I ask whether post-socialist urbanism is a variant of post-modern urbanism – a concept of paradigmatic urban change that has been applied almost exclusively to "threshold" Western cities such as Los Angeles (see, e.g., Jencks 1993; Dear 2000). Is post-socialist urban transformation related to the well-documented processes of contemporary global urban restructuring, whether labeled post-industrial, post-Fordist, or post-modern? Or is it grounded in local historic and geographic continuities and thus autonomous from them? Further, if post-socialist and post-modern urban restructuring are inherently related, does this suggest that the end of socialism was a variant of an imploding Western modernity (Bodnar 2001)? Does it indicate that post-socialism in Eastern Europe and post-modern-ism[1] as an ostensibly new epoch in global development have an "elective affinity" for each other (Kumar 1995)? These questions are not tangential to any debate on privatism and urbanism. On the contrary, the "rise of the public" as discussed in Chapter 2 coincides both temporally and con-ceptually with the rise of Western Enlightenment–Modern thought. Post-modernism, as a societal stage, a cultural-epistemological shift or a type of architecture and urbanism,[2] is inherently related to privatization – the

Iron Curtains, First Edition. Sonia A. Hirt.
© 2012 John Wiley & Sons, Ltd. Published 2012 by John Wiley & Sons, Ltd.

reduction of public assets, the decline of ideologies centered on beliefs in collective emancipation and, ultimately, spatial fragmentation and the decline of urban publicness (e.g., Harvey 1989a; Jameson 1991; Loukaitou-Sideris and Banerjee 1998).

Like post-modernity, post-modern urbanism has inspired intense debate in the literature over the last quarter of a century.[3] While some declare it a new model of urban development that marks a clean break with the modern past (e.g., Relph 1987; Dear 2000), others label it a mere shift in façades rather than foundations – a shift of "all sail, no anchor" that leaves the basic structural elements of the modernist city intact (see, e.g., Harvey 1989a; Lewis 2003). Either way, though, the concept has been analyzed almost exclusively in Western (especially US) cities with the presumption that the cities of the "less developed" world, including those of post-socialist Eastern Europe, would follow in the footsteps of the Western avant-garde.[4] My take on this is quite the opposite. I argue that post-modern urbanism is on an equal if not stronger footing right there in the post-socialist East, where, many scholars believe, modernism came to an end. Like Robinson (2006), then, I seek to question the privileged relationship of Western cities with modernity (and post-modernity, for that matter).

(Post-)socialism, (Post-)modernity

The thesis that the fold of East European socialism marked the death of Western modernity is not new. Bauman (1992: xxv) called socialism's end the "last nail in the coffin" of "modern ambition." This thesis follows from another: that state socialism and its ideological basis, scientific communism, were unequivocally embedded in Western, Enlightenment–modern thought (e.g., Scott 1998; Inglehart 1997). Marx, Engels and Lenin did not hesitate to position themselves as heirs to the Enlightenment intellectual tradition (as followers of Comte and Owen, for example), and the point certainly did not escape a long series of thinkers like Polanyi (1967 [1944]), Adorno and Horkheimer (2002 [1947]) and Berman (1983),[5] who argued it as well. Scientific communism's core claim that it had discovered the objective laws of history was far from a stand-alone phenomenon in the Enlightenment-born social sciences. In fact, it was a part of the broader modern movement to make an exact science out of everything: Comte's social physics, Renan's science of religion, Mill's science of human nature, Smith's science of commerce, Zola's science of literature, etc. (Stevens 1990). Bauman put the socialist–capitalist overlap in perhaps the strongest terms: communism and capitalism, he said, were the "the two legs on which modernity stood" (1995), and their confrontation, which most people know as the Cold War, was merely a "family squabble" (2000; also Lyon 1999).

62 *Iron Curtains*

Table 4.1 Two transitions with an "electivity affinity" for each other (Kumar 1995)

	The socialist regime	The Fordist regime
TRANSITION	Extensive accumulation through state-led industrialization; industrial gigantism.	Fordist economies of scale (state- and private-sector-led); industrial gigantism.
	Redistributive state.	Keynesian welfare state.
	Pursuit of limitless technological progress; bureaucratic and scientific administration; reliance on meta-narratives.	Pursuit of limitless technological progress; bureaucratic and scientific administration; reliance on meta-narratives
	The post-socialist regime	*The post-Fordist regime*
	Intensive accumulation through commodification and mercantilization.	Economy of scope; flexible specialization; post-industrialization.
	Marketization and *laissez-faire* state.	Post-Keynesian post-welfare neo-liberal state.
	Departure from meta-narratives.	Departure from meta-narratives.

Source: The table is based partly on Wu (2003).

Bauman's interpretation of capitalism and socialism as alternative modernities can be justified not only by pointing to their common Enlightenment roots, but also by identifying the basic premises that socialist and capitalist regimes shared throughout most of the twentieth century. These include: their common reliance on Fordist scale economies (Lenin in fact deeply admired both Ford and Taylor; Murray 1992) and a general taste for industrial gigantism; their common embrace of limitless technological advancement; their sheer fascination with newness and disdain for tradition; and their common belief in the scientific administration of society. Whether achieved through rational planning or through the equally rational, if invisible, hand of the market, the scientific administration of society was secured through strong state intervention (either Marxist-Leninist redistribution or the Keynesian welfare state). Both Fordist capitalism and state socialism depended on universalistic and ostensibly scientific, objective theories (in Lyotard's terms, meta-narratives; 1979) that sought to comprehensively improve the human condition and impose order on a seemingly chaotic world (Berman 1983; Anderson 1984; Murray 1992; Scott 1998; Wu 2003; Table 4.1).

In his famous address upon receiving the Philadelphia Liberty Medal in 1994, Havel spoke of the collapsing modern era as an era marked by the "dizzying development of science, with its unconditional faith in objective reality and complete dependency on general and rationally knowable laws." He attributed these characteristics to capitalism and socialism without making a distinction. Following Havel, then, we can take modernism as the belief in perpetual collective betterment achieved through the application of enlightened technocratic reason (also Berman 1983; Scott, J. C. 1998). As such, it spanned the political spectrum, from the far left to the far right. In either case, it was up to the potent state and its benevolent bureaucracies to implement the brave modernist doctrines.

Assuming the overarching similarities between capitalism and socialism, one can then argue that the end of socialism is the particular, local manifestation of the general (global) crisis of the Fordist accumulation regime. This crisis is marked by the advent of decentralized and flexible economies (in lieu of Fordist mass production), by post-industrialization and the advent of the consumer society (in lieu of the modern manufacturing-based mode of production), by a shrinking public sector (drastic privatization of public assets and weakening of state regulatory mechanisms), and by a cultural turn toward pluralism, subjectivism, privatism and "small-is-beautiful" worldviews (in lieu of modern discipline and totality; see, e.g., Crook et al. 1994).[6] Lyotard (1984) put the latter point most succinctly: post-modernism is "incredulity toward metanarratives." All of the above aspects of change make good definitions of post-Fordist economies (Amin 1994) and post-welfare-state, post-modern politics (see, e.g., Ost 1990). Castells (1998) famously interpreted the Soviet fall as the "expression of the structural inability of statism and of the Soviet variant of industrialism to ensure the transition to information society." His is essentially a similar argument for socialism's end as industrial modernity's end, even without using the term "modernity" per se.

The thesis of state socialism as a variant of modernity – and by the same token, the thesis of socialism's collapse as modernity's crisis and post-modernity's dawn – has its critics, for some good reasons. To begin with, it glosses over the obvious fundamental contrast between socialism and capitalism: that even though both adhered to the idea of benevolent public-sector domination to ensure perpetual progress, in the former the state played a dominant role in organizing production and consumption, whereas in the latter it intervened only to correct market failures and inefficiencies (e.g., Wu 2003). Furthermore, the balance between state-imposed collectivist order and individual liberties under the two regimes were quite different, to say the least. Even more fundamentally, though, the thesis of socialist–capitalist overlap has been challenged on the grounds of whether socialism was even *modern*. Holmes (1997: 41–2; also Dingsdale 2001) distinguishes between socialism as theory and practice: "in theory, communists were quintessentially modern," but in practice they enforced structures and relations that were "atypical" of modern states and were thus essentially pre-modern, for example autocracy and personality cults, the persistence of traditional, "demi-Orient" values, and informal, personal, clan-based and "feudal-like" networks in material production and distribution that were thinly veiled behind layers of scientific planning and technocratic management (also Ray 1995, 1996, 1997). Fehér et al. (1984: 210) argued that socialism manifested a "de-Enlightenment process" by enforcing "loyalty and obedience to the sovereign as supreme values [that] belong to a world prior to Enlightenment." But if this argument is correct, if socialism was *not* modernity, then the argument for its end as modernity's close and post-modernity's dawn becomes weaker. An alternative thesis of post-socialism as a return to modernist tenets of development (in this case, neo-liberal tenets) emerges. This proposition is famously associated with Habermas (1990, 1994) who termed the 1989 East European departures from socialism "revolutions of recuperation": the East's return to Western modernity.

In summary, then, we have two alternative interpretations of socialism: as modernity or not (and therefore, two interpretations of post-socialism as post-modernity or not; see also Burawoy and Verdery 1999: 1–18). Can the two be reconciled? Much of the verdict rests, of course, on how we define modernity and post-modernity – a difficult task to begin with. Dingsdale (2001: 3–14) proposes a compromise by suggesting that East European socialism and its successor, post-socialism, are cross-sections, amalgams produced by historic and geographic continuities. Each was embedded into the intellectual wells of modernity and, later, post-modernity (i.e., each is the heir of a particular Western tradition); in practice, however, each is grounded in the locally or regionally specific (and thus spatially, geographically dependent) trajectories of East European development.

I do not dispute this thesis per se, but what strikes me about it and some of the other interpretations mentioned above is the extent to which they seem to imply certain time-linear or space-linear trajectories. First, these interpretations share an implicit notion of temporal progress, a historic march of epochs from pre-modernity through modernity toward post-modernity. This is, of course, why post-modernity is *post*-something to begin with: it comes *after*, it is the cultural logic of "*late* capitalism," to borrow from Jameson (1991); it appears at a certain *moment* of historic development (e.g., at the advent of post-Fordist capitalism as an ostensibly new economic stage). Such an approach strikes me as being universalistic, evolutionary and therefore quintessentially modernist. Second, these theories share an implicit notion that both modernity and post-modernity follow a clear spatial trajectory: from West to East, as if cities and societies from around the world have all merely "borrowed" Western modernity in some incomplete manner (see also Robinson 2006). Combined, these two assumptions underlie much theory on socialism and modernity (and post-socialism and post-modernity). For example, the notions of socialism as anti-modernity and socialism as modernity in theory (but a failure in practice due to the "primitive," autocratic traditions mentioned earlier) both rely on a certain idea of Eastern Europe as backward, lagging behind, not *ready* for modernity. The same image underpins the view of post-modernism as something that originated in the West, developed in pioneering US cities, and is only now catching on elsewhere (e.g., in Eastern Europe) as a result of economic and cultural globalization.

My view on this is slightly different. Socialism, in its unyielding dedication to social and material transformation in the name of the collective good, was not only a variant of modernity; it was modernity's *sine qua non*. The modern idea of heroic development, perhaps best epitomized by Goethe's Faustus (Berman 1983), may have originated elsewhere – but it found fertile ground in Eastern Europe not despite its traditions but because of them. Socialist modernity was the perfect and perhaps even the only vehicle to overcome the East's nagging "backwardness"; it was also an inherently autocratic vision that was easier to impose in the East (Scott 1998). Not only was state socialism "modernity in its most determined mood and most decisive posture" (Bauman 1992), it was "modernity's most devout, vigorous and gallant champion"; "it was under communist ... auspices that the audacious dream of modernity, freed from obstacles by the merciless and omnipotent state, was pushed to its radical limits" (Bauman 1991). I disagree, however, with Bauman's assertion that state socialism was also modernity "purified of the last shred of the chaotic, the irrational, the spontaneous."[7] I think there was plenty of chaos and irrationality in socialism or, at least, what would *seem* like chaos and irrationality to a modernist. Take, for example, the much-maligned "feudal-like," kin-based and personal relationships that undermined socialist planning and management.[8] In socialist Bulgaria, these were known as *vruzki*, or connections. In a world of scarce material commodities, they were the most coveted resource for anyone seeking success. They sabotaged the modern, faceless bureaucratic state (from what I could tell, they *were* the state) and made it into the joke that it deserved to be. They flourished in the "lamplight of the private world," to use the words of Marx again, because the "universal sun" was down (although it perpetually maintained that it was up). They impregnated socialism with the seeds of its demise – doubt and disbelief in the collective modern utopia – an endeavor that seems to me utterly post-modern.

Bauman (1992) goes on to say that socialism's downfall marked the "most resounding defeat of the modern project," as well as "the most spectacular triumph of post-modern values." I think this is correct if we take post-modernity, as he puts it elsewhere (1993), to be "modernity coming to terms with its impossibility." Because socialism took the modern dream to its extreme, it also showed its impossibility in the most obvious, irrefutable terms. Socialism suppressed the post-modern *within* – personalism, spontaneity, fragmentation – at least on the surface, to such a degree that when released it devoured any decency that the modern dream had to begin with. Such an interpretation of post-socialism as modernity's ultimate demise and post-modernity's most visible eruption runs contrary to the theories of uniform spatial and temporal trajectory: from West to East, from the most advanced industrialized societies to their less advanced neighbors. But trajectory theories are premised on a notion that post-modernism as a cultural paradigm is somehow inadvertently linked to post-Fordist industrialism as an economic state – a thesis that is inherently Marxist *and* modernist. But what if it isn't? What if culture and economy, post-modernism and post-Fordism can be decoupled (e.g., Leontidou 1993)? What if postmodernism is an attitude (Allmendinger 2001), a "state of mind" as Havel called it (1992b, 1994)? What if it does not follow modernism temporally – it is not post-, not after – but it is what is within that gets released? Could it be, as Kharkordin (1995, 1997) said of Russia, that in their chaos and fragmentation, in their radical nihilism and aggressive privatism, and in their "avalanche-like collapse of officialdom," post-socialist societies are in fact more post-modern than the societies that invented the term? I cannot pretend to answer this question unequivocally. But I will argue next that much as the socialist city epitomized modernity, the post-socialist city presents us with material displays of post-modernity as paradigmatic as those found in the most "advanced" Western cities, such as London and LA.

Modernity and the Socialist City[9]

David Harvey (1989a: 66) defines modernist urbanism as the reliance on "technologically rational and efficient urban *plans*, backed by absolutely no-frills architecture (the austere 'functionalist' surfaces of 'international style' modernism)" – planning's own meta-narrative (Beauregard 1989). This philosophy was first applied in the wholesale demolition and rebuilding of Paris in 1853–70. By the end of the nineteenth century, it had reached a level of intellectual coherence that was well exhibited in Otto Wagner's 1895 tractate (Wagner 1986 [1895]) on why architecture should embrace "*modern* life" (as opposed to history and tradition) and in Ebenezer Howard's 1898 tome (Howard 1946 [1898]) on "garden cities," in which he insisted on abandoning old cities and building modern ones on a clean slate. A very long line of the world's most renowned builders working from the late 1800s to the 1960s and 1970s fit into this tradition: Arturo Soria, Louis Sullivan, Tony Garnier, Patrick Geddes, Josep Luis Sert, Nikolai Milyutin, Frank Lloyd Wright, Mies van der Rohe, Walter Gropius, Le Corbusier, Robert Moses, and Lucio Costa, to name just a few. The peculiar thing about these talented men is that their ideological affiliations crossed the political spectrum. What united them was their enchantment with start-anew transformations, the total domination of nature, and the imposition of structure over chaos and enlightened reason over popular ignorance in the name of perpetual progress (see, e.g., Scott 1998; Gandy 2002). The architects of the landmark Soviet avant-garde and German Bauhaus[10] schools were clearly on the left, but Le Corbusier – deemed modernism's patriarch, as well as the "Lenin of architecture" (Scott 1997) – leaned heavily to the right.[11] A champion of scientism and standardization who went so far as to write an ode to statistics and to declare that "a house is a machine for living," Le Corbusier did not shy away from offering world dictators from Pétain to Stalin his revolutionary vision of a city of giant skyscrapers built in place of what he viewed as remnants of past cultures. Tellingly, the last page of his book *The City of Tomorrow* (1987 [1929]) displays neither a plan nor a rendering, but rather a portrait of Louis XIV – the "master planner."

Brazil's capital Brasília, built between 1956 and 1961 on a clean slate after the monumental clearance of rainforests, is often called the climax of modernist urbanism. Its architectural cousins, however, span the globe: from India's Chandigarh to the Parisian *grands ensembles* and the housing "projects" erected during the Urban Renewal era in the United States. Brasília exhibits the quintessential features of modernist urbanism: enormous public parks and plazas, vast industrial sectors, a clear separation of functions, a rigid spatial hierarchy, and a strikingly simplistic aesthetics. These features were articulated in the *Athens Charter* (CIAM 1973 [1934]) – the most authoritative statement of the International Congress of Modern Architecture, written largely by Le Corbusier himself. Brasília was envisioned and constructed by Brazil's President Juscelino Kubitschek, who by all accounts had no sympathy for the left, yet entrusted the design of his capital city to Oscar Niemeyer, an architect who later served as President of Brazil's Communist Party. Modernism, again, united the right and the left (Holston 1987; Scott 1997; Banerjee 2004).

Kubitschek, though, built only one Brasília; the Soviets and their East European allies built many: the gigantic standardized housing projects that surround every large city in the Eastern bloc. Of course, capitalist countries like the United States built many similar projects as well under the auspices of the federal Urban Renewal program in the 1950s and 1960s.[12] But whereas US public projects comprise a minuscule portion of the national housing stock, in socialist cities districts of this type often account for almost the entire fabric built from 1960 to 1990, as I mentioned in the previous chapter. The socialist districts were the ultimate outcome of the "technologically rational and efficient urban *plans*, backed by absolutely no-frills architecture" that Harvey mentions. Of course Stalin, like Hitler, detested modernist architecture and insisted on "socialist realism" (a peculiar name for something that was in essence Russian neo-classicism – a grand imperial tradition that he restored after prematurely burying the excellent Soviet constructivist school; see, e.g., Aman 1992). But upon Stalin's death, modernism with its unyielding dedication to scientism and standardization became the credo of socialist urbanism. The Balkans were no exception. One of my interviewees in Sofia, an older architect whose career spanned several socialist decades, summed up his experience as follows:

> I think most of us [Bulgarian architects] had a portrait of Corbusier somewhere .... I mean he was the grand master, you wouldn't doubt this, it seemed at the time .... [E]verything had to be very carefully pre-planned .... [W]e were buried in data, calculating and recalculating the ratios, the proper land-use balances and this and that; the state codes for green space per person, allotted residential spaces per person, we had these things certainly .... Everything was per person .... Well now they say it [the architecture] is boring and not good, but at the time the idea was that everyone [must] have the same conditions. And this would have been very hard without [prefabricated] panels.

Looking at archival photos of the socialist housing projects under construction, say Novi Zagreb (New Zagreb) or Novi Beograd (New Belgrade), leaves one wondering whether they are images of Brasília. They certainly *could* be. Their layout and aesthetics – vast public green spaces, Herculean civic structures, collectivist residential towers, hierarchy, orderliness, uniformity – are strikingly similar, and can all clearly be traced to the prescriptions of the *Athens Charter*. Brasília of course is bigger, but there is only one Brasília; there are hundreds of socialist districts. Havel detested the *socialist* look, but the look itself – and the principles and aspirations that inspired it – were those of global modernism. The idea of the socialist city as an autonomous model, as I presented it in the previous chapter, is not without merits. Still, many of the characteristics of the socialist city – spatial grandeur, orderliness, primacy of public spaces, aesthetic minimalism – were those that modernists cherished around the globe (why else would modernism be called the *International* Style?). Some differences were more a matter of design degree than design logic. The key contrast was that in the socialist city, petty private interests and popular distaste for modernist monotony did not stand in the way; there, in the socialist city, as Bauman (1991) said, "the audacious dream of modernity" was "free from obstacles [placed] by the merciless and omnipotent state." Kornai (1997) called the socialist state "the premature welfare state." But perhaps it was the mature welfare state. Maybe, as Harvey once suggested (1989b: 196), the socialist state and its planners could do everything their bourgeois colleagues *wanted* to do but could not.[13]

Post-modern Urbanism Defined

If the modernist city was defined by mega-spaces, industrialism, mass housing, rational planning order, functional separation, and assembly-line architectural anonymity, then the post-modern city is marked by fragmentation, small plans, commercialization, consumerism, sponta-neity, informality, and architectural eclecticism, neo-classicism and pastiche (e.g., Jencks 1984; Hassan 1985; Relph 1987; Harvey 1989a; Leontidou 1993; Dear 2000; Table 4.2). There are multiple driving forces behind this shift in city-building: economic (e.g., de-industrialization and commercialization), political (e.g., deregulation and the shrinking role of the public sector) and ideological (loss of belief in total order, re-appre-ciation of tradition and greater acceptance of pluralism; Table 4.2). Several Western cities, such as Las Vegas (Venturi et al. 1977), London (Raban 1974), Baltimore (Harvey 1989a), Atlanta (Jameson 1991) and Cleveland (Hirt 2005b), whose downtowns have changed from produc-tion sites to spaces of tourism and entertainment and have turned to embracing architectural pastiche, have been used as examples of post-modern urbanism. Ellin (1996) identifies a post-modern direction in con-temporary French, British and US urbanism and architecture in general. In terms of overall metropolitan form, edge cities (Garreau 1991) – commercially dominated new towns at the rim of US metropolises – have been said to function along post-modern tenets of form composition in the sense that they do away with the clear urban–suburban hierarchy established during the modern era (Dear 2000). And in terms of aes-thetics, a case in point is New Urbanism, a popular trend involving the construction of new (and often gated) communities that resemble charm-ing old towns and are ridden with nostalgic architectural references such as Greek gazebos and Victorian gingerbread houses (Hirt 2009b). Clearly, we are talking about diverse phenomena, sometimes driven by economic and political processes (e.g., the emergence of new spatial forms such as edge cities) and sometimes driven by cultural changes (e.g., the emer-gence of new architectural fashions). To the extent that both represent a rupture with the established order, spatial or aesthetic, they could be interpreted as parts of a common, post-modern paradigm shift, as Ellin (1996) suggests.

Los Angeles remains the most-cited exemplar of post-modern urbanism; in fact, it is widely accepted that there is an "LA school" of urban geography and sociology that counters the ostensibly modernist Chicago school of the early twentieth century.[14] Several of the basic tenets of post-modern urbanism have been explored in LA with varying theoretical and empirical depth. Loukaitou-Sideris and Banerjee (1998), for instance, have pointed

Table 4.2 Contrasting modernism and post-modernism

Modernism	*Post-modernism*
Large-scale, comprehensive and scientific plans; machine-like efficiency; "big is beautiful" outlook; strict plans and regulations; meta-narratives; planning for social transformation, renewal.	Incremental, piecemeal, pluralist planning; "small is beautiful" outlook; deregulation; entrepreneurship; planning for rehabilitation, historic preservation.
Vast public improvement projects; generous public spaces; public sector plays key role in city-building. Mass standardized housing; open accessible space; attempts to provide housing egalitarianism.	Reduction of public funds for city improvement; public sector begins to plays secondary role. Individualist solutions; spatial privatization; enclosures; differentiation; increasing social and spatial polarization.
Domination of production over consumption; assembly-line industrialism; the City Functional.	Domination of consumption over production; post-industrialism; commercialization; carnival city; the City Spectacular.
Order, structure, hierarchy; land-use segregation; discipline, totality, anonymity.	Urban spontaneity; urban bricolage; informality, marginality, spontaneity and diversity; mixed use.
Aesthetic unity and simplicity; International Style without reference to local context; fascination with newness; rejection of historic styles; Cosmopolis.	Aesthetic pluralism; mixing of local and global styles; fascination with (some) traditions; revival of historic architecture; copy-and-paste architecture; Heteropolis.
Elitist architecture; avant-garde architecture; "less is more"; "form follows function"; role of architecture is to transform society (e.g., provide mass housing).	Populist architecture; "less is more but is a bore"; form follows finance, fantasy and fear; role of architecture is to decorate; architecture for fun.
Hard surfaces, straight space and blank canvas.	Soft surfaces, textured space and collage.

Sources: Relph (1987), Harvey (1989a), Ellin (1997) and Dear (2000).

to a substantial shift in the scale of urban planning and the scale of public projects in the city. In the 1960s and 1970s, urban planners looked at LA comprehensively and strived to implement large-scale, systematic public improvements. In contrast, recent efforts following from the slashing of public funds focus on small areas of the city in a disjointed fashion, and most new open spaces that appear to be public are in fact produced by private firms or public–private partnerships and are not widely accessible.

Dear and Flusty (1997, 1998) and Jencks (1993) have shown the radical commercialization of LA's built environment that typically occurs at the expense of civic and industrial uses, as well as the intense social polarization of the metropolis, and the spread of heterogeneous, frivolous architecture reflecting increasing ethno-cultural fragmentation and a growing popular taste for fantasy landscapes (e.g., urban carnival places). The most controversial aspect of LA's new spatial order, however, is the solidification of physical barriers that break apart previously accessible spaces (Davis 1990, 1992). Practices of this type include the closing off of public streets, residential fortification, enhanced security and surveillance in parks and other public spaces, and the construction of securitized malls and even libraries. Indeed, the prison look has become an architectural fashion easily identifiable in buildings designed by star architects such as Frank Gehry (for example, the somewhat infamous Frances Howard Goldwyn Regional Branch Library in Hollywood). Ellin (1996) refers to these trends as post-modern urbanism driven by finance, fear and fiction – the spatial outcome of a culture of privatism, escapism and narcissism, or what she calls "the post-modern temper." But are these trends limited to avant-garde Western cities?

The Post-socialist City as a Variant of Post-modernity

In the previous chapter, I summarized physical changes in the post-socialist city as follows: the end of compact spatial form; a decrease in the scale of development (especially in terms of public spaces and public housing developments); a tilting of the land-use balance toward commerce; an emergence of stark social contrasts, informality and marginality; and the end of visual uniformity. Wu (2003) puts these slightly differently. He describes the new spaces of "transitional cities" as spaces of consumption, marginalization, differentiation and globalization. Either way, as he aptly points out, these phenomena are neither new nor unknown to the Western world (regardless of some differences in urban form between the United States and the countries of the European Union) and to other parts of the globe. Rather, Wu claims, they seem to be "familiar processes" leading to "familiar outcomes," even if they take different forms in post-socialist and contemporary capitalist cities. Of the five aspects of change that I outlined, only suburbanization has not been linked to post-modern capitalist urban restructuring per se, for the simple reason that it has accompanied the history of capitalism for decades. It is only the latest suburban variation – the commercially dominated edge city and the quaint New Urbanist town – that seem to fit the post-modern label (Ellin 1987). But in the post-socialist case, intense suburbanization and sprawl became possible because of the total collapse of strict socialist (modernist, that is) planning rules that had for decades inhibited growth in the urban peripheries. Furthermore, a closer look at post-socialist sprawl reveals that it proceeds with such a breathtaking speed as to seemingly skip the usual stages of suburbanization that took place around Western cities: first residential, then commercial suburbanization. Rather, commercial uses – upscale hotels, multi-national corporate headquarters, entertainment complexes – often appear to follow residential uses closely (or even lead the way), giving rise to speculation that post-socialist (or post-modern) edge cities are already emerging in an extremely time-compressed manner (see, e.g., Nuissl and Rink 2005 on Leipzig, Dimitrovska-Andrews et al. 2007 on Ljubljana). One good example is Belgrade's Airport City, a glitzy commercial node near a planned golf community, which according to its developers will likely be gated and guarded (Hirt 2009a).

Regarding the other four aspects of post-socialist urban spatial change, the affinity with the post-modern urbanism of Davis and Ellin is even more apparent. For example, take the functional change of de-industrialization and commercialization of the urban fabric, in Belgrade. As I mentioned earlier, commercial spaces in Serbia's capital have quadrupled since 1990, but nearly 60% of the city's old industrial lands lay underused, according to the latest Master Plan. This is certainly an example of extreme de-industrialization. The trend is obviously well underway across Eastern Europe, and more prosperous cities like Budapest have already taken the lead in converting old industrial sites into places for shopping and entertainment (Kiss 2007). Although this has yet to happen in poorer cities like Belgrade, it is telling that the first renovated industrial block in the city was turned into a super-private, super-securitized luxury residential compound. Equally telling is the name of the city block, which changed from *Partizanka* (a heroic female participant in the anti-fascist movement) to *Oasa* (oasis; Figure 4.1).

Or take the shift in the scale of urban planning and public projects. Since the 1970s, the United States has seen an obvious trend toward incremental planning and away from the kind of ambitious, transformative planning that Robert Moses practiced in mid-twentieth-century New York and civic activists like Jane Jacobs fought against (see Flint 2009).[15] The termination of the federal Urban Renewal program, which was responsible for massive demolition of historic buildings in many US cities and the construction of hundreds of International Style public housing projects, is often deemed the end of the modern era, at least in urban design.[16] Since then, the US federal government has been slashing funds for public housing. Existing projects have been replaced by smaller ones with medium-sized buildings and semi-enclosed yards following the prescriptions of Oscar Newman (1996 [1972]) for "defensible" (i.e., private) space. The trend is not limited to the United States. Sudjić (1993) argued that in the 1970s and 1980s the governments of the United States and several West European countries, such as France and the United Kingdom, concluded that the

Figure 4.1 This once-industrial building in Belgrade was refurbished to become a supersecuritized residential complex with a large interior yard and luxury common sports facilities. Entering the building poses significant challenges. One must first ring the intra-phone and talk to a guard through a small window. The guard decides whether the person should be admitted to the foyer and calls the residents to see whether further permission should be granted. The foyer is equipped with multiple security devices.

very idea of modernist-type mass housing was a fiasco. He sees this as evidence not only of a crisis in modernist design, but also as a broader crisis in the core concept of social, public housing.[17] Still, in few other parts of the world were public funds for social housing slashed as severely as they were in East Europe after 1989. It is stating the obvious to note that East European governments abolished their social housing programs at a time when they were nearing bankruptcy. The larger point is that in the Eastern bloc the modernist dream of solving the housing problem by erecting innumerable standardized "machines for living," just as Le Corbusier had imagined, came to its fullest fruition. And it is there that it came crashing down most abruptly – not literally of course (physical demolition can hardly be an option when millions of dwellings are at stake), but at least conceptually, as an ideal. As one architect in Sofia put it, while the large collectivist buildings from the socialist past are here to stay, most people who continue to live in them seem to be doing so out

Figure 4.2 A new residence in Belgrade's Dedinje. The prison look is definitely in.

of necessity. According to the interviewee, "whoever can get out, will"; "*panelkite* [the panel buildings] have a bad name"; "people these days want something different, something of their own – a house and a yard."

In the more liberal socialist states like Hungary and Yugoslavia, the "house-and-yard" notion has in fact been gaining steam since the 1980s, if not earlier. About that time, the construction of large, state-sponsored mass-housing projects came to a halt, and obtaining bank loans for individual housing construction was purposely made easier (see, e.g., Bodnar 2001; Hirt 2008a). By the late 1980s, about a third of new dwelling units produced in the Yugoslav capital annually were in fact single-family homes (Vujović and Petrović 2007). Ever since, fascination with the "house-and-yard" idea has only spread.[18] Belgrade, much like Sofia, Bucharest, Tirana or Skopje, may not have any prison-like libraries designed by Frank Gehry, but urban securitization around private homes is well underway,[19] and the prison look is definitely in. A full-blown withdrawal from the public street is underway in many urban areas; in fact, it is not too difficult to find large early-twentieth-century villas whose decorative wrought-iron fences have been replaced by two-meter-tall solid walls (Figures 4.2, 4.3 and 4.4).

Figure 4.3 More of the prison look. The iron rods that make the top portion of this fence around a large family residence in Dedinje, are being taken down to be replaced by taller solid brick walls.

Figure 4.4 A multi-family residential structure built in the early 1990s in Sofia. Unlike its socialist-era predecessors, this building, which sits on formerly public green space, is surrounded by a wall. The wall was the first element constructed on the site.

The extent to which the idea of mass, publicly sponsored, egalitarian housing was discredited after 1989 paralleled the extent to which the very idea of strong, modernist public intervention in the built environment (i.e., planning and regulation) lost credibility as well.[20] There is of course significant variation among East European countries. Still, if Western nations have been shifting from large-scale toward incremental planning as part of the post-modern shift since the 1980s, in post-socialist nations the trend has been toward resisting planning altogether. Not only did most East European nations function without national programs for housing or urban development throughout most of the 1990s, but even their state capitals proceeded without new master plans: Bucharest adopted its first post-socialist citywide plan in 2000, Ljubljana in 2002, and Belgrade and Zagreb in 2003 (Hirt and Stanilov 2009: 45). Sofia managed to postpone adopting its first post-socialist plan until 2007. The delays were typically blamed on organizational and procedural difficulties and lack of funding but, as Stanilov (2007) observed, the lack of urban policy has been "the policy itself" – one that appears to have gained broad political support across the region, especially during the early years of the transition. In theory, cities were supposed to function under the legal auspices of their last master plans, but since these plans dated back to the socialist 1960s, 1970s and 1980s, they were viewed as obsolete and were thus, perhaps correctly, ignored. Typically, development permits were linked not to a citywide vision or program but to a particular neighborhood-scale plan that could be easily modified without extensive legal wrangling to suit the aspirations of any private developer. Coupled with the popular contempt for planning rules, even where they existed, this process laid the groundwork for the extremely piecemeal, fragmented and thus inherently post-modern urban development patterns we see today. (This partially changed only after some semblance of comprehensive urban planning was restored after 2000.) The new rules of the game (or lack thereof) had an obvious consequence: a sharp rise in urban spontaneity in the form of impromptu places, including entire subdivisions in urban parks and on peri-urban greenbelts. In the Balkans, urban informality linked to statutory secession reached epidemic proportions, as mentioned earlier. As Leontidou (1993) speculated for Europe's South and Southeast, perhaps the process has been fed by deeply held cultural attitudes that resist modernist order and discipline in the city as in everything else – the South's long-standing tradition of undermining central authority and interpreting laws and regulations loosely and "creatively" (Newman and Thornley 1996: 39–41). Spurned for decades under state socialism, this tradition – both proverbial and post-modern (Leontidou 1993) – seems to have erupted in the post-socialist Balkans like a genie from a bottle.

In architecture, the post-modern obsession with historicism and surprising aesthetic combinations appears to have prospered in post-socialist conditions no less than in the Western world.[21] Russian architecture seems to have moved most decisively in the direction of modernist negation, historic nostalgia and post-modern classist revival (Boym 2001b; Chipova and Feuer 2007; Makarova 2009). "Forward comrades, we must go back!" cried one of post-modernism's greatest, the Luxemburg-born architect Leon Krier (1981). In New York, Philipp Johnson's ATT building – a skyscraper whose top resembles a cupboard in the eighteenth-century Chippendale furniture style – is often deemed the ultimate post-modern structure for its seemingly random, frivolous adoption of a historic style in the arts. The Russian equivalents, however, go even further. One fine example is the residential building that looks like a Fabergé egg. Other notable examples include the monumental neo-Gothic residential skyscraper dubbed the Eighth Sister (Stalin built seven similar skyscrapers, one of which houses Moscow State University), the Pompeii House, a cheerful symphony of colors and columns that grow like flowers from Roman-like frescos, and the bright yellow super-classicist residential building called The Patriarch (Kurkovsky 2009).

Russian neo-imperial grandeur is of course hard to replicate in Balkan conditions, where the scale of spaces and structures tends to be much smaller. But, walking through the *nouveau riche* areas in Belgrade, Bucharest, Sofia or Skopje, one sees just as startling a vanity fair of shapes that include revived old Balkan architecture along with neo-Gothic, neo-Venetian and neo-Tudor elements – styles that never played a significant part in the Balkan architectural vocabulary. (I discuss Sofia's new architectural styles in greater detail in Chapter 9.) Some houses convey rich narratives of a walk through time – houses whose first, second and third stories are decorated with Doric, Ionic and Corinthian columns, respectively. Popular architectural details include gilded eagles, marble balustrades, and representations of Apollo and Aphrodite placed strategically on the Ottoman-like stone walls right next to the guard houses and security cameras. One smart architectural critic referred to the new architecture as Turbo Pop, alluding to the populist Balkan neo-classicism that in some cases includes folksy elements (Weiss 2006). (The term Turbo Pop refers more specifically to the somewhat misguided but beloved music style that combines Western pop with Balkan folk.) My preference, though, is for the term Mafia Baroque (Hirt 2008a). Neo-Baroque was the style of choice across the Balkans in the late nineteenth and early twentieth centuries. It was used primarily in grand public buildings (Stalin and Ceausescu of course carried on the tradition in the later part of the 1900s). In the early

1990s, the style gained considerable popularity across the Balkans among those whose quickly acquired wealth was generally of unknown origin. A decade later, it spread in a more modest form to upper-middle-class homes as well, although its popularity now seems to be waning.

So where does this all lead? Here is my proposal. If we accept that post-modern urbanism entails characteristics such as commercialization, fragmentation, securitization, a reduced role for public planning, and architectural pluralism and historicism, not only can we find these in post-socialist cities, but we can find them there in more intense forms than in Western cities. Dear and Dahmann (2008) have identified the reversal of center and periphery as an integral part of post-modernity. They meant this in the specific context of post-modern urbanism in the United States.[22] But perhaps we can imagine another still braver post-modern center–periphery reversal. Perhaps post-modernism is not a Western "innovation" exported abroad, but rather a phenomenon that erupted with greatest vigor precisely in the places where modernity reigned supreme, places which until recently were considered peripheral: those in the post-socialist East. Judging from the collapse of Soviet-era totality and hierarchy, the spread of cultural values of "an almost unrestrained personalism and privatism" that brought about the "avalanche-like collapse of officialdom" (to cite Kharkordin once again), and the related rise of private-led, hotchpotch urbanism and architecture, we can perhaps infer that post-socialist societies and cities exemplify the post-modern in clearer hues than we find in Western settings. Or, at least, that an excursion through the post-socialist world leaves us with a taste of an alternative post-modernity that the key scholars on the subject seem to have missed.

Notes

1   It can be argued that there is a distinction between the terms post-modernism and post-modernity. The first is often referred to as a cultural or epistemological shift; the second is typically used to denote a historic period – a new "epoch turned to the future" (Therborn 1995; the future-oriented nature of post-modernity, though, is a bit paradoxical since the term itself is oriented toward the past; i.e., it is modernity with a prefix). In this book, however, I have used the terms post-modernism and post-modernity interchangeably.

2   Post-modernism is an extremely complex construct which I will not be able to explore here in the depth that it deserves. In Michael Dear's interpretation (2000), for example, we can detect at least three main interpretations: (1) post-modernism as a new economic and political epoch in human development affiliated with post-Fordist and post-industrial capitalism; (2) post-modernism as an epistemological and cultural shift that entails skepticism toward the

modernist faith in science and linear progress and thus a turn to pluralism, subjectivism and phenomenology; and (3) post-modernism as change in the arts and architecture that includes the rejection of large-scale, science-inspired, hierarchical and standardized ways of constructing urban forms and their replacement with more frivolous, pastiche and informal means of city-building. As I have tried to suggest in this chapter, the three are intertwined. For example, in urban planning, we observe the proliferation of smaller-scale, private-led efforts at city-building which reflect disbelief in the idea of planning as a rigid scientific activity and produce a more colorful and unruly type of built environment.

3 For some, both modernity and post-modernity remain a mirage. On the non-existence of modernity, see for instance Bruno Latour's *We were never modern* (1991). There is a much longer line of scholars who believe that post-modernity is illusionary. The line includes Habermas, Harvey and Giddens. Some argue, for example, that we live in an era of augmented, hyper- or super-modernity (e.g., Spretnak 1999).

4 This is ironic having in mind that even though the term post-modernism is traditionally associated with "advanced" Western contexts, it was first used and gained prominence in Hispanic America, as Anderson (1998) has shown.

5 Berman (1983: 50) argued that the modern aspiration for limitless development is "equally central to the collectivist mystique of twentieth-century socialism" as it is to capitalism.

6 Here of course I intertwine two of the main interpretations of post-modernity – as a historic stage, and as a cultural and epistemological shift.

7 Here is a fine example of irrational outcomes of Soviet rational (modernist) planning. One Soviet factory had to meet a quota of 100,000 men's shoes. However, since the state planners misallocated the amount of leather that was required for the job, the factory managers took a creative approach. They did secure the production of 100,000 shoes, only not for men but for little boys. Still, the quota was fulfilled and planning triumphed while Soviet men went out of luck (Kelleher 2004: 60).

8 On the importance of the household as an economic unit during socialism, see for example Smith and Stenning (2006).

9 This section is in a sense my attempt to further explore one of the two main theories on the socialist city discussed in the previous chapter: that despite its specific characteristics, the socialist city represented the spatial outcome of communism as a variant of industrial modernity.

10 On the history of the German modernist school *Bauhaus*, see for example Droste (2006). The school opened in 1919 and was closed by Hitler in 1933.

11 Le Corbusier lobbied (unsuccessfully) the Soviet leadership to adopt a new, transformational plan for Moscow. He designed the landmark headquarters of the Central Union of Consumer Cooperatives and the Palace of the Soviets (the latter was not built) and was somewhat sympathetic to Soviet dreams of total social and spatial metamorphosis. In the 1930s, however, he moved increasingly to the political right led by French politicians such as Hubert Lagardelle. He later worked for the fascist Vichy government. James Scott (1998: 88–103)

provides a good account of how Le Corbusier reconciled two seemingly contradictory philosophies by pointing to his obsession with hierarchy and
authority.

12 Public housing projects are certainly not the only legacy of modernist planning,
    although they may be the one that has been most vilified. The American
    suburban housing stock erected after World War II, epitomized by places such
    as Levittown, can also be regarded as an example of assembly-line modernism.

13 Harvey's statement is that "socialism seemed to hold out the possibility of doing
    everything that the bourgeois state wanted to do but could not."

14 The LA school claims to have found the markings of a new model of urbanity
    that may throw light on the future of global urbanism (Soja 1989; Dear 2000;
    Dear and Dahmann 2008). This is an example of post-modernism taken as an
    epistemological turn in the social sciences.

15 In 1973, Douglas Lee summarized the pending paradigm shift in US urban
    planning and policy as a "requiem for large-scale models."

16 Charles Jencks (1984) in fact claimed that urban modernity's end came
    somewhat violently with the implosion of a particular residential project in
    St. Louis. This project once received design awards yet eventually became a
    symbol of mass-housing nightmares around the country.

17 Such housing, however, continues to comprise a significant share of the housing
    stock in some West European countries (e.g., Scandinavia).

18 In fact, a recent survey showed that the idea of private territoriality seems to
    be driving residential gating in Serbia's capital even more than concerns about
    crime (Hirt and Petrović 2010).

19 As of 2005, an estimated 23% of US households had some type of security
    device at home; the number was projected to grow to about 29% in 2009
    (Parks Associates, 2005, *Home Security Update*, www.parksassociates.com/
    research/reports/tocs/2005/security.htm; accessed October 21, 2009). A
    survey of 405 households in areas undergoing significant housing growth in
    Belgrade found that 52% of residences had at least one security device (e.g.,
    video camera, alarm system, guard).

20 This statement though is to be taken with some caution. Whereas in the Balkans
    the influence of the public sector was dramatically weakened, in Russia there is
    evidence for the persistence of strong public intervention in city-building. This
    intervention has occurred less through traditional instruments such as public
    infrastructure investment and building regulation and more through the
    emergence of powerful coalitions between municipal authorities and private
    capital. In Moscow, Pagonis and Thornley (2000) speculated that the socialist
    tradition of state-led urbanism goes on.

21 In some countries, of course, the trend can be traced to the 1980s. Ceausescu's
    grand boulevards in central Bucharest are the most notable example (in fact,
    the boulevards strongly resemble the architecture of iconic post-modern
    Western masters like Ricardo Bofill).

22 They meant that peripheral, edge cities are now taking primacy over old city
    centers.

5

Sofia: Wither the Socialist City

"Our city grows on auto-pilot."
                    Excerpt from an interview with an urban planner, 2002

"Every theater a mall, every gallery a pub!"
                    Graffiti decorating a downtown building

Sofia became the national capital in 1879 following Bulgarian independence from five hundred years of Ottoman rule. Although it is among Europe's oldest cities and used to be a key regional node during the Roman Empire and the medieval Bulgarian Kingdom (see, e.g., Tashev 1972; Labov 1979), in 1879 Sofia was but a sleepy town with some 12,000 inhabitants and 3,000 houses. The choice of Sofia was based primarily on its geographical location: it was the approximate center of the relatively large Bulgarian state that was formed after Russia's triumph in the Russo-Ottoman War of 1877–8. But as the 1879 Berlin Congress shrunk the borders of Bulgaria and returned many of its new southwest territories to Ottoman jurisdiction, Sofia lost its central location, the single advantage that it had once held over other Bulgarian cities.

Sofia's provincial nature seems to have been a source of serious embarrassment to the ambitious new Bulgarian ruling class, who dreamed of making their country, albeit shrunken, an important regional player. In their view, one obstacle to this goal was the "oriental" appearance of the town, with its multiple mosques and its narrow, curvilinear streets. One of the first acts of the new government was to straighten and thus "Europeanize" Sofia's street system. Some of the new administrators still perceived the old town as irredeemably "oriental" and thus proposed its abandonment in

Iron Curtains, First Edition. Sonia A. Hirt.
© 2012 John Wiley & Sons, Ltd. Published 2012 by John Wiley & Sons, Ltd.

favor of a new capital to be designed along modern, European principles
(Jeleva-Martins 1999). Pragmatic considerations led to the rejection of this
proposal, but ambitions to upgrade old Sofia did not subside, and feverish
planning and building activity quickly commenced.[1] This involved removing
most Ottoman artifacts, redesigning the street system, erecting new civic
buildings in line with the European architectural fashions of the day, and
upgrading some of the housing (Hirt 2007a). Numerous French, Russian,
German and Italian architects and engineers were promptly put to the task,
followed by a generation of Bulgarian professionals educated abroad. Sofia's
remodeling adopted the dominant Western ideas of the time by incorporating Parisian-style boulevards and a Viennese-style ring road, albeit in a
very modest fashion (Jeleva-Martins 1991; Slavova 2003). Perpetual scarcity
of resources undermined any schemes to endow Sofia with citywide glamour.
Still, the city center was radically transformed to include several gracious
civic streets, squares and landmark buildings in neo-classical, neo-Baroque
and Art Nouveau styles, sometimes mixed with references to traditional
Balkan architecture.

By the 1930s, Sofia was a virtually new city. Its population increased from
12,000 to 400,000, and its territory expanded from 3 to 42 sq km, making
it the fastest-growing Balkan capital. Its second-rate status almost forgotten,
it had become the undisputed industrial and cultural center of the nation
(Labov 1979; Lampe 1984). By this time, its contemporaries saw it as a
modern, European city, at least in the official commemorative books that
marked its fiftieth anniversary as state capital (Stolichna Obshtina 1928).
Sofia's new modernity, however, was mostly a surface phenomenon. Exiting
the fancy downtown and the petit bourgeois neighborhoods that surrounded
it, one entered a sprawling periphery of slums that housed the peasant and
proletarian armies, as well as the thousands of recent war refugees expelled
from the territories Bulgaria lost in the Balkan Wars. Most homes in these
areas were in an appalling state; access to urban infrastructure was non-
existent. The problems had been painfully obvious to both the national and
the municipal governments for many years. Perhaps no one summarized
them more clearly than Sofia's pre-World War II Mayor, Ivan Ivanov, who
outlined the rationale for the first Master Plan of Sofia by pointing to the
desperate conditions in which most of the citizenry lived, especially in the
peripheral neighborhoods (Ivanov 1938). The first plan of Sofia was prepared between 1934 and 1938 by Adolf Muessman, a Nazi-backed German
architect who won an international design competition under somewhat
dubious circumstances but was gladly accepted by Bulgaria's fascist-leaning
government. Muessman sought to further modernize Sofia by upgrading
its transport system, introducing functional zoning, building a gigantic civic
center, and converting Sofia's periphery into a ring of garden suburbs – all
mainstream Western planning ideals at the time. He also proposed the first

comprehensive system of large public parks. Muessman's plan was adopted, but few steps toward its implementation were taken – not only because of the impending war but also because Sofia's political and professional classes viewed the plan's central elements as plainly foreign. The plan seemed to call for the construction of a mini-version of Hitler's monumental designs for Berlin on Sofia's soil; it also envisioned dispersing Sofia's upper and middle classes to quaint single-family housing in a new suburbia, whereas they preferred to stay closer to the city center (Lampe 1984; Jeleva-Martins 1998, 2000; Hirt 2005a, 2007a). Thus, the dream of citywide modernization had to wait a bit longer, until a revolutionary, socialist regime came to power in 1945.

Building Socialist Sofia

The nationalization of urban land, large real estate and means of production, which was completed in 1948, three years after the new regime took power, set Sofia on a new course. Lyuben Tonev (1987 [1945]), the author of Sofia's first socialist Master Plan, wrote a passionate exposé of the "grave errors" of Muessman's vision, especially regarding the intention to clear many areas occupied by proletarian housing in order to convert them to parks and single-family homes (the latter was clearly condemned as "bourgeois").

Although initial plans for Sofia, including the plan by Tonev, were relatively modest and focused on rebuilding its bombed-out areas,[2] by the early 1950s the city-building paradigm had shifted to embrace a new monumentality. The first striking example of large-scale, socialist-type public planning and building in central Sofia was the Largo – a group of impressive government structures in the style of Stalinist socialist realism that replaced a dozen downtown city blocks. The buildings and the vistas that connected them dwarfed any public spaces created in the pre-socialist era (Figure 5.1). Upon the death of Bulgaria's first socialist leader, Gyorgi Dimitrov, the public complex was expanded to include his white marble mausoleum – an unmistakable imitation of Lenin's mausoleum in Moscow. (Dimitrov's mausoleum was the first thing to go after 1989; the first post-socialist government reduced it to rubble in a spectacular implosion and replaced it with a small garden dedicated to the European Union.) Thirty years after the Largo, the socialist state made its last attempt to commemorate its Herculean powers in space: another equally monumental downtown public complex, crowned by the People's Palace of Culture (Figure 5.2).

The socio-spatial structure of Sofia changed fundamentally during the socialist period. Between 1963 and 1989, Sofia's population expanded from about 400,000 to 1,200,000 as a result of both natural growth and massive migration from the countryside following the construction of large industrial

Figure 5.1 The Largo in Sofia. Erected in the style of Stalinist "socialist realism," this 1950s complex of civic buildings, which replaced several old city blocks, was the largest downtown project ever built in Sofia – a prime example of the power of the Party to shape society and space.

facilities in both central and peripheral urban areas. The commercial significance of downtown was dramatically reduced (see, e.g., Carter 1979), as most private stores were either uprooted or nationalized. Industrially zoned lands, on the other hand, kept expanding to eventually reach 27% of Sofia's territory (Bertaud 2004; Hirt and Stanilov 2009). The urban borders increased from 42 to 190 sq m to include vast green and agricultural fields. The spatial generosity of the socialist regime was also on display in its ambitious program for constructing large public parks. During the sixty-six-year period between independence and the end of World War II, Sofia acquired only about 130 ha of public greenery; during forty-five years of socialism, however, that number increased by twenty-one times to reach 2750 ha, making socialist Sofia one of the greenest capitals in Europe (Local Development Initiative 2004; Kovachev 2001; Radoslavova 2008).

Housing the fast-growing population remained the main urban challenge for decades. The initial solution was to upgrade the existing urban neighborhoods and build new medium-scale apartment structures in keeping with the traditional spatial structure of old city blocks. From the 1960s

Figure 5.2   The People's Palace of Culture – the last large public space built under socialist auspices. Even though it did not match the spatial splendor of Ceausescu's Palace constructed about the same time in Bucharest, Sofia's Palace also required the demolition of multiple old city blocks. Today, the main building functions as a mall; it includes a cinema and various upscale shops and restaurants.

on, however, following the Soviet lead, Sofia turned increasingly to a more revolutionary approach by embracing industrialized building methods. Economies of scale required territorial conquest, and many of the former farms and green fields at the urban edge were turned into construction sites.[3] Liulin and Mladost were the first two vast housing districts comprising collectivist buildings made of prefabricated panels (for the location of all administrative districts, please see Figure 5.3). Initiated in 1963, these districts expanded continuously until 1989. Over time, a full necklace of similar districts was erected around the historic heart of the city, including Iskar, Nadejda and Studentski Grad. Together, they now house about 700,000 people, or 60% of the metropolitan population (Hirt and Stanilov 2009).

The organization of the socialist districts followed the tenets of modernist urbanism precisely as they were outlined in the *Athens Charter* and embodied in, say, Brasília. Instead of incorporating traditional streets and interior neighborhood courtyards framed by continuous façades, the mass-housing districts

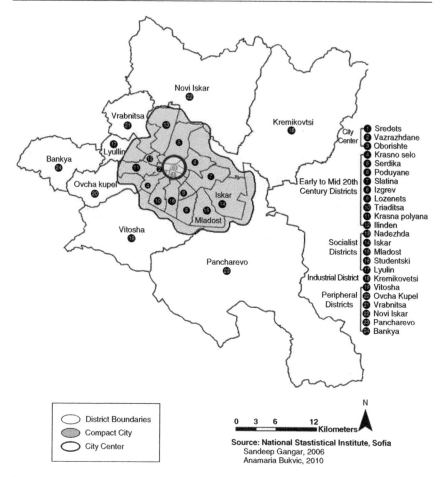

City
Center { ① Sredets
        ② Vazrazhdane
        ③ Oborishte

Early to Mid 20th { ④ Krasno selo
Century Districts   ⑤ Serdika
                    ⑥ Poduyane
                    ⑦ Slatina
                    ⑧ Izgrev
                    ⑨ Lozenets
                    ⑩ Triaditsa
                    ⑪ Krasna polyana
                    ⑫ Ilinden

Socialist { ⑬ Nadezhda
Districts   ⑭ Iskar
            ⑮ Mladost
            ⑯ Studentski
            ⑰ Lyulin

Industrial District { ⑱ Kremikovetsi

Peripheral { ⑲ Vitosha
Districts   ⑳ Ovcha Kupel
             ㉑ Vrabnitsa
             ㉒ Novi Iskar
             ㉓ Pancharevo
             ㉔ Bankya

District Boundaries
Compact City
City Center

N

0   3   6   12
            Kilometers

Source: National Stastistical Institute, Sofia
Sandeep Gangar, 2006
Anamaria Bukvic, 2010

Figure 5.3 Map of the region (oblast) of Sofia showing its 24 administrative districts. There are nine such regions in Bulgaria. Almost all territories beyond the urbanized part (which in official documents is somewhat misleadingly labeled as the "compact city") are only technically part of Sofia. They include small towns and villages and vast undeveloped territories (e.g., mountains and water bodies). The census releases almost all its data using this administrative division.

comprised modernist super-blocks of free-standing structures. The buildings were oriented to obtain maximum sunlight rather than provide street enclosure and legibility; they were also far larger than any residential buildings erected in the past.[4] In theory, the housing estates were planned as self-sufficient neighborhoods, meant to provide their residents with a full range of services, hence their official name "residential complexes" (*jilishtni kompleksi*). The most vital services, the schools, the kindergartens and the hospitals, were built simultaneously with or immediately after the residential buildings. But, as resources were always tight and providing services was never a priority for the socialist regime, most of the stores, restaurants, cafés and sports facilities shown on the plans were never built (hence the districts were often mocked as the "un-complex complexes"). Until 1990, Mladost, home to 100,000 people, never had a single cinema, swimming pool or tennis court.

Regardless of their many functional deficiencies and rather bleak architecture, for three decades the socialist estates were coveted as the modern residential alternative, one much preferred to housing in most central urban areas where comprehensive renovation never took place. The standardized housing units in the urban periphery were assigned according to quotas linked to people's places of employment and were sold after construction at discounted prices (this process led to the exceptionally high homeownership rate of socialist Bulgaria, mentioned earlier). Families often waited for many years until their dream standardized apartment was finally complete. Thus, the socialist "middle class" was gradually pushed toward the new periphery, while most of Sofia's traditional areas acquired a slightly worn-out look. Only a few select downtown neighborhoods, which were occupied by socialist elites (often residing in the same fancy apartments once owned by their bourgeois predecessors), retained an aura of prestige and desirability. Socio-spatial segregation in Sofia thus exhibited some historic continuity, but was notably softened during the forty-five years of socialism (Hirt and Kovachev 2006; Hirt and Stanilov 2007).

By 1989, after more than four decades of socialist city-building, Sofia conformed well to the spatial model of the socialist city as French and Hamilton (1979) described it. It comprised eight zones: (1) an ancient core including the Roman and medieval buildings; (2) an inner, capitalist-era downtown and central neighborhoods; (3) a zone of early socialist-era, quasi-traditional/quasi-modern neighborhoods built in the 1950s; (4) a zone of 1960s districts with increasingly modern characteristics; (5) a very large zone of post-1960 housing constructed on former green fields with indus-trialized building methods; (6) generous greenbelts; (7) industrial zones; and (8) countryside and recreational zones (Figure 5.4). The zones were not as neatly concentric as Hamilton proposed them because the socialist planners certainly did not reject all planning legacies of the past and had to deal with metro-Sofia's old hotchpotch spatial structure (for example, Muessman's parks, which acted as radials, were kept where he envisioned them, and the industrial zones had to be inserted between some old villages to avoid mas-sive demolition on land that continued to be held in private hands). Still, the model represents reality fairly accurately.[5]

Consistently with Hamilton's model, Sofia lacked signs of sprawl: its vast mass-housing estates ended abruptly, providing the city with a clearly defined edge framed by concrete towers. Furthermore, even with the significant

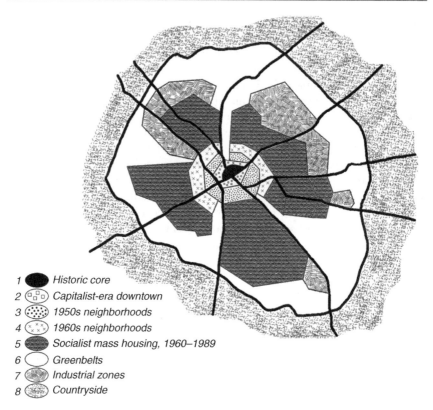

1 ● Historic core
2 ⊙ Capitalist-era downtown
3 ⊙ 1950s neighborhoods
4 ⊗ 1960s neighborhoods
5 ● Socialist mass housing, 1960–1989
6 ○ Greenbelts
7 ◉ Industrial zones
8 ◉ Countryside

Figure 5.4 The eight zones of the socialist city (the graphic uses a simplified version of Sofia's spatial structure as its basis). Based partially on Hamilton (1979) and Stanilov (2009). Map by Anamaria Bukvic.

urban expansion undertaken during the 1960s and 1970s, Sofia, like other socialist cities, remained relatively dense and compact. Density in metropolitan Sofia was about 57.5 persons per ha; in the built-out areas of the city (the "compact city"; Figure 5.3), it averaged 105 persons. This far exceeded the densities of cities in Western Europe and the United States: 42 persons per ha in London, 46 in Paris, 48 in Amsterdam, 53 in Stockholm, 16 in Chicago and 12 in Boston (Kenworthy et al. 2001; Buckley and Tsenkova 2001). The industrial zones were located mostly near the railroad terminal on the north side of the city (following the early-twentieth-century pattern of development). On all other sides, the urbanized areas were surrounded by farms and green fields where construction was either prohibited or severely limited. Beyond the green fields was a string of old-fashioned villages. Some of these villages had attracted the attention of bourgeois elites in the 1920s and 30s and, later on, their socialist successors in the 1970s and 1980s as

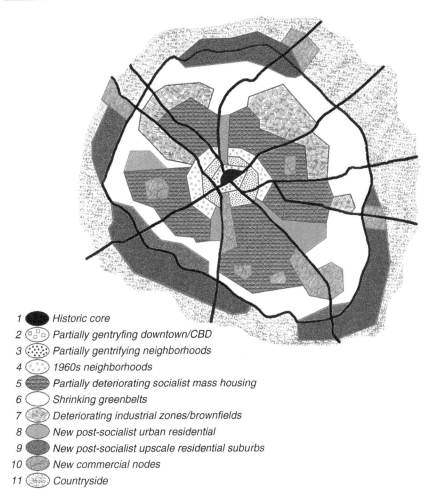

1 Historic core
2 Partially gentryfing downtown/CBD
3 Partially gentrifying neighborhoods
4 1960s neighborhoods
5 Partially deteriorating socialist mass housing
6 Shrinking greenbelts
7 Deteriorating industrial zones/brownfields
8 New post-socialist urban residential
9 New post-socialist upscale residential suburbs
10 New commercial nodes
11 Countryside

Figure 5.5   The post-socialist city in eleven zones. Map by Anamaria Bukvic.

places for the construction of secondary homes (in Bulgarian, *vili*). These semi-rural areas were eventually designated recreational or villa-zones (*vilni zoni*). But the process remained rather limited, as I reiterate in the next chapter. A ring of permanent low-density residential settlements – suburbs, that is – never developed. It was not until the 1990s that Sofia truly attained its ninth, suburban ring (Figure 5.5).

In short then, by 1989, Sofia had a compact urban edge, plentiful public spaces, limited commercial services and large industrial areas, softer social divisions, and a rather monotonous architecture. In other words, it had acquired the five typical characteristics of the socialist city as I outlined them in the previous chapter.

Enter Post-socialism

The end of socialism sparked a severe crisis in Bulgaria. The heavily industrialized, state-run economy collapsed. In the early 1990s, inflation ranged from 40% to 300% annually. GDP fell by about a third from its 1989 level, and unemployment neared 20% (Tables 3.2, 3.3, 3.4 and 3.5). More than half a million people left the country to look for a better life elsewhere, mostly in Western Europe, and the country's population declined by 12%.

Recovery began in 1998 and continued more or less unabated for ten years, until the latest global recession. Inflation and unemployment were constrained to single digits, and GDP grew by 5% to 6% annually – twice the EU average. The economic profile of the country changed fundamentally, with the percentage of persons employed in the service sector shifting from only 19 in the year 1990 to 56 in the year 2000 (the 2007 figure is 57; US CIA undated). Still, it took twelve years to return to the 1980s-level GDP per capita, and the country's income per capita continues to be only about a third of the EU average. Post-2000 Bulgarian governments have adhered strictly to neo-liberal principles, even though one of them was actually dominated by the Socialist (i.e., the former Communist) Party. In addition to securing much-coveted NATO and EU memberships, these governments have taken pride in recent developments such as the near-completion of privatization reforms,[6] the relatively high Foreign Direct Investment levels (about $6 billion per year), the notable increase in living standards (household income doubled between 1999 and 2007), and the fact that the public sector has operated in an environment of such fiscal austerity as to make Bulgaria one of the few European countries running a public-sector surplus in 2008.[7]

In terms of privatization of assets and services, post-socialist Bulgaria generally followed the path of most other East European states, although with some brief initial delay. The only significant deviation is that housing privatization had a limited effect on homeownership rates, since they were already high (they increased from 84% to 92% after restitution and privatization in the early 1990s). Like other governments in the region, the Bulgarian public sector withdrew from the production and distribution of housing, and the annual production of housing units decreased to a fraction of its earlier level. By 2001, the ratio between average housing price and annual household income increased to 6:1, posing monumental challenges to homebuyers at a time when mortgage financing was still a rarity and most homes were purchased in cash (Hirt and Stanilov 2007).[8] Urban programs at the national level were no longer passed, and many planned large public infrastructure projects at both national and urban levels were put on hold (this, however, has changed since Bulgaria entered the EU). The municipal governments unloaded all sorts of activities (e.g., waste collection) onto the private sector, and municipal planning efforts virtually ceased all over the country. Bulgarian towns did not prepare new Master Plans during the 1990s (the only exceptions were municipalities along the Black Sea, whose plans were funded by the World Bank). In Sofia, where the adoption of a new Master Plan is especially complicated since it requires an act of the National Parliament, the planning process was especially byzantine, and as noted above the new plan was not adopted until 2007. In the meantime, the city was supposed to function under its latest legally valid Master Plan from 1961, which was completely irrelevant and thus implicitly disregarded. This meant that growth in Sofia was legally enabled through changes in the regulatory planning schemes that exist only at the city block level. These schemes, as I noted earlier, could easily be modified in piecemeal fashion in response to requests by private investors.[9] The capital city thus functioned without any long-term comprehensive vision for its development for almost twenty years. As one planner I interviewed succinctly put it, for nearly two decades Sofia was "the investor's dream city"; it grew "on auto-pilot" (Hirt 2006). This language implies both the fact that planning was put on the back burner and the fact that, often, planning permits were not even sought. [10] Estimates of the percentage of buildings erected in Sofia without municipal sanction are not available. Yet the phenomenon has been so widespread as to prompt the city's Chief Architect to write an unusually strongly worded piece titled "Zashto?" (Why?), which was published in Bulgaria's largest newspaper (Dikov 2009). Rather than sharing his views on new architectural styles – a topic to be expected from a Chief Architect – P. Dikov chose to discuss illegal usurpation of and construction on public spaces (statutory secession, as I have termed it). Starting his piece with the seemingly trivial question of why a large number of private automobiles were found illegally parked in new bike alleys the morning after the alleys first opened to much municipal fanfare, the Chief Architect went on to ponder why people prey on public space generally and why Bulgarians subvert public rules routinely. He pointed to two chief factors, both of which I alluded to in Chapter 2: the sharp diminution of the notion of public interest in post-socialist laws, and the fact that even when laws do exist to protect the public interest, they are commonly broken by the very elites who passed them. In Dikov's view, these elites then serve as behavioral role models for the rest of the population. Dikov, of course, is not a social scientist, but his ideas seem quite similar to those offered by V. Ganev in *Preying on the State*: that public assets became widely perceived as "objects of extraction," especially by actors who had the greatest opportunity to take advantage of the "extraction" (i.e., post-socialist political elites), thus only contributing to further mass skepticism toward the idea of a benevolent public realm.

The laws Dikov refers to were passed within a few years of the collapse of socialism. They guaranteed a privileged position for private property. The key law on restitution, passed in 1992, postulated that any chunk of land can and should be returned to its pre-World War II owners, as long as no "improvement" had taken place, that is, as long as "an activity for which the land was expropriated [in 1948] had not been initiated."[11] The word "activity" was time and time again interpreted to mean the construction of a substantial structure. Since playgrounds and gardens had only slides, swings, gazebos and benches (rather than "real" structures), they were immediately subject to restitution claims (Kovachev 2001). This applied to both green spaces in the central urban neighborhoods (unless they were labeled as public green spaces before 1948) and to green spaces between residential buildings in the socialist-era districts. The latter were especially vulnerable to restitution claims. As a result of the socialist spatial generosity, the green spaces typically exceeded by far the green-to-built-area ratios required in state land-use ordinances; thus, they were assumed to be "too" green and became ripe territory for private development. For fifteen years, the media routinely published letters to the editor written by residents of socialist districts in all large cities of Bulgaria – letters that expressed shock and outrage at the perpetual conversion of their neighborhood playgrounds to paid parking. The process even acquired a name: construction terrorism (*stroitelen terrorism*).[12] Still, it was sometimes legal as long as the green-to-built-area zoning standards were not violated. The large public parks built in cities after 1948 were technically not in the same category, since they were viewed as having undergone some "improvement," and most were subject to stricter preservation standards based on existing cultural heritage laws. But this did not stop private construction in the large parks, including the city's Botanical Gardens, through various legal loopholes (Local Development Initiative 2004). The topic became so politically contested that in 2003 the National Parliament was forced to pass a moratorium (but not a ban) on construction on green spaces, especially spaces between buildings in the socialist districts of all Bulgarian cities (Hirt and Kovachev 2006). The moratorium, however, did not apply to greenbelts and farm-belts on the periphery of cities. In fact, the rules for the conversion of agricultural land to urban uses have only become more relaxed over time (Stanilov and Hirt forthcoming).[13]

Because of Sofia's undisputed primacy in the national urban hierarchy, which further solidified after 1990 (Buckwalter 1995), the city's economic collapse during the 1990s was slightly softer than elsewhere in the country. Indeed, during the post-socialist period, Sofia has consistently produced nearly 30% of the Bulgarian GDP and attracted close to 50% of all Foreign Direct

Investment (Hirt and Stanilov 2007). Thus, unemployment rates have been consistently lower, and wages consistently higher, than national averages. Still, the first decade of post-socialism was a time of economic quagmire, with poverty peaking at 37% in the mid-1990s (Buckley and Tsenkova 2001). The city economy transitioned from manufacturing-based to service-based (between 1991 and 2001, the percentage of persons employed in the service sector increased from 55% to 70% in the metropolitan region and reached over 80% in the central urban districts; Stolichna Obshtina 2003). Because investment and construction activities were concentrated in the capital city, the spatial privatization processes described above proceeded more intensively in Sofia than anywhere else in the country. Not surprisingly, the 2003 parliamentary moratorium on the conversion of public space to private uses cited Sofia as the nation's most extreme example.

Sofia: Wither the Socialist City

It would be safe to say that during twenty years of post-socialism, Sofia has lost the definitional characteristics of socialist spatial structure as French and Hamilton (1979), Szelényi (1996) and others describe them. Following the taxonomy identified in Chapter 3, I discuss changes in five elements of urban form: overall spatial articulation, spatial scale, functional balance, social character and aesthetic character (Table 3.1; some of these changes are discussed in further detail in the following chapters as well).

One of the most obvious changes was the blurring of the clearly articulated socialist-era urban edge – a process made possible after the undeveloped fields around Sofia were restituted, and the strict building regulations that applied to the pre-socialist-era peripheral villages and the socialist-era recreational zones were lifted.[14] The process started in the 1990s with sporadic residential and commercial construction and intensified immensely after 2000, when economic growth returned to Sofia. In twenty years, the compact city and the ring of villa-zones and villages almost "met" as the greenbelt that had once separated them was consumed by growth.

The legal environment significantly facilitated urban decentralization: there were far more land-ownership conflicts in central Sofia (where several parties often claimed the same small piece of land) than in the urban outskirts (where land was undeveloped before 1948 and private claims of much larger chunks of land could be proven more easily). Furthermore, unlike in the city itself, land in the old villages in the vicinity of Sofia was not nationalized in the mid- to late 1940s, so these villages became prime sites for private construction fifty years later.

Decentralization was initially driven by upper-class residents who chose to secede from central Sofia, ostensibly to seek a higher quality of life

(I return to them in the next chapter). Improvement in living standards after 2000, along with the introduction of mortgage financing, accelerated this exodus (Stanilov and Hirt forthcoming). At about the same time, the decentralization process was further propelled by the need of commercial and industrial facilities for relatively large pieces of land, especially land for parking (these facilities included malls, hypermarkets, warehouses and constellations of new office buildings). By 2003, for the first time in Sofia's history, the outskirts of the city had more high-quality office space than downtown (Colliers International Bulgaria 2004a, 2004b). The largest edge-city-type commercial node today is Business Park Sofia, which was developed by the German Linder Group at the rim of the socialist district of Mladost. The Linder Group was the first firm to acquire First-Class Investor status under a 2004 law that put large, typically multi-national investment firms in a privileged position.[15] Business Park Sofia is touted as the largest business park in the Balkans and a "city within the city" (although "city outside the city" might be more accurate). Located on 22 hectares of former green space, it includes 35 buildings and 300,000 sq m of commercial space housing 150 firms (Business Park Sofia undated).

Business Park Sofia provides a good illustration of how spatial scale and organization have shifted in the transition from socialism to post-socialism. The largest new developments in Sofia are commercial and located outside the city center (therefore, they are accessible largely by private car).[16] Comparable large-scale central-city public projects – like the 1950s Largo or the 1980s People's Palace of Culture – are no longer erected (in fact, the People's Palace of Culture itself is now a commercial building owned by the municipality but rented out to various private tenants). The Business Park is nicely landscaped; with its 22 hectares, it is the largest green space recently developed in Sofia. Although it cannot offset the massive loss of public green space throughout the capital city, it has become a focal point, a meeting place frequently visited by people from Mladost and elsewhere in the city (Figure 5.6). Yet there is a catch: the "park" is not only privately owned but also operates as private space. It is fenced off and accessible only through a few entry points. Its barriers lift for cars only after a visitor slides an employee ID card or receives authorization from a guard (Figure 5.7). It is closed on the weekend and after business hours. Asked how he decides whom to admit, one of the guards explained that he exercises "face control," meaning that he lets in respectable-looking people, mostly in automobiles: men and women in business suits, nicely dressed parents with children, and polite retirees – "people who will not create problems."[17] Others, like unruly teenagers, are not allowed to disturb the peace. "Face control" has no local translation; in Bulgarian it is pronounced phonetically "feis kontrol."

The most obvious element of the functional transformation of post-socialist Sofia has been the decrease of public uses, especially public open

Figure 5.6   The grounds of Business Park Sofia – the largest and, arguably, the best landscaped and maintained new greenery in Sofia created after the end of socialism. Despite its popularity and seeming openness, the Business Park is actually a tightly monitored private space.

space. Although a precise inventory of green-space loss has never been carried out, municipal sources estimate that about 870 to 900 ha have been (to put it casually) "lost in transition" – a striking number that comprises about a third of all such spaces in the city (Local Development Initiative 2004). According to data from 2004, the municipality designated public funds for maintaining only 1000 hectares of the remaining green spaces that it continued to own (Local Development Initiative 2004); this left another third (or about 900 hectares) on "auto-pilot." Privatized lands now include nearly 20% of the South Park, 10% of the West Park and 5% of the North Park (Kovachev 2001; Hirt and Kovachev 2006). Landmark examples of the fate of privatized large green spaces include the massive Hilton Hotel complex, which now occupies parts of the South Park, and the four-hectare site of the new American Embassy, which, ironically, received a certificate of Leadership in Energy and Environmental Design (LEED) from the US Green Building Council (USGBC) in 2007. In socialist districts like Mladost, losses also stand at 20% to 30% (Kovachev 2001). In many cases, the first thing property owners install on their new territory is a fence. This fashion

Figure 5.7 One of the few entry points of Business Park Sofia.

has spread not only among upscale residential buildings but even to some new supermarkets, whose fences usurp former public green spaces and even parts of the adjacent roads and sidewalks (Figure 5.8).

An equally important functional change has been the shifting balance between industrial and commercial land uses in Sofia, following the restructuring of employment. An estimated half of Sofia's once oversized industrial territories lay underused fifteen years after the end of socialism (Stolichna Obshtina 2003).[18] In contrast, commercial areas have grown considerably. Although the number of retail outlets remained steady during the last socialist decade, it quadrupled in about a dozen years after 1989, despite limited population growth (Figure 5.9). The process has been most intense in the socialist housing districts, where retail uses were most scarce during socialism (Figure 5.10), and in the downtown area, which has gained what it lost during socialism: the flavor of a Central Business District (Figure 5.11). The downtown landscape has been transformed by countless new retail spaces, some of which were formerly used as small libraries, galleries and theaters. Graffiti on a downtown building, perhaps written by some angry member of the shrinking intelligentsia, described the process succinctly, if sarcastically: "Every theater a mall, every gallery a pub!"[19] Official statistics actually underestimate the feverish commercial activity that spread through

Figure 5.8 The entrance of the German-owned hyper-market HIT. The store is surrounded by a light fence, which is locked after business hours. The billboard says "Welcome! We work for you." The smaller sign on the guard's kiosk says "Attention: permanent video-surveillance."

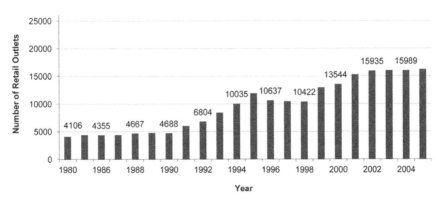

Figure 5.9 The retail revolution of post-socialist Sofia. The number of retail outlets remained stable through the 1980s but quadrupled in the 1990s, even though population growth was marginal. Growth has lately levelled off, likely because of both market saturation and the high rates of small business bankruptcy, which followed the entry of Western super-stores like HIT.
Source: National Statistical Institute, Sofia. Chart by Anamaria Bukvic.

Figure 5.10   The first floor and even parts of the second floor of this drab socialist-era residential building became shops in the 1990s. Not only ground-floor apartments but even common entry halls became selling spaces (here, we see a pharmacy, a video game store, etc.).

the city in the early 1990s. At the time, much commerce was conducted not in officially designated structures but in open public spaces, in sidewalks and in parks, adding a patina of liveliness and informality to what was once a rather boring urban environment. The explosion of retail leveled off after 2000, probably because of market saturation as well as the bankruptcy of hundreds of the small family businesses that dominated the 1990s, which could not survive competition with the new multi-national big-box retailers (Stolichna Obshtina 2003; Figure 5.9).

Post-socialist spatial restructuring in Sofia both continues and augments socialist (and pre-socialist) inequality patterns. Several researchers have identified growing social-spatial inequality as integral to Sofia's post-socialist transition (Staddon and Mollov 2000; Vesselinov and Logan 2005; Valkanov 2006). However, we lack comprehensive data such as that available for other large Central and East European cities like Berlin (see, e.g., Häussermann and Kapplan 2005). The problem is that the Bulgarian census conducted by the National Statistical Institute does not provide data on the classic attributes of social status (e.g., income, education, occupation) at the neighborhood level or at any other fine-grained level such as a city-block or groups of city blocks. Rather, some data is provided at the level of the

Figure 5.11 Old Sofia in new clothes: this mid-20th-century, formerly residential downtown building has had several of its units converted to commercial use and has thus been suitably redecorated. The fast commercialization of the urban landscape is sometimes semi-jokingly referred to as "ground-floor capitalism" (also Sármány-Parsons 1998).

administrative districts shown in Figure 5.3 (data on income is provided only for Sofia as a whole). But some of these administrative districts, especially those in the urban periphery, are very large, sparsely populated and diverse (for example, they have upscale suburban populations in some places, and very poor rural populations in other places). This renders any analysis meaningless. An alternative, if imperfect, way of demonstrating inequalities is to look at housing prices, since these are reported by real estate firms at a finer-grained scale for the urbanized areas of Sofia (the "compact city"; Figure 5.3). This data shows extremely large price differentials (Figure 5.12). Average asking prices for housing in the center of Sofia and south of it (including in the new suburbs discussed in Chapter 6) are 1200 or more Euros per square meter. In the northern parts of the city, they are under 200 Euros per square meter (data is unavailable for some areas, including the Roma ghettoes, since few formal property transactions occur there). This stark contrast well exceeds what could be found in socialist Sofia, and it has only been increasing in recent years.[20] The pattern builds on the traditional, pre-socialist lines of socio-spatial segregation in Sofia: the south facing the green hills of Mount Vitosha has always been the serene, desirable place to live, whereas the north is the site of the railroad and the city's largest and most polluting industries (Staddon and Mollov 2000; Hirt and Stanilov 2007). Still, the division has been exacerbated in recent times, as informal terms for these areas suggest. While the north is said to be made of "black spots" (*cherni petna*; this refers particularly to the Roma neighborhoods), the south is said to be made of "golden ghettoes" (*zlatni geta*). Of course, this neat dichotomy oversimplifies matters. For example, the "golden ghettoes" are perpetually infiltrated by poor construction workers, many of them Roma, since they happen to build the very houses in which the *nouveau riche* live. (The presence of "roaming" construction workers is sometimes identified as a reason for gating and securitization in the suburbs, as I discuss in Chapters 7 and 8.) Furthermore, downtown has for twenty years been the territory of desperate Roma boys and girls who, despite draconian police efforts, never seem to go away. (One resident of the "golden ghettoes" described the major difference between pre- and post-1989 Sofia as follows: "Well, now the gypsies are everywhere.") Finally, the ring road, which divides the city from its growing suburbs, is flanked by as many signs of new wealth (e.g., new upscale furniture stores) as signs of new marginality (e.g., young girls selling their bodies).

Finally, any account of the spatial structure of post-socialist Sofia would be incomplete without a mention of its changing architectural traditions. I attempt to classify the architectural styles that have emerged in Sofia since the end of socialism in Chapter 9; thus I offer only a brief note here. In a nutshell, as one Bulgarian sociologist put it, after 1989 the building paradigm moved from a "state of full-blown collectivism to a state of full-blown individualism" (Dandolova 2002). This transformation entails not only the spread of diverse and often peculiar styles, but also the very process by which buildings "appear" on the ground. The once orderly fabric of the city, especially the fabric of its socialist-era neighborhoods, has been penetrated by new structures in unexpected locations. New buildings have appeared between existing buildings and sometimes even upon them (e.g., the self-built commercial extensions located on the second floor of a socialist housing tower, shown in Figure 5.10). These ad hoc structures – roof additions, lateral extensions, semi-enclosed selling stands, kiosks, cafés, shops, small restaurants – are sometimes derogatorily referred to as "mushrooms" (*gubi*) or "popcorn" (*pukanki*) precisely because of the way they quickly (and often illegally) pop up. Regardless of their aesthetic deficiencies, they seem to have filled some of the land-use vacuum left over from socialism, and they have created a pluralist environment. One long-term resident of the Mladost socialist housing district, who is an architect, described the new environment as one rich in "delightful, medieval-like surprises."

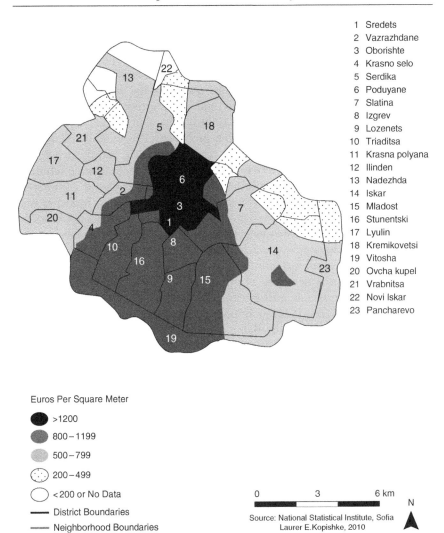

1 Sredets
2 Vazrazhdane
3 Oborishte
4 Krasno selo
5 Serdika
6 Poduyane
7 Slatina
8 Izgrev
9 Lozenets
10 Triaditsa
11 Krasna polyana
12 Ilinden
13 Nadezhda
14 Iskar
15 Mladost
16 Stunentski
17 Lyulin
18 Kremikovetsi
19 Vitosha
20 Ovcha kupel
21 Vrabnitsa
22 Novi Iskar
23 Pancharevo

Euros Per Square Meter
● >1200
● 800–1199
● 500–799
⬚ 200–499
◯ <200 or No Data
━━ District Boundaries
━ ━ Neighborhood Boundaries

0   3   6 km
N

Source: National Statistical Institute, Sofia
Laurer E.Kopishke, 2010

Figure 5.12 Average asking prices per square meter for housing in the urbanized areas of Sofia, 2010. Based on real-estate magazines such as Imoti, June 2010. Price differentials are quite dramatic and the majority of expensive housing is (and traditionally has been) located in and south of the city center.

In conclusion, the recent transformation of Sofia's spatial structure well illustrates the general features of post-socialist restructuring as outlined in the previous chapters. A modified, post-socialist version of Hamilton's (1979) urban model might contain the following elements: (1) an ancient core including the Roman and medieval buildings; (2) an inner, pre-World War

II downtown, which has undergone intense commercialization since 1989 and has acquired the characteristics of a capitalist-style Central Business District surrounded by some of the most expensive housing in the city; (3) a zone of early socialist-era, quasi-traditional/quasi-modern neighborhoods built in the 1950s; (4) a zone of 1960s districts with increasingly modern features; (5) a very large zone of post-1960 housing districts, many of which have deteriorated significantly since 1989 but have also been diversified in terms of land-use balance; (6) shrunken greenbelts; (7) generally dilapidated industrial zones; (8) new urban in-fill residential zones, mostly in place of former greenbelts that were close to the central areas; (9) an upscale suburban periphery of mostly single-family homes; (10) new peripheral commercial nodes; and (11) a chopped-up countryside (Figure 5.5) The model is only roughly concentric – the new periphery is to a large extent built onto the greenbelts and the old-fashioned villages that survived the socialist period without much change.

Whereas the overall structural composition of the city (i.e., its current eleven rings) can be generalized as a post-socialist model, the visual character of the city, I believe, has a distinct Southeast European or, perhaps more accurately, Balkan feel. It is much more colorful, unruly, than anything one finds in Central Europe or the Baltic region. This urbanism resulted at least in part from the following factors: (1) the extraordinary weakness of Bulgarian public institutions in the 1990s (including their near-total withdrawal from planning and development control, which sparked an assortment of private, self-styled strategies); (2) the extremely aggressive application of land privat-ization laws; and (3) the strikingly predatory attitudes toward public assets, including space, of elites and middle classes, precisely as Ganev (2007) and Dikov (2009) describe them. Regardless of how we position Sofia's contem-porary urbanism in reference to urbanism in other parts of post-socialist Europe or other world regions where the characteristics of spatial modernity are being challenged, it is clear that Sofia is being dynamically reshaped by multiple spatial secessions: secessions from common urban space entailing its seizure and usurpation for private purposes; secessions from rules and from the common styles that define the architectural heritage of Sofia; and secessions from the city altogether, as residents withdraw to isolated and explicitly private settings on the urban fringe. No part of Sofia exhibits these spatial secessions better than the gated homes of its sprawling new suburbs. I turn to these suburbs and their residents in the next chapter.

Notes

1   A new design for some downtown extension or remodeling was prepared about every five years between 1880 and 1928 (Kovachev 2001; Hirt 2005a).

2 About 12,000 buildings in Sofia were destroyed by bombs during World War II (Tashev 1972; Labov 1979).

3 As one of the planners in charge of the socialist housing estates put it in a media interview: "We could not have stayed within the borders of the existing city – the cranes and the lines of panels demanded expansion" (Mushev 1992).

4 For example in Mladost, the average number of dwelling units per building constructed during the 1980s was fifty. Certainly no such buildings existed in Sofia before the introduction of industrialized building methods (Hirt 2006).

5 It is not hard to see that Hamilton's model can to some extent be used to represent the twentieth-century capitalist city just as well, at least in Europe. Zones 1 and 2 (the ancient core and the early capitalist downtown) can be certainly found in most older European cities regardless of which side of the Iron Curtain they once were. Some of the rings (e.g., the modernist housing estates and the industrial districts) were proportionally larger in socialist cities, but their general location was similar to that in capitalist cities. The lack of low-density residential periphery remains an undisputed difference between the socialist city and its capitalist counterpart, but differences in this respect may be actually greater between the American and the European city (assuming these can used as models) than between the East and the West European city. This outcome can be partially explained in terms of the role of the public sector vis-à-vis the private sector in the production of housing, as well as by some differences in housing preferences between the European and the American populations. Once again, this leads us to the question posed at the beginning of Chapter 3: was the socialist city an autonomous urban model, or did industrial modernity – capitalist or socialist – produce broadly similar spatial results?

6 According to the Bulgarian Privatization Agency, as of December 31, 2008, 99% of all state assets which were designated for privatization were indeed privatized. This comprises two-thirds of all socialist-era state assets.

7 Based on *Resume: Ikonomikata na Bulgaria v nachaloto na 2008 godina* [Summary: *The Bulgarian Economy at the beginning of 2008*; in Bulgarian], unpublished report provided to the author by the Ministry of the Economy. Since the start of the global recession in 2008, however, the Bulgarian government is no longer running a surplus.

8 Since most households in Bulgaria owned their homes, lack of housing affordability was not among the most pressing issues of the transition period. However, it should be noted that the socialist mass-produced dwellings were very small by European standards and overcrowding in such dwellings continues to be routine.

9 These schemes were always changed *after* a private investor's proposal instead of proactively as a result of considering what potential changes may be desirable. The first private construction project that was halted because there was no comprehensive plan for an area came in 2008 in the district of Studentski.

10 Despite asking for years, I have never been able to find an estimate that I could corroborate. An interesting "black list" of the largest firms which have built illegally (and the names of government officials who have turned a blind eye) has been compiled by citizen organizations. See http://bgnature-blacklist.bravehost.com/index-en.html (accessed November 17, 2011).

11   Another key law was the Law on Municipal Property of 1996. This law
      introduced the idea that municipal property can be either public or private.
      "Public municipal property" included the structures necessary for the
      municipalities to continue operating (e.g., the municipal buildings) and other
      properties which are vital to the "public interest." Such property could not be
      subjected to restitution and privatization. The second category, "private
      municipal property," included all other municipal holdings. This type of
      municipal property could be restituted, sold or rented to private parties in order
      to increase municipal revenues. It typically included all municipally owned
      green spaces, excluding the large urban parks.

12   The newspaper *Novinar*, for example, published an article calling on the
      municipal authorities to finally stop "construction terrorism" (Delijska 2008).

13   A recent report by the Directorate of Agriculture and Forestry noted that no
      more than 1% of the thousands of applications for changing land designation
      from rural to urban status have been declined since the year 2000. In 2004
      alone, 460 sq km of agricultural land were rezoned for urban expansions
      (Stanilov and Hirt forthcoming).

14   There were discussions in the 1990s to preserve a London-style greenbelt
      around Sofia by offering the pre-1948 owners either compensation or land in
      the compact city. Ultimately, however, the greenbelts were fully restituted.

15   The law guarantees government support to large-scale (and therefore generally
      suburban) developments. The support entails faster project approval and financial
      breaks (e.g., permitting the fast conversion of agricultural land to commercial
      zoning and securing government help for land acquisition; Stanilov and Hirt
      forthcoming). Since 2004, several mighty foreign investors have received this
      privileged status for large-scale sprawling developments: the French Carrefour
      (for several hypermarkets in the periphery of Sofia), the Greek Danaos, the
      Austrian Shopping City and the Austrian Forum (all three for new suburban
      malls), and the Spanish Ferry Group (for a monumental 160-hectare golf
      community in the outskirts of the capital city; Stanilov and Hirt forthcoming).

16   Over the last twenty years, the number of cars in Sofia has quadrupled, whereas
      the population has increased only marginally. Official statistics put the number
      of cars at 800,000 in 2005. In 2010, the number got closer to a million. This
      makes Sofia fourth among European capitals in cars per person. Traffic jams
      are now a constant companion to urban life, especially along the roads
      connecting the city center to the suburban areas. The problem may be partially
      mitigated in the future, since Sofia's authorities finally mustered enough will
      and resources to start the construction of a citywide subway system (see also
      Stanilov 2009).

17   In Bulgarian; "*Tia deto niama da mi praviat problemi.*"

18   Thus, in 2003, the municipal authorities counted only 13% of Sofia's territory
      as designated for industrial purposes as compared to 27% during late socialism
      (Stolichna Obshtina 2003).

19   In Bulgarian: *Vseki teater mol, vsiaka galleria kruchma!*

20   For example, the same type of data but for 1999, cited in Vesselinov and Logan
      (2005), shows a much smaller range.

6

The Ninth Ring: Suburbanizing Sofia

"Sofia is a madhouse and now an opportunity has opened for me to escape it!"
Excerpt from an interview with a new resident
in Sofia's growing southern suburbs, 2004

Sofia is sprawling. Has it happened before? Some hundred years ago, its periphery comprised the unplanned proletarian and war refugees' huts, which were spread out too amorphously and too far from the city center to be efficiently served by its infrastructure (or so at least thought Mayor Ivanov, who commissioned the 1934 Master Plan in part to address this issue). Some fifty years later, during socialism, the periphery began to grow intensely again, this time as a result of intense planning. The goal was to make a home for the socialist middle class in the modern high-density standardized housing blocks.

I believe, however, that the twenty-first-century peripheral expansion is Sofia's first "real" sprawl; it is a low-density and relatively upscale expansion that is now "eating up" the once clear-cut edge of the city. Not only does this expansion look different from its predecessors but, I argue, it involves social processes and reflects cultural preferences that are new to Bulgaria's capital. Sofia is now undergoing a process in which parts of its upper and middle classes are intentionally exiting the city to settle in its greener outskirts; thus, they are suburbanizing (at least according to the specific definition of suburbanization I offer on the next pages). In this way, Sofia is far from unique among the large cities of Central and Eastern Europe: as Ladányi and Szelényi (1998) noted some dozen years ago, urban decentralization of this type is perhaps the "most striking new phenomenon of post-communist urban development." For Sofia, though, it is the first time.

Iron Curtains, First Edition. Sonia A. Hirt.
© 2012 John Wiley & Sons, Ltd. Published 2012 by John Wiley & Sons, Ltd.

In this chapter, I interpret the process of residential decentralization partially as a function of cultural change, specifically changing residential preferences regarding how to live, where to live and with whom to live. I make my case by offering a close look at the views and lifestyles of people residing in the fastest-growing parts of Sofia, its southern outskirts, as well as by reviewing select documents and media materials related to this new type of peripheral development. My interest is driven by the observation that the very absence of this type of suburbs was one of the most fundamental distinctions between the socialist city and the capitalist city as outlined in the previous chapters; thus, the intense development of Sofia's ninth, suburban ring (to use Hamilton's typology of the eight socialist urban concentric rings for the last time) has made the burgeoning suburbia a paradigmatic compo- nent of post-socialist urban spatial restructuring. My interest is also driven by my belief in the intimate relationship between suburbanization and the search for private and exclusive family lifestyles: suburbia is, to quote Mumford once again, "the collective effort to live a private life" (1938: 43). I do not suggest that the causes of post-socialist residential suburbanization are solely or even primarily cultural (nor do I suggest that culture is the sole driver of any other aspect of post-socialist urban change). On the contrary, the process of post- socialist suburbanization has been enabled by a series of legal and economic factors contributing to both the supply and the demand sides of the equation, many of which I identified earlier. To summarize, these include: the mass restitution and privatization of land in the urban periphery; the privatization of the building sector, which led to the emergence of actors seeking to profit from converting agricultural land to urban uses; the weakening of planning rules pertaining to the urban rim; commercial pressures on downtown, which resulted in a notable residential exodus toward distant locations; a shortage of public investment in older urban areas and the socialist districts, which made them less desirable over time; and the dramatic increase in the number of private automobiles, which not only aggravated pollution (thus making central Sofia a less attractive place to live) but also made possible, for the first time in Sofia's history, daily commuting between the center and the periphery. After the Bulgarian economy stabilized at the dawn of the new millennium, Sofia experienced additional impetus for suburbanization. Standards of living rose, and the building and housing industries experienced significant changes. The building industry underwent consolidation and became dominated by larger firms, including a number of transnationals with the capacity to erect bigger housing subdivisions and provide them with the necessary infrastructure. This process was facilitated by recent laws such as the one mentioned earlier that grants preferential status to large investors. Finally, home mortgage financing became much more widely available.

My argument, however, is that this long list of suburban prerequisites, many of which have been already extensively discussed in the literature on suburbanization across post-socialist Europe, is incomplete. To it we must add the current fascination with private, single-family living in increasingly exclusive settings, a lifestyle that seems to have captured the imagination of post-socialist elites, at least in Sofia. My thesis is thus similar to the one advanced by Robert Fishman (1987) on the origins of bourgeois suburbia in eighteenth- and nineteenth-century England: that although economic, institutional and technological factors were indispensable enablers of the suburbanization process, suburbia was in part a cultural creation – the outcome of collective upper- and later middle-class distaste for dense and messy urbanism. It was, in part, a cultural phenomenon because it involved a rethinking of the relationship between home and work, family and community or, in other words, private and public. Without forcing unnecessary parallels between the eighteenth and nineteenth centuries and the twenty-first century, I argue that contemporary suburbanization in Sofia has not been propelled, on the demand side, merely by the practical quest for larger, higher-quality dwellings that are difficult to obtain in dense urban settings, as some scholars have suggested (e.g., Valkanov 2006). Nor is it some objective, inevitable outcome of rising living standards (see, e.g., Timar and Varadi 2001). Rather, like suburbanization in Western settings, it has been an active exercise in spatial secession, urban escapism, and renegotiation of the place of the individual and family in the city. I further contend that it is a process distinct from any other peripheral growth in Sofia's history (including during socialism). It is a process driven at least partially by a not-so-subtle dislike of city life, as well as a conscientious rejection of socialist residential collectivism, and a romantic yearning for the private family lifestyle that socialist ideologues tried to suppress in large cities across socialist Eastern Europe. (Of course, the socialist elites exempted themselves from some of the rules as they enjoyed their luxury weekend villas.) The romance is on display not only in the promotional literature written by those who directly benefit from building suburbia (the real estate industry), but also in various media discourses and even in official urban policy documents. If Sofia's socialist planners condemned the idea of the suburban single-family home as "bourgeois-fascist" on the grounds that "[i]t is the yard that makes the bourgeois," post-socialist planners seem to have welcomed it as part of the larger project of converting Sofia into a "normal" (i.e., Western-like), "civilized" city. I propose, then, that the building of post-socialist suburbia can be viewed, in part, as a purposeful effort to secede from and deconstruct not simply the city, but the *socialist* city.

Defining Suburbanization: Capitalist Versus Socialist Contexts

I should start by discussing what I mean by suburbanization. The term is more complex than its common use implies. Throughout history, cities have of course expanded by conquering new territories at their rim, especially in times of population growth. Whether all these expansions can be qualified as suburbanization very much depends on the definition we choose to employ. Even during the twentieth century, cities around the world have grown by a variety of processes that, depending on our definition, may or may not constitute suburbanization. One such process, associated mostly with contemporary cities in the developing world, is rural-to-urban migration, sometimes referred to as rural urbanization. This process involves the relocation of residents from the countryside, including the immediate urban hinterlands, to large urban centers. A variation on the same theme is stepwise migration (the relocation of residents from provincial towns to urban nodes that occupy the higher tiers of the urban hierarchy). Along with population growth, rural-to-urban migration was the main mechanism by which cities in the Western world expanded during the Industrial Revolution (see, e.g., Knox and McCarthy 2005). East European cities experienced the same pattern of growth as a predictable outcome of industrialization in the late 1800s and early 1900s. Early twentieth-century Sofia – the city surrounded by the proletarian and refugees' slums – was certainly no exception. Rural-to-urban migration continued, in a different, more intense and organized form, after the advent of socialism. The new regime embraced urban industrialization as a key state objective, an objective that could be accomplished by enveloping the historic urban parts of the city in massive standardized districts. As I have already noted, however, the latter had little to do with the type of upper- and middle-class, low-density, single-family-home-dominated suburbs that one finds at the rim of Western cities, especially in the United States, in terms of either formative processes or spatial features.[1]

The edge of East European cities during socialism expanded in at least two other ways as well. Socialist regimes normally imposed strict restrictions on urban citizenship, ostensibly to achieve balanced growth and prevent housing shortages. Thus, citizens could not freely settle in a city of their choice without a government permit, although some spontaneous rural-to-urban migration still occurred. When aspiring urbanites searching for access to urban jobs and services failed to secure government approval, they had little choice but to settle in old villages and small towns on the outskirts of big cities, which caused some peripheral metropolitan expansion.[2] Some peripheral growth also occurred through the construction of modest cottages with garden plots in rural or recreational zones (e.g., the Russian *dacha*, the Bulgarian *villa*, the Yugoslav *weekendica* and the Czechoslovak *chata*). Many of these part-time cottages enabled their lower- and middle-class owners to supplement their diets with home-grown fruits and vegetables. Other "cottages," however – especially those belonging to party leaders and favored members of the intelligentsia – were used for recreational purposes and had all the markings of important status symbols. Such cottages became increasingly popular in the 1970s and 1980s.

Neither of these development processes, however, amounted to suburbanization as I use the term in this chapter. Neither had much to do with purposeful attempts to secede from city life. Following Jackson (1985) and Fishman (1987) among others, I take suburbanization to mean urban decentralization, that is, the outflow of population from an urban center to its periphery (see also Hirt 2007b). The process has historically been driven primarily by upper- and middle-class households who permanently settle in the urban outskirts in order to improve their quality of life (e.g., by leaving urban crowding and pollution behind and finding more "family-oriented" lifestyles in greener, more private and socially homogeneous settings), while continuing to depend on the central city for jobs and services.[3] This is not a universally accepted definition.[4] Indeed, some authors classify other processes of urban or metropolitan expansion, including rural-to-urban migration and stepwise migration, as suburbanization.[5] The suburbanization I discuss here, though, is a specific type of metropolitan expansion: it is the only one that involves a conscious urban escapism, a conscious secession from the chaos and complexity of urbanity, a conscious pursuit of a private family lifestyle in a green setting.[6] Before socialism, this process burgeoned in only a few East European cities such as Budapest (Kovacs 1994; Kok and Kovacs 1999). Sofia was not among them: as I mentioned, the very idea of building "garden towns," as Muessman proposed in 1934, was at the time perceived as distinctly foreign. The socialist villa, the one owned by privileged bureaucrats and intellectuals, was perhaps the closest prototype of a suburban home,[7] but it did not evolve into a place of full-time residence until the post-socialist 1990s, at least in Bulgarian cities.[8] The scenic southern outskirts of Sofia, where most of the upscale new growth is now occurring, remained well into the 1980s not much more than a string of rundown villages, only sporadically penetrated by the villas of the party apparatchiks.

Theories on Suburbanization

Scholars have long portrayed the type of suburbanization I discuss here as a logical stage in the process of modern metropolitan growth (e.g., Fielding 1982; Van den Berg 1987; Vartianen 1989; Kok and Kovacs 1999). In this interpretation, middle- and upper-class actors find residences in greener settings and escape the disadvantages of urban living, while retaining proximity to urban jobs and services; thus they combine the best of both worlds, and their decisions represent rational behavior in response to external circumstances. These locational choices are made possible by a number of supply-side prerequisites, including the availability of land and infrastructure in the urban periphery, the active presence of a profit-seeking private building industry, and various advances in transportation technology.

Although we can hardly question the presence of these prerequisites, overemphasizing them risks obscuring the extent to which suburbanization is underpinned by specific changes in attitudes, preferences and lifestyle ideals – changes that do not follow invariably from "objective" economic or technological preconditions.[9] On the contrary, as Fishman (1987), Spain (1992), Hayden (2004) and many others have shown, in England and the United States, for example, the suburbanization process entailed several substantial reversals in commonly held views of what is possible, what is proper and what is desirable. The new views attained a dominant position in society after decades of advocacy in a variety of sites of public discourse, from novels to popular media to professional journals. These reversals include: a rethinking of the relationship between the urban core and the periphery (i.e., the periphery came to be seen as a place of prestige, as opposed to backward and undesirable); a rethinking of the relationship between home and city, private and public, family and community (i.e., the nuclear family came to be seen as the quintessential, autonomous unit of society that could and should exist apart from city life – an ideal best materially exemplified by the single-family suburban home)[10]; and a rethinking of the role of women in society (i.e., women came to be seen as "ministers of home" (Beecher 2006 [1865]) who should secede from messy urbanity and, therefore, from business and political life). Scholars have demonstrated the latter point time and time again even in contemporary conditions, decades after women joined politics and business in substantial numbers in the Western world (e.g., Cristaldi 2005; Crane 2007), much as they did in socialist societies. Furthermore, high-power opportunities continue to be concentrated in central nodes, so suburbanization tends to reinforce gender inequality by presenting women with yet another obstacle to their advancement – this time, a spatial one. In this sense, suburbanization tends to convert women's "social entrapment" into "spatial entrapment" (Stimpson et al. 1981; Hanson and Johnson 1985; Oberhauser 2000). These gender inequalities were of course more prominent in the exclusively residential suburbs of the nineteenth century, in which women were literally spatially confined. The continuous relocation of jobs from cities to suburbs during the twentieth century across the Western world and the more active role of women in society today have mitigated this spatial effect to an extent. However, there is persistent evidence of a gender gap in all life spheres: occupational segregation by gender persists (see, e.g., Hanson and Pratt 1995) and women continue to spend more time in household work and child care (Bittman et al. 2003; Schwanen 2007). Furthermore, they travel much shorter distances to work than men and their private and work spheres remain confined in narrower boundaries (Blumen 1994; Cristaldi 2005; Crane 2007). Thus, low-density, suburban patterns continue to reinforce gender inequalities (Wyly 1998). Clearly, the ideal of private family living away from the urban bustle is far from gender-neutral.

Suburbanizing Sofia

To this day, the word "suburbanization" has no translation in the Bulgarian language. The term closest to "suburbs" is *predrgradia* ("in front of the city"). In the past, it referred sometimes to the most peripheral socialist districts and sometimes to the older edges of the city, mostly on the poorer northern side. Never before 1990, however, did the term imply higher-status settlements in the urban periphery. Lacking an appropriate term to capture the dynamics of post-socialist growth, especially growth on the south side of the city, most Sofia citizens refer to these settlements simply as *novite kvartali* (the "new neighborhoods") or, less subtly, as *zlatnite geta* (the "golden ghettoes"). Sofia's newly rich (*novobogatashi*) are in fact often called "those from the new neighborhoods" (*onia ot novite kvartali*),[11] even when the speaker has no idea of where the described person resides. This is an interesting example of how space itself – in this case, new suburban space – has become a key formative component of group identity in the collective imagination.

The absence of terminology should not obscure the fact that the suburban family home – a housing concept neither possible nor widely coveted during socialism – began to appear routinely in a romantic light right after 1989. This happened on the pages of both popular and professional magazines such as *Nash Dom* (Our Home), *Arhitektura* (Architecture) and *Jenata Dnes* (The Woman Today), which began to present family homes as both a logical and a desirable alternative to socialist living. (Socialist housing was promptly dubbed "the architecture of totalitarianism"; Klassanov 1992.) Take, for example, a 1991 *Arhitektura* article by a team of sociologists and architects on the changing needs of the Bulgarian family. The article praised the virtues of the traditional family home located in a spacious setting, a home that could be found in old Bulgarian towns, yet one that, as the authors correctly argued, was "brutally attacked" during the socialist period with all the instruments of the state. Going so far as to dismiss not only the large socialist residential tower but even the medium-scale apartment building – the type of residence that defined Sofia's center in the 1920s and 1930s – the authors argued that autonomous family living is an important prerequisite for a democratic society. By the mid- to late 1990s, the city's streets (especially on the south side) were decorated with renderings of "dream" single-family homes, often advertised in English as much to attract foreign buyers as to evoke the "American Dream" on Bulgarian soil (Figure 6.1). Also around that time, architectural and planning journals took a sudden interest in Muessman's sixty-year-old plan for Sofia, partially because it advocated a green single-family periphery. Once an obscure, half-forgotten figure, Muessman not only attained near-hero status in professional circles, but also became virtually a household

Figure 6.1 A billboard located by Sofia's Ring Road advertising new suburban homes.

name. Moreover, the suburban ideal received serious official endorsement in all major planning documents prepared at the time. For example, the first draft plan for Sofia's southern outskirts, which was created six years after the end of socialism, not only acknowledged burgeoning suburban growth but recommended it as the most appropriate model for the city's rim. This growth was enabled by the repeal of the area's few remaining socialist-era building restrictions (Hirt 2007a, 2011).

Sofia's first post-socialist Master Plan, the one adopted in 2007 after several years of political wrangling, took these recommendations several steps further. Initially, the master-planning process involved two competing scenarios for Sofia's development, each developed by a multi-disciplinary team of experts. The first team argued for a compact Sofia. The urban greenbelts would retain some legal protection, while the authorities would focus on finding ways to develop Sofia's internal, underused urban territories, including its multiple brown-fields. (In fact, the team's analysis showed that vacant urban territories could accommodate up to 260,000 new dwellings – far more than the city would need in the foreseeable future.) In contrast, the second team lamented that Sofia continued to be denser than Western capitals and sought to implement the "dispersed city model." In this scenario, the municipal authorities would not only permit but actively encourage suburbanization through regulatory and (so far as possible) financial means. The new Master Plan ultimately adopted the goals of the second, pro-suburban scenario; these goals were echoed in yet another policy document, Sofia's regional plan, a couple of years later. The final version of the 2007 Master Plan included language such as the following:

Dispersed living amid nature, an expression of new forms of spatial organization inherent to the information society and enabled by advanced communication technology, should be encouraged …. It is not necessary to utilize the whole potential of the existing urban territory. The growth of residential areas should be related to the growth in the standards of living rather than population growth. The already populated existing urban areas should only be renovated keeping in mind that the correlation between urban density and urban poverty is so obvious that it needs no further proof.

The goals of the plan were justified on multiple grounds. The plan was seen, for example, as a creative mechanism for preserving green space without investing public funds in it. The basic argument was that Sofia lacks the resources and the logistical capacity to keep and maintain its socialist-era greenbelts and should thus transfer them to private parties who have the resources to preserve them in the form of lush green private yards. Through the privatization process, the city would thus save money, while providing its middle-class population with opportunities to live in a more private and ostensibly healthier manner – a win–win situation for both the public and the private sectors. Interviewed at about the time the plan was adopted, three leading experts responsible for the "dispersed city model" scenario explained how the compact city represents the unfortunate legacy of socialism – a legacy that a contemporary, democratic society must reject and deconstruct. Suburbanization, in this view, took on the bold mission of civilizing Sofia, converting it into a Western-style city.

The time of totalitarian control is gone. The time when people [could] be told where to live is finished. We can't tell people anymore how big an apartment [to get] and who their neighbors should be! This is now a free country and a market economy …. So it would be improper for the municipality to have a policy that constrains people's choices as a policy of telling them where or how to live and thus either encourage or discourage this social mix that still exists. There must be freedom of movement. This is the foundation of the new system. The market will decide where people will live. The goal of keeping a social mix [a goal advocated by the team proposing to keep Sofia compact] smells too much like a totalitarian state …. And, in fact, the whole thing seems to me to be a win–win situation. You have money – you buy land in the urban out-skirts! The money goes to a poor person who can then move to a cheaper place and use the remainder [of the money] for a better lifestyle. It's good for both!

By all means, the dispersed model should be encouraged …. The dispersed model can save the compact city from crowding and congestion. Thus far … during the early years of the transition, we have not been able to fund this [model]. But now the situation is improving, things will be changing …. We all know that large cities all over the world have developed peripheries, and often it is the affluent people who live in them in many cities. People who can

afford it naturally try to leave the city and live in a greener environment ....
So our long-term goal is to create the conditions to enable parts of the
population to do that, so that Sofia can catch up with the global tendencies.

We want to encourage new types of dwellings, in a new type of environment
of a totally different character, and encourage a lifestyle that is closer to
nature. People are totally fed up with this over-urbanized environment that is
now the compact city .... Our people ... long to live amid nature. In socialist
times, the government had an interest in cramming people in high-density
housing estates because it saved money. But in a market economy, in an
information-type society, in a democracy, the compact city is no longer the
right choice.

By about a decade after the end of socialism, the suburban ideal had acquired
a prominent position. This is evident in the fact that the only two surveys
addressing the housing preferences of city residents showed a substantial
shift: in the mid-1980s, the ratio of people preferring a single-family home
over an apartment building was 20/80; by the mid-1990s, it had flipped to
80/20, even though it was still difficult for most people to obtain single-family
homes (Dandolova 2002). Preferences translated into trends. By the end of
the 1990s, it was already clear that systematic relocation from the city
center to its periphery was underway, probably driven by the suburban
ideals described above (Figure 6.2). We can draw some inferences from the
1992 and 2002 censuses[12] (Nacionalen Statisticheski Institut 1993, 2003).
The census data shows that during this time period, the population of metropolitan Sofia remained almost unchanged. Yet significant population and
housing growth occurred in all peripheral districts, with the exception of the
heavily polluted industrial district of Kremikovtsi on the north side of the
city,[13] while serious losses occurred in the neighborhoods in the central areas
(Figure 6.3). The data also indicates that the fastest-growing administrative
districts are along the southern urban rim (e.g., Vitosha and Pancharevo,
the most picturesque parts of the region, in the foothills of Mount Vitosha).
    Additional data (Nacionalen Statisticheski Institut undated) shows how the
built patterns in these peripheral areas differ from those in the denser parts
of the city, especially the socialist districts. Whereas densities in socialist districts such as Mladost and Nadejda reach up to 400 persons per hectare,
in the newly built areas of Bankya and Vitosha they are only about 25
persons per hectare. Whereas the average number of dwelling units per
building erected in Mladost in the 1980s was 50, the average number of
dwelling units per building erected in Vitosha after 1990 was only 1.9.
These numbers suggest the dominance of single- and two-family residences
with private yards – residences typically much larger than any in the central
city. Initially, during the first dozen or so years of the post-socialist period,
the process was largely informal. New homes – including those belonging to

Figure 6.2 Under construction: building suburbia, Sofia-style. The area in which this fancy single-family home is located, on the south side of the city, is called the Vitosha Collar (see Figure 6.3 for exact location). It is also commonly referred to as the "golden ghettoes" or the "new neighborhoods."

the top echelon of post-socialist society – were constructed on an individual scale, often without permits or after a piecemeal amendment to a detailed regulatory plan. In fact, Sofia's southern rim became a prime example of the ad hoc development (or statutory secession, to use my term) that defined post-socialist growth, especially during the 1990s. In some areas, this spontaneous expansion led to the near-collapse of existing public infrastructure. Many roads disintegrated into strings of giant potholes[14] (in fact, some of the new neighborhoods came to be known as *Djiplend* – "Jeep Land" – as residents needed SUVs to navigate the rough terrain). The new homes were connected to the existing water lines by illegal hook-ups, which overloaded the systems. Waste was routinely dumped into nearby creeks in defiance of rules requiring a septic system. In fact, an estimated third of the sewer lines and a quarter of the water lines in Sofia were never authorized – a phenomenon particularly common in the fast-growing southern periphery (Stanilov and Hirt forthcoming). Illustrating the attitudes that lay beneath the informal growth of the 1990s, one new resident, Peter, a manager of several gas stations in his forties, explained how he built his fancy home on what was once a family garden plot with a modest cottage:

> My father, you understand, built a very small hut so he could come on the weekend for the vegetables. He also wanted to make it bigger for us kids in

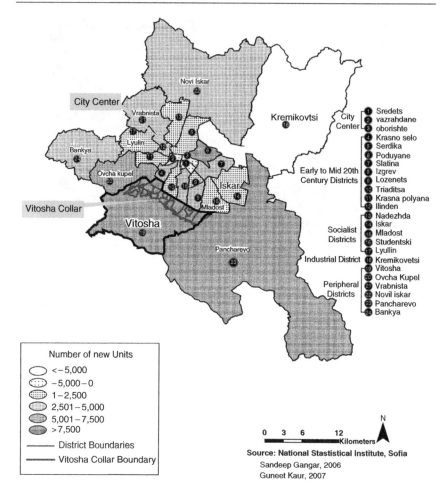

Figure 6.3 Changes in the number of dwelling units in the Municipality of Sofia, according to the last two censuses. The Vitosha District has added the greatest number of units, a majority of which have been built along its northern edge, in the Vitosha Collar, commonly referred to as the "new neighborhoods" or the "golden ghettoes."

the summer. He said he asked for a permit for what … several years. Well, there must have always been something, a rule or something; he never got it. And he wasn't the type who would have many connections …. Now I would be sure not to repeat this [mistake] …. Everybody is building what they want these days, eh? Gee, some people are building in the forest; I built on my own lot …. I mean, isn't this what it's all about? I own the place and I will build what I want and no government bureaucrat will tell me about what is mine.

And he went further to expresses his unambiguous contempt of the current public authorities:

> Now if they [the government bureaucrats] would get their act together as in normal countries and improve things here, I wouldn't mind going through their process .... Maybe I wouldn't have to be dumping my garbage out [in the creek]. But they don't because they are all busy building themselves .... There is no way I can get myself what I need within a reasonable time. So I will do what I have to and I will like it too, my house with the birds and the trees all around.

Peter's views are instructive. Building illegally (in this case, without a septic tank) is not simply a way to avoid expense or inconvenience; rather, it is a quasi-rebellious gesture in which he takes pride. What Peter's father could not do, Peter can; what socialism prohibited, post-socialism propels. This is the pride and pleasure of subverting a public authority that appears to be failing, the pride and pleasure of feeling that "I can do it alone," the pride and pleasure of privatism. Welcome to freedom!

Peter's story is one of many. But who exactly are they, "those from the new neighborhoods"? What motivates them to leave Sofia and settle permanently in its outskirts? What are their lifestyles, preferences, aspirations? Are they really seeking to secede from the city? Are they really suburbanites according to the definition used here? We lack systematic, metropolis-wide data to unequivocally answer these questions, because of the limitations of the census identified earlier. There are other limitations too: the census gives no data on residents' place of origin (are they coming from central Sofia or from elsewhere?) or the year of their relocation. It says nothing about their views or motivations. (Thus, we cannot use it to assess whether suburbanization is occurring, since we define suburbanization as population outflow from the city center toward its edge, led by the upper social strata in search of a higher quality of life.)[15] The best clues are offered by a dataset provided by the Institute of Sociology at the Bulgarian Academy of Sciences. The data is the result of the only known survey to explicitly target Sofia's new rim.[16] The survey, which used a standardized questionnaire administered in person, was conducted in 2006–7. It included 550 randomly chosen residents of the Vitosha Collar – a sliver of land covering several former villages and villa-zones in the immediate vicinity of the heavily urbanized parts of the city, right on top of its shrinking greenbelt (Figure 6.3).[17] I used the survey database to select subjects for follow-up open-ended interviews (I selected 55 and was able to talk to 39). I chose interviewees who represented a spectrum of socio-economic profiles (in terms of, for example, gender, age, income, education, and family status), as well as year of relocation, place of origin, and housing characteristics. As I mentioned in the

Introduction, the interviewees were asked to reflect on the current state of the city, their neighborhoods, their neighbors and their homes. (Those who lived in gated homes were also asked about their specific reasons for gating; I discuss these responses in Chapter 7.) Furthermore, they were asked to share their views of public institutions, to elaborate on how they participate in civic activities, and to describe how their experiences today differ from what they remember of their experiences during socialism.

It is important to emphasize that the Vitosha Collar is precisely the area that most citizens of Sofia refer to as the "new neighborhoods" or the "golden ghettoes." (Still, it is not as uniformly exclusive as these names suggest, because some of its residents and their families have lived there for decades. They are long-term residents or "villagers," rather than suburban newcomers.) It is widely perceived as the most desirable and prestigious part of metropolitan Sofia (Genova 2000), and it has some of the area's steepest property values (comparable to those in the heart of downtown). In the next sections, I discuss what I learned about the "new neighborhoods" and their residents from the survey and the follow-up interviews.

"Those from the New Neighborhoods": Attempting a Portrait

The principal goal of the Institute of Sociology's survey was to identify differences in the social characteristics, lifestyles and motivations of people who moved into the southern outskirts of Sofia before and after socialism (i.e., differences between the long-time residents and the newcomers). The survey revealed that despite some basic similarities in types of housing and in ownership status,[18] there are fundamental and, for the most part, statistically significant differences in the socio-economic status of the two groups. The post-socialist newcomers are, predictably, younger. They are also much wealthier. Twenty-six percent of the newcomer households in the sample have monthly incomes of more than 2000 Bulgarian leva ($1345), which in 2007 was around four times the national average (European Social Watch Report 2010). Only 5% of the long-time residents had such high incomes. Less than 10% of the newcomer households had monthly incomes of less than 250 leva (which was around half the 2007 national average), as compared to nearly 40% of the long-time residents. The newcomers also had much higher levels of educational attainment.[19] There were significant differences between the two groups in working status. Since the long-time residents are generally older, it is not surprising that this group has a higher proportion of retirees.[20] Of those working outside the home in both groups, most work in the densely urbanized parts of Sofia and commute regularly. This provides evidence of a daily economic dependency on the city that has historically defined suburban areas around

Western cities but is novel for Sofia.[21] There were also statistically significant differences in ownership of material goods. For example, the average dwelling size was much larger for newcomer households than for households of long-time residents: 162 sq m as compared to 115 sq m.[22] Furthermore, whereas 80% of newcomer households owned cars (often more than one), among long-time resident households the figure was 57. Of those newcomers who worked outside the home, 56% commuted by private automobile and only 28% by public transit. Among the working long-time residents, the figures show a much higher reliance on public transport: 42% used automobiles, while 43% used mass transit.

The survey further revealed substantial differences in previous place of residence and in lifestyle aspirations. For the long-time residents, the decision to live in the outskirts of the capital city had little to do with escaping big-city life or finding a suitable family setting in a green environment. Nearly 30% of them had never made a deliberate choice to move from one place to another – the house they currently lived in was the very house in which they were born and raised. Asked in the survey's open-ended questions to briefly explain why they live where they do, many expressed bewilderment and said that they had never considered an alternative. Typical remarks included the following: "Where else can I go?"; "This is my home"; "I've always lived here"; "My family is from here"; and "We are locals." And whereas 30% had in fact moved out of central Sofia, sometimes for quality-of-life or quality-of-dwelling reasons, an even greater number, 34%, moved to their present residence from a home in the same neighborhood, another neighborhood in Sofia's periphery or a provincial settlement elsewhere in Bulgaria, primarily for either family reasons (e.g., moving in with a spouse's family) or economic ones (e.g., moving from a small town to Sofia to work in the city). Lydia, a long-term resident in her eighties, shared the story of how she moved to Sofia's outskirts during socialism:

> When we came here with my husband from Radnevo [a small provincial town] ... we had relatives here and we could buy a piece of land and build cheaply .... I used to really enjoy living here. I used to go to Cherni Vruh [the tallest mountain peak] on Sunday. And I liked having a decent job in the city and yet having a garden here .... Then [in 1989] the changes came. My husband passed away. I retired and it all became very difficult .... Before, I could walk and take the bus to Sofia and it wasn't a problem – that's how I went to work for years.

And she shared how her life changed since she retired from her job at a local kindergarten:

> But now, as you can see, I have trouble walking and if you don't have a car these days, you can't get around here at all .... The nearest stores are too

much of a walk for me, and I can't afford most of the things they sell .... Maybe the best thing for me to do is to sell this place. Some rich person from Sofia will come; he will demolish it and build a large house with a tall fence like the ones you see everywhere. And then I may be able to find a small apartment in the city.

The motivations of people who moved to the Vitosha Collar after 1989 are substantially different. A very strong majority, 72%, relocated to the Collar from central Sofia, whether from the historic or the socialist districts, as compared to only 30% of the long-term residents. For two-thirds of the newcomers, the dominant reason for moving away from central Sofia was their distaste for urban living and their desire for a higher quality of life in a greener, cleaner setting. Size and quality of dwelling, as well as economic factors, played only a minor role in their decision to relocate. Comments from the newcomers included the following: "Sofia is too polluted for normal people to live there"; "Nadejda [one of the socialist districts] became too noisy and dirty for my taste"; "I feel free here. Finally, I don't have annoying neighbors"; "I don't like city life. It is overcrowded"; "It's cleaner here"; "It's better, healthier for the family"; "It [the city] is too crowded for my taste"; "Can't live with that kind of noise and pollution [in the city]"; "I like it here, now I have a house with a garden"; "I like privacy"; "I escaped my neighbors from the apartment building. Here I can't even see my neighbors"; "One can't find privacy in an apartment building"; and "Sofia is a madhouse and now an opportunity has opened for me to escape it" (see also Hirt 2007b, 2008b). Some referred directly to their new living environments as a welcome antithesis to what socialism had to offer: "My parents lived in one of those concrete monstrosities; they could not live in a house with a yard .... But I can."

Alexander, a successful lawyer and a new suburban resident who grew up in one of the socialist districts, told a story of leaving Sofia that differs greatly from the stories of older residents like Lydia.

And I guess it was normal then [during socialism]; it [the socialist district where he grew up] was a neighborhood .... But now we live in different times. There is more crime .... So I think when my wife and I got this place, we did better than my parents. We sold the apartment to buy the land here .... Both of us have good jobs [in the city] .... We enjoy the place; it's a big house; we built it as we wanted it, with a nice big yard so the kids can play. It's private and cleaner .... It's a better place, really, for the family.

Alexander's wife, Natasha, seconded his opinion:

[G]enerally I am very pleased [with the move]. We like the air, the space, the house and the yard, the freedom, really. Honestly, I don't miss having neighbors and all sorts of neighborly events like having to go to the [homeowners'] association meetings.

The different aspirations and lifestyles of the older population and the post-socialist newcomers are producing a splintered suburbanism – a world in which two groups of people, one poor and one rich, pass by each other yet barely talk to each other, a world of spatial proximity and social distance. The poorer long-time residents walk the narrow beat-up sidewalks to the nearest small store to get their bread and milk, while the wealthier newcomers drive home through their highly securitized gates and garages without ever setting foot in public space. Here is how new homeowner Stephan, a busy young professional who works for the local branch of a Greek bank in Sofia, described his experiences in the neighborhood:

> Well, it's an interesting area to live in. Certainly, there are many benefits .... But there are also some things you don't get in the city. Like, seriously, I am in a hurry for a meeting [in downtown Sofia] and [must] stop for someone walking their entire herd of sheep right in front of ... my car. And when I say walking, I mean that if they went any slower, they'd stop! Now, I don't really have anything bad to say about these people. I mean, most seem friendly and nice enough, I mean that, although they seem to move through life at a slower speed ....

But even though he thought of his neighbors as friendly, he had security problems:

> [W]hen we first moved in, we had a lot of people peeking in the yard ... and trying to start a conversation and sometimes [telling] some tear-jerker story, asking for money. And then we got robbed twice! So, finally, we built the fence and installed the camera and the alarm system. Now, I am not into the prison look, but how else can I protect my property?

On the other side of the fence, Vera, Sasha and Tatiana, women in their seventies and Stephan's not-so-distant neighbors, had little good to say about their interactions with newcomers like Natasha and Alexander:

> We [the new residents and I] have nothing in common. We are "we" and they are "they." For me, they may just as well be from another planet .... And I barely see their faces anyway. I walk around quite a bit .... But they only ... [get] from the cars right into the garage .... If I see them, I say "good day," they say "good day," and that's all there is to say.

> I used to be the local tax inspector. I was here for twenty years [until 1990]. I used to know who lived in every single house. But now I don't know the people even right around us. Many of the old owners sold their houses to richer people

so that they can have money …. Or very often, when the old owner dies, his children sell it. In ten years, there will be no place here for people like us.

[I]f you are talking about some of the new people, these people with the big cars with the dark windows, I think they live in another place …. I don't sit at their table and they don't sit at mine.

A Better Place for the Family?

As the above-cited interview with Alexander illustrates, many newcomers believe that the green environment and their private homes are more suitable than the city for family life.[23] Anton, another suburban resident, echoed this sentiment:

> Look … it is very difficult to raise a family in the city these days, if you want to have a normal life that is, it is difficult. It's true it can be convenient [to live in the city] – you know your kid can take the bus or even walk to school. Here, the wife and I, we are like chauffeurs is what we are …. But to be honest, there are many places these days I wouldn't want them [the kids] to take the bus to. I mean it is very different than when you and I, right, were growing up …. Once they come back from school, I don't have to think about where they [the kids] would go, because I will be the one driving them there, right? Not that they can't still get themselves in trouble, but less …. So purely as a parent I say that I think it's better here.

This view appeared to be shared widely by interviewees from the newcomer group, regardless of their gender. There were, however, notable differences in the ways suburban family living seemed to affect men's and women's lifestyles. This is hardly surprising if we keep in mind that regardless of heavy socialist propaganda touting gender equality, males' and females' lifestyles remained different across the Eastern bloc. Women never became equal to men, either at home or at work.[24] And while they benefited from a number of progressive laws[25] and a generous system of maternity and child-care benefits, they carried a heavy "double burden" of paid work *and* household work (see, e.g., Corrin 1992). Arguably, the position of women only worsened after socialism, due to the decline of public funds for maternity support, the privatization of child care, and the weakened enforcement of gender-equality laws, in Bulgaria as well as in all other post-socialist states.[26] The trend was bolstered, especially during the 1990s, by a not-so-subtle admiration of the ideal of the woman as homemaker – an ideal that was unattainable during socialism but is omnipresent in new novels, [27] TV shows and popular magazines.

The survey data shows that women are less likely than men to reside in the suburban areas for lifestyle reasons.[28] There were also obvious gender differences in work and mobility patterns. Relatively few working-age women consider themselves full-time homemakers.[29] However, the women in the sample had a slightly lower educational status than the men, and those who were in paid employment were less likely to work in Sofia, where the high-power opportunities are concentrated.[30] Women also depended to a greater extent on public infrastructure, whereas men tended to commute by individual car. Whereas two-thirds of men used an automobile to get to work, just over a quarter of women drove; whereas over half of women relied on public transit, less than a quarter of men did. Given the rather sorry state of mass-transit connections between Sofia and its burgeoning suburbs (with travel times sometimes approaching two hours), it is not surprising that female respondents found it much harder than men to get to the city.[31]

New restrictions in mobility imposed by the suburban family lifestyle are making women choose: some between family and work, others between household work and leisure – choices that tend to restore a more patriarchal mode of family relations. One educated young woman named Athena shared her decision to become a full-time mom in the suburbs as follows:

> When he [our 3-year-old son] was born, we [my husband and I] decided together that I was going to stay home .... It's not that I think that my career is less important, but from a family point of view it made more sense for my husband to have a career at the moment. If I had to work and he stayed home – I mean, this is totally hypothetically speaking – there is no way I could make us the same income .... But there are some issues. Like we have one car at the moment. My husband goes to work early and comes back late. So I am generally here – it's rather difficult to move around with a little kid if you live here. It's actually worse because his job requires quite a bit of travel. So on the days when he is traveling, I am really stuck here. Then I can only go places if I arrange it in advance with a friend. Which does happen, but it is a hassle.

Liliana, a professional woman in her late forties, explained how her new life constrained her free time after her family moved from the city center to the suburbs in 1995 (her son had asthma, so the family was trying to escape urban pollution for his sake).

> My husband and I agreed on this and I still think it was the right thing to do. Now, these are the problems. Like, we have one car and I am not a very good driver anyway. So my husband uses the car to go to work. Sometimes he takes me to work and brings me [home], but sometimes I take the bus.

And acquiring a focused, slightly worried look she began to think aloud about what this meant for her social and family life:

Now if I take the bus, it takes me at least about an hour [to go to Sofia] and at least an hour to come back. So, an eight-hour working day and some two hours commuting .... Of course, my husband is glad to drive me, but I generally must keep his schedule in mind .... [If] I am coming back by myself, I need to plan exactly what I need for dinner and make sure I buy it. I can't forget something because it will take more time on the bus .... Can't be deciding things on a whim; can't just decide I am going to stroll downtown when I feel like it ... with my girlfriends. I can still meet them, say, over lunch or right after work, but if I plan to go home with my husband, I need to do this in a way that works for him too.

Settling in the suburbs is of course not the primary cause of women's changing lifestyles. More importantly, the shrinking of the public sector, including the severe reduction of public benefits for child care and education and the removal of state guarantees for employment, has transferred many tasks back to the household. And in a patriarchal model this means transferring them primarily to women. A middle-aged resident, Marina, who had worked for twenty years as a store-manager but quit her job and moved to the suburbs in the mid-1990s, shared her view on the position in which families (and particularly women) find themselves today:

Before [when I had a job], my husband and I would go to work and come back home at about 5:30 and then my second shift began. He never worked much around the house .... But, still, he did the shopping for food and other things .... But it became rather difficult when the state firm he used to be with closed down and he started working in the private sector. He couldn't just leave at 5. Today, nobody is guaranteed to stay in business, so they all have to do whatever it takes – travel, work on the weekend and all. So he stopped helping me altogether .... [A]bout that time, I quit my job .... I think this old family model, the one from before 1945, you know, from biblical times, if I may say so, with the woman staying home and running the household, works much better for everybody these days. Without me in the house, he couldn't really make it at work, nor could the family ....

And things are different for us as parents too. Look, the state school system is not nearly as good as it used to be, as I'm sure you know. So parents have to spend time with their kids to make sure they learn .... And then, you must look after your kids like, like a policeman. With so many drugs, you have to be on their case all day long. It didn't used to be this way when I was growing up, but now it is as it is. So now someone – and by someone I mean myself since otherwise who else – must do that. And it seems to me a good enough reason [for me to stay home].

This is not to say that some women (and men) did not appreciate their new life situation. Some welcomed it as an improved focus on the family.

A contented husband, Todor, who had recently moved from the socialist districts to the suburbs, shared the following:

> I personally like it very much .... There are certain things that are simply natural. I mean women are better at some things; you know, they make better parents – I am the first to admit it. We [men] have our responsibilities .... Well, for over ten years [during socialism], we ... worked and worked. We were very young then of course; we had the first kid there [in one of the socialist districts] .... And you know it does not have to be that way. We have our own home now, so we don't have to listen to other people's quarrels through the panel walls .... And now my wife [who became a part-time interior designer working from home] can spend more time on our family stuff, but she also has more free time .... People missed that [during socialism] because the idea was to somehow change how families live. And for what?

His wife, Albena, seemed equally satisfied:

> I wouldn't trade it [my life here] .... I worked for years day after day and took care of my household and the kids. Now, since we moved, I finally have the time to spend on myself. True, there are few places to go, and if I need to go shopping or meet my girlfriends or go to the salon, I have to take a taxi or the bus. We have two cars, but my husband drives one to work and my [19-year-old] son... takes the other. So it does take me some time to get to where I want, but hey, gee, I have the time! My kids are grown and now I am finally free .... Honestly, I think some of my girlfriends are jealous. One tried to brag a few days ago that she became a vice-president of her company. I say, "Great!" But I don't care .... Why should I, [if] my husband makes plenty?

Some of the authors of the Master Plan expressed similar appreciation for traditional family living. Asked whether the new plan could have negative implications for gender equality because it encourages suburbanization, one of the authors of the "dispersed city model" explained:

> Now really, I thought we tried that already. Back in the day [during socialism], the government had all these ideas about the socialist man and the socialist woman and tried to impose them on people, on families .... Look, if women want to work, let them work; if they want to stay home, let them stay home. If a family wants to live in the city, more power to them; but if they want to live in the outskirts, we should make this available to them as well. These are private people's choices and only a totalitarian, communist government can aspire to reform people and reform family life .... Not that I disagree here that we should try to organize our situation, our city is what I mean, so that everyone can access the jobs, but trying to influence family choices? This is like the old regime, I can tell you that right now.

Yet regardless of this expert's assessment that governments should be "neutral" on private, family matters and that women are completely free to make choices, the empirical evidence suggests that women's opportunities, civic, social or business, do get influenced by the place they live. In fact, these opportunities – as many scholars have argued in other regions of the world – get constrained, even in the twenty-first century, when women move away from the city and begin commuting longer distances.

From Solo Homes to Standard Subdivisions: A Glimpse into Sofia's Newest Suburbia

By all accounts, the suburbanization of Sofia has continued and only intensified over the last few years.[32] But its patterns have changed. The most visible difference between the 1990s and the post-2000 period has been the shift in building scale and morphology. The 1990s were characterized by a fragmented development mode,[33] in which the most common new form was the individual family home, tucked in between socialist-era "villas" in order to take advantage of the existing infrastructure, thus producing an architecturally (and socially) eclectic environment. With economic stabilization after 2000 and the emergence of larger homebuilding firms, the scale of development shifted significantly. In a few short years, a string of large subdivisions emerged in Sofia's outskirts. Examples include Orchid Hills with 200 units, Simeonovo River Park with 250 units and Residential Park Sofia with about a 1000 units, all in the Vitosha foothills and all gated, as I further discuss in Chapter 8. The layout of the new subdivisions – with their smooth, wide, automobile-friendly roads, ample parking, cul-de-sacs, and artfully manicured common spaces inaccessible to outsiders – is another novelty for Sofia. So is the building process in which a private firm initiates a large new development and pre-sells standardized luxury units that allow future homeowners a limited selection of finishing touches and façade treatments along with meticulously maintained shared spaces and infrastructure. The new model of development enables a different kind of retreat from the city and a new kind of lifestyle. During socialism, individual households removed themselves from urbanity and entered a world of semi-rural villages. In today's suburbanization, individual households leave the city to join a suburban community of like-minded (and like-paying) others. In 2009, I re-interviewed Stephan, the young banker who had to stop for a herd of sheep while rushing to Sofia. By then, he had moved to one of the new (gated) suburban subdivisions. He likes his new area very much:

> This is a very good place. And I don't mean just that it is pretty and maintained and all that. What I want to say is that there no surprises .... The electricity

works [he laughs], the water pressure [is good], the grass is always cut, and I am not worried that someone is going to break in …. And the people, the people are the kind of people that I work with in the city.

In the next two chapters, I continue studying the suburbs and their residents but with a focus on gating. Indeed, why is it necessary to add another layer of separation between oneself and the city – not only by living far from the city but also by surrounding oneself with heavy walls?

Notes

1 See, for instance, Tammaru (2001) and Bernhardt (2005) on the principal differences between peri-urban growth in socialist and capitalist contexts.

2 In the Russian context, Ioffe and Nefedova (1999) refer to this process as stepping-stone suburbanization. In their interpretation, whereas in Western cities suburban settlements grow because residents choose to leave central cities, in socialist Russia suburban settlements grew because people wanted to move into the central cities (i.e., the settlements served as stepping stones for people's eventual permanent relocation to the city). As a rule, settlements of this type were occupied by the lower middle classes and the quality of their housing was notably lower than that in the standardized socialist housing districts (see, e.g., Ladányi 1995).

3 This statement should be taken with some caution. As Nicolaides and Wiese (2006: 99–101) point out, suburbs in the United States have always displayed socio-economic diversity – there were wealthy enclaves, but there were also workers' enclaves. The picture is more complex in Western Europe where elites have been more attached to the city and workers have participated in suburbanization from earlier on (White 1984). Yet, as Fishman's (1987: 39–72) and Muller's (1981: 33–5) classic works have shown, suburbanization is typically led by the upper social strata, at least initially.

4 A current multi-million-dollar research project, which includes two dozen scholars from around the world and is led by Dr. Roger Keil from York University, is specifically looking into what constitutes suburbanization in varied global contexts (the project is appropriately entitled Global Suburbanisms). As one of the scholars involved in the project, I can attest that deriving a definition for "the suburbs" was one of the hardest tasks undertaken by the research team. In fact, I doubt that a single definition is possible.

5 An excellent attempt to dissect the meaning of suburbia has been offered by Richard Harris (2011). He argues that there are three main characteristics which make a settlement a "suburb": its peripheral location vis-à-vis the city, its newness, and its low density (again, vis-à-vis the city). This definition clearly allows urban expansions such as rural-to-urban migration and stepwise migration to be considered suburbanization. I am not advocating that Harris (2011) is wrong. I am only proposing to investigate a particular type of urban expansion: the type that entails the deliberate decentralization of the upper and upper-middle classes; i.e., the type which I believe is occurring for the first time in Sofia's history. Once again, my definition is consistent with definitions used by K. Jackson and R. Fishman.

6   In this sense, suburbanization is a process opposite to rural-to-urban migration; suburbanites are motivated by a desire to secede from urbanity and find more peaceful lifestyles elsewhere, whereas rural-to-urban migrants seek to enter the city typically for economic reasons.

7   That secondary homes or summer cottages predate full-fledged suburbanization is not surprising. Fishman (1987) has shown that such summer cottages were the essential suburban prototype in industrial England as well.

8   In cities such as Budapest, however, there was limited suburbanization during the last socialist decade (Kovacs 1994; Kok and Kovacs 1999).

9   Fishman (1987) showed that upscale suburbanization developed in England in the eighteenth and nineteenth centuries in large part because the English bourgeoisie came to 'idealize' private single-family living in the countryside. Such rethinking did not occur in France. There, the bourgeoisie chose not to withdraw from the central city, but rather reclaimed it through the rebuilding of Paris undertaken by Baron Haussmann. Thus, two societies responded to similar economic conditions in very different ways, once again highlighting a role for culture as an important explanatory variable.

10 Havel's dream of Prague dominated by family houses as opposed to "gigantic public housing developments" cited earlier alludes to this type of rethinking of the relationship between family and community. For a critique of Havel's vision, see Leach (1998) on the "re-domestication of Eastern Europe."

11 The term has a negative connotation at least when used by people who cannot afford to move to the "new neighborhoods".

12 Data from the next census will be available in 2013.

13 Of the central districts, there is high growth only in the administrative district of Poduyane. However, the high growth figures for Poduyane are due to the fact that its administrative boundaries were recently redrawn to include areas which before 1992 were part of adjacent districts. Thus, this data for growth in Podyane is misleading.

14 Never lacking a sense of humor, residents informally renamed one of these badly damaged roads as "Pathway to Europe" (*Put kum Evropa*), referring to a slogan used by many Bulgarian politicians prior to the country's entry into the European Union. The name was clearly meant to make fun of the sorry state of the road as much as of the sorry state of the country in general. Another popular anecdote of the time was that the very large potholes were the result of NATO missiles, which mistook Sofia for Belgrade.

15 Establishing social status and motivation for relocation is crucial to determining whether suburbanization, as I defined it, occurs in Sofia. This is because scholars have shown that an alternative process of peripheral growth occurred in some post-socialist cities during the 1990s. Because of the radical decline of manufacturing and the high unemployment rates of the 1990s, some residents left central cities to settle in their once part-time summer cottages and use their garden plots as their primary source of subsistence (Ladányi and Szelényi 1998). This process is sometimes referred to as urban ruralization. It is part of a package of "survival strategies" of poor households during the initial years of the 1990s economic collapse (Smith 2000; see also Clarke et al. 2000 and Seeth et al. 1998 on the Russian "garden plot" or "food jars" economy). Data on this

process in Sofia is limited because of the crude nature of the Bulgarian census and the scarcity of metropolis-wide surveys. Anecdotal evidence suggests, however, that the process developed only to an extent in the poorer, northern parts of the metropolis.

16 The survey was implemented by the Institute of Sociology under the guidance of Dr. Emilia Chengelova as chief field researcher. I secured the funding with grants from the National Council for Eurasian and East European Research, the International Research and Exchange Board, and the American Councils for International Education.

17 The survey was conducted among a random sample generated from a full list of household addresses in the Vitosha Collar. The list was obtained from the municipality. The survey can thus be considered statistically representative of the population of the Vitosha Collar which, as earlier said, is the largest and most paradigmatic of the post-socialist "golden ghettoes." It is of course not easy to generalize from this particular suburban area to all suburban areas of Sofia. To participate in the survey, respondents had to self-qualify as either household heads or persons with significant participation in household decision-making.

18 Strong majorities, 80% of newcomers and 73% of long-time residents, reside in single-family homes. Overwhelming majorities, 92% of newcomers and 99% of long-time residents, are homeowners. These results are not surprising. The Vitosha Collar is dominated by privately owned single-family homes to an extent greater than almost all other parts of Sofia.

19 Sixty-four percent of newcomers have college degrees as compared to 38% of the long-time residents.

20 Retirees comprised 55% of long-time residents as opposed to 21% of newcomers.

21 However, the city commuters are a stronger majority among the working newcomers, 83%, as opposed to 71% among the working long-time residents. In contrast, larger minorities of the long-time residents work either in the same neighborhood (7%) or in a nearby area outside of central Sofia (22%). The corresponding figures for the newcomers are 3% and 11%, respectively.

22 There was a notable difference in household size. Thus, the average dwelling space per person in newcomers' dwellings was 56 sq m compared to 36 sq m for the long-time residents – a statistically significant difference.

23 The survey data shows that the post-socialist newcomers are more likely to be nuclear families with children.

24 The claim of gender equality in socialist nations was based on the fact that over 80% of working-age women were fully employed – a level unmatched anywhere else in the world (Brainerd 2000). In Bulgaria, 90% of working-age women were employed and the state provided months-long paid maternity leave. It also guaranteed the right to return to work after maternity leave (Koeva and Bould 2007). Women fared well in fields such as health care and education and, to an extent, in engineering and the sciences. But top political and managerial positions were male-dominated (Metcalfe and Afanassieva 2005). Furthermore, traditional gender divisions in the household persisted. Women's "emancipation by employment" was enabled by the system of

entitlements provided by the paternalistic state rather than by increased male responsibilities at home (Daskalova 2005). The image of the woman as worker *and* mother and wife was deeply embedded in all socialist institutions (Koeva and Bould 2007; Rudd 2006).

25   I refer here to the state-guaranteed rights to employment, free education and health care for all.

26   See for example Mayer et al. (1999), Smith (2000), LeFont (2001), Badjeva (2002), Stoilova (2006).

27   Take for example the critically acclaimed memoir *Street without a Name* (*Uliza bez ime*) by K. Kasabova (2008), a Bulgarian author living in New Zealand. The book tells Kasabova's story of her childhood in a grim housing district in socialist Sofia, her emigration to Western Europe and later New Zealand right after 1989, and her bittersweet rediscovery of Sofia in 2006. Kasabova tells a moving personal story and levels many legitimate complaints at the totalitarian regime. Interestingly, however, one of her complaints has to do with the role of women. While pitying her mother who had to carry the "double burden" of being an engineer and a wife and mother in socialist Bulgaria, Kasabova praises the fact that in Western societies women had the "freedom" to be homemakers.

28   According to the survey data, 49% of men believed that they moved to the suburbs for lifestyle reasons, whereas the corresponding figure of women was 33%.

29   Still, 8% of women described themselves as homemakers as compared to 2% of men.

30   Whereas 74% of surveyed women worked in Sofia, for men the corresponding figure was 81%. In contrast, whereas only 1% of men worked close to home (in the same suburban area in which they live), for women the figure was 9%.

31   Specifically, whereas 36% of men thought that getting to Sofia was either "very easy" or "somewhat easy," the corresponding figure for women was just half of that, 18%.

32   We will have to wait until 2013 to provide census evidence for this statement.

33   There is only one residential subdivision constructed in the 1990s: Bokar in southern Sofia. Even though it was far larger than anything else produced at the time, Bokar has in fact only 100 units.

7

Iron Curtains I: Gated Homes

"[T]here is this new gated compound over there down the road. All fenced off with a two-meter-tall wall. I bet you can't get in. But if you can, you ask them, you ask them for me: who are they and why are they building the walls? And then come and tell me because I want to know."

Excerpt from an interview with an older resident of
Sofia's suburbs, 2006

Danka, a woman of 79 who lives in a small house in the Vitosha Collar, was once a school teacher who taught Bulgarian language. Her next-door neighbor and friend, Petya, a postal employee, recently passed away. Petya's children sold their family lot with the house on it. A family from Sofia bought it, demolished the old house and built a new, much larger one. Danka found herself in the company of new neighbors. During socialism, a thin metal net covered with plants had separated the two neighbors' lots. The thin net did not last, says Danka:

> [O]n both sides [of the net], we [Petya and I], we grew raspberries. Then we picked them without thinking much about whose raspberries grew on which side. But when these, the new people came, they uprooted the raspberries, got rid of the net and built this thing [a brick wall] instead. My raspberries are now withering; they are now all in the shade.

Asked what she thinks of her new, wealthier neighbors, Danka says, "Well, they are polite people," even though "we don't talk much, mostly just hello and how are you." She doesn't dare talk much to them, nor can she: "You can't talk to the wife much. She goes into the garage in the car …. And the

Iron Curtains, First Edition. Sonia A. Hirt.
© 2012 John Wiley & Sons, Ltd. Published 2012 by John Wiley & Sons, Ltd.

nanny says she is at the fitness salon if I ask." Once, Danka wanted to ask
her neighbor if she could borrow some sugar. Back when Petya was alive,
all Danka had to do when she needed to borrow something was to yell to
her neighbor. But it stopped being so simple:

> First, I can't ask easily because I can't see who is at home or not .... So I am
> not going to be yelling [to ask for sugar] if I can't see .... I don't know their
> phone [number], so I go to the front to ring [the bell]. Then I wait for the
> guard to open the little window so that he can show his nose. [H]e goes back
> [to the house] to ask for the sugar, if the wife is at home, of course. Then he
> gets a sack but it cannot go between [the bars of the window]; so he has to
> get some key ... so that he can pass it [the sack] through another opening [in
> the gate], so this is what he does .... I don't see much of a human face this
> whole time .... Well, but they spared the sugar, so that was nice. I gave it back
> of course.

Danka's story has been replicated throughout the southern rim of Sofia, as
new people have streamed in over the last few years, building their large
homes with large gates and transforming the area from a modest, semi-rural
one to a higher-class, suburban one. In this chapter, I ask why fancy new
homes, mostly in the suburbs but also in the other, older parts of Sofia
where they have recently mushroomed, have such an exceptional propen-
sity to be surrounded by tall walls and be equipped with multiple security
devices. To borrow the words of Steven Flusty (1997), who wrote about
the Los Angeles of the 1990s, why has the "simple act of entering" (or the
simple act of handing over a small sack of sugar) become such a "dauntingly
complex" task? Why are tall gates now built around some of the old homes
as well, especially those purchased by new owners and renovated? How
did one architectural element, the solid wall, become – as one Bulgarian
sociologist and art critic put it – the defining element of post-socialist residential architecture (Dandolova 2002)? (This is true to such an extent that
information on just one variable – the type of fencing surrounding a home –
goes a long way in predicting whether it was built during or after socialism.)
With the exception of the villas of a few top-tier socialist bureaucrats, almost
all homes built during socialism had either no fencing or low fencing that
permits visibility from the street, whereas those constructed (or renovated)
in recent years tend to be surrounded by much taller, less permeable enclosures (Figure 7.1).

The tall solid gates have become a material artifact that serves as a
social-group identity-marker. Much as passing taxi-drivers often refer to
the *nouveau riche* as "those from the new neighborhoods," long-time residents of the very same neighborhoods refer to their new neighbors as
"those with the gates." They often volunteer comments on the new houses

Figure 7.1 The type of massive gates that surround new homes in the Vitosha Collar. The gates are typically supplemented by several security devices.

and their tall enclosures, without being prompted by the interviewer. Take, for example, Pena, another retired older resident who reflected on her changing surroundings as follows:

> Some changes [*laughs*] .... I tell you want I want to know ... who came up with these gates? Why are they hiding all these beautiful new houses? Aren't they beautiful enough? We never had fences like these before. You can see what we [the old residents] have .... Everybody can see us from the street and we can see. Now they are building fences as if they are making a prison, a medieval fortress or this or that, or a sultan's harem, I don't know, I am saying we have never seen such a thing. This is how it was in Turkish times, eh? Then people had to hide because they were afraid and that is why they were hiding.

She goes on with growing anger:

> But what are they afraid of now? Is it me – the old woman – they are afraid of, eh? Or maybe they are not afraid. Because they are ashamed. Just ashamed ... [of] how they live with the pools and the saunas and whatnot and how I live here with my 170 leva [a monthly pension of about $115] .... They don't want me to know, eh? I don't know how it doesn't bother them [to live this way]; that's what I can't understand. I will never do it .... And I have told the sons: you build them [walls like these] when I am dead. Then, then and only then.

Or take Anna, another older long-term resident whom I also quoted in Chapter 2. When asked about her new neighbors, she sent me on a research mission: "[T]here is this new gated compound over there, down the road. All fenced off with a two-meter wall. I bet you can't get in. But if you can, you ask them, you ask them for me: who are they and why are they building the walls? And then come and tell me because I want to know." Burning curiosity mixes with resentment in such questions. For the long-term residents, the gates around the new homes represent the borders of an unknown and impenetrable world. What lies behind the gates is the stuff of legends. Farther down the road from the gated compound that Anna wants to know about is another, even larger and more spectacular one. There are rumors of a marble sculpture garden inside; no, it is an exotic zoo; no, it is a "swan lake." I doubt that any of this is true, but since nobody – certainly not a researcher – is allowed inside this compound, nobody knows. Gates like these play a dual role. They veil and they reveal. They veil reality and make it into mystery, inviting outsiders to imagine what cannot be seen. And what they would reveal, if ever they opened, may be more prosaic than what passers-by envision.

So back to the question: why the gates? The literature on gated housing has noted a complex set of both supply- and demand-side explanations, as I briefly noted in Chapter 3. On the demand side, several key behavioral explanations have been offered. People choose to live behind gates because (1) they try to protect themselves from crime, (2) they strive to display their high status, (3) they seek access to certain amenities that the public sector fails to provide, and (4) they want to live in socially homogeneous communities (see, e.g., Blakely and Snyder 1997). These explanations have been applied mostly in the context of the large, gated residential community rather than the individually gated, securitized "block-home" (as Steven Flusty calls it). This is the kind of gated home most commonly built in Sofia's new neighborhoods, especially during the 1990s. Arguably, it presents the most unambiguous antithesis of the open-entry collectivist residential building from the socialist era. (As a matter of fact, the latter two demand-side explanations, control of shared amenities and desire for an exclusive community, cannot meaningfully be applied to the individual "block-home.") My argument is that while the first two explanations, the search for security and the search for status, certainly matter, other variables engrained in the local socio-cultural context (i.e., the post-socialist Balkan context) play an important role as well. In this sense, I agree with Setha Low that universalistic explanations for gating are always insufficient, and that the phenomenon is always "evolving from local architecture and sociohistorical circumstances and is always embedded within specific cultural traditions" (2003: 16).

Theories on Gating

As I discussed in Chapter 3, cities throughout history have always been marked by divisions, walls and gates; only the types and causes of gates have varied (Kostof 1991; Marcuse 2002).[1] Without delving into the complex history of gating, we should note that many scholars view a particular gating form, the bourgeois housing compound that emerged in the nineteenth-century Western city, as the true predecessor of the contemporary gated community (see, e.g., Vesselinov et al. 2007). Gating around mansions of wealthy individual house-holds, for reasons of both protection and status, was also a common nineteenth-century phenomenon. Arguably, the practice was even more widespread in Islamic cities (as compared to, say, Central and Western Europe), where the spatial enclosure of extended well-to-do families had long been a traditional feature of urban life (Raymond 1989; Glasze 2006). The Balkans, which were dominated by the Ottomans between the fourteenth and the nineteenth centuries, were certainly no exception: the most representative streets in Ottoman cities were often flanked by tall and solid walls surrounding the household compounds of local elites well through the 1800s (Gutkind 1972).

The majority of contemporary literature that has theorized gating around the world has focused on the gated community, which is typically defined as a "residential area that is enclosed by walls, fences, or landscaping that provides a physical barrier to entry," an area that includes "streets and neighborhood amenities" and is run by a homeowners' association (Vesselinov et al. 2007). This focus can be explained in several ways. First, although many parts of the world have deeply entrenched traditions of residential enclosures at the family level,[2] the large gated community is a relatively new form of urbanism – one that has spread with a remarkable consistency and intensity in every world region.[3] Second, and partially stemming from the above, certain structural conditions associated with worldwide neo-liberalism (e.g., a diminished public sector and increasing social stratification) have been linked to the proliferation of gated communities around the world, thus prompting many scholars to interpret the phenomenon not only as a direct offshoot of neo-liberalism but also as one of its most iconic spatial expressions (e.g., Genis 2007). And third, gated communities are commonly presented as the ultimate "private cities" (Glasze et al. 2006), as the highest form in an intricate hierarchy of urban privatization strategies – the one that entrenches social divisions in the most extreme spatial form and, thus, the one that is most threatening to the public realm (see, e.g., Blakely and Snyder 1997; Low 2003; Vesselinov et al. 2007).

The reason I bring this up is to point out that, by emphasizing the link between gated communities and globalization, the literature has tended to underestimate the role of local factors in gating. Furthermore, by focusing on the "official" gated residential community, especially in post-socialist Balkan conditions, scholars have sometimes reached an erroneous conclusion: that because there were few large gated communities in cities such as Bucharest, Belgrade and Sofia by around 2000, gating itself has been limited in the region (see, e.g., Stoyanov and Glaze 2006 on Bulgaria, Hristić 2005 on Serbia). Remarkably, scholars sometimes draw this conclusion about cities that contain a plethora of gates. As noted in Chapters 3 and 4, in Sofia it is easy to find supermarkets and business complexes with gated entrances, and it has become extremely common to establish a controlled point of entry in all types of residential buildings. According to interviewed experts, not only are new single-family homes gated, but "almost every apartment building is now locked and has a guard." Even though "back in the day [during socialism], everyone could enter the [socialist-era apartment] buildings ... now their entrances are locked, too, and the people who live in these buildings have hired a security guard – some old retired policeman who sits there and watches who comes." Finally, the literature has failed, at least in my view, to capture the symbolic meaning of the gates that surround individual homes – the type of homes that socialism scorned, at least in large cities. The gates around these homes do not merely protect their residents from criminals or display their residents' high status (although both motivations certainly exist, as the literature has repeatedly confirmed). Rather, my argument, based on my interviews, is that the gates are also a cultural reflection, a reflection of a widespread idolization of private property, private rights, private ownership and private territory (see also Hirt and Petrović 2010, 2011). This syndrome is particularly acute in post-socialist conditions in the Balkans. There, individually gated homes often reflect people's desire to express their autonomy from and even their outright hostility to what they view as a broken public world outside. They represent a withdrawal from the messy public realm as potent and intense as the withdrawal associated with the classic gated community that has so fascinated scholars around the world.

The Gates of Sofia: A Brief History

In Sofia, the post-socialist gates are called *duvari* (this is the term used by Anna, Pena and Danka; Figure 7.1). The older, early- and mid-twentieth-century gates are called *ogradi*. There is a subtle but important difference. *Ogradi* literally means a fence – something that can be low, light and see-through. *Duvari* is a word of Turkish origin – it means a tall, solid, prohibitive enclosure, typically made of stone. *Duvari* is the term used to describe the enclosures around historic, Ottoman-era homes in old Bulgarian towns, homes in the so-called Bulgarian National Revival style (discussed

Figure 7.2 Ottoman-era duvari in the historic town of Bansko. All homes still standing from this period are set several meters away from the public street. Heavy walls frame the entire street length, penetrated sporadically by dark-wood gates marking the individual entrances.

in Chapter 9), which are under the protection of culture heritage laws around the country. A good example is the Town of Bansko in the Mount of Pirin – one of Bulgaria's most popular tourist resorts. In Bansko, the old homes, many now pubs and hotels, are all separated from the street by massive stone walls and tall, handsome dark-wood gates (Figure 7.2).[4]

If there were many *duvari* in Sofia, they were systematically taken down at the dawn of the twentieth century; their elimination, like the destruction of the mosques and the straightening of the street system, was part of the process of "Europeanizing" the new Bulgarian capital.[5] *Ogradi* were another matter. They consisted of a low, roughly 20-centimer-tall solid base and an ornamental upper section of elegant iron rods, often covered in flower bushes. *Ogradi* proliferated throughout the "European" Sofia of the early 1900s and served to mark private space while at the same time engaging it in a dialogue with the outside (Figure 7.3). The semi-private yards they framed were arguably a good example of the interim spaces that Jane Jacobs (1961) advocates – spaces that provide a "balance between people's determination to have essential privacy and their simultaneous wishes for different degrees of contact, enjoyment or help from the people around." These fences are still common everywhere in the historic parts of the city, in neighborhoods such as Oborishte and Lozenetz. Interior courtyards of middle-class apartment buildings were also commonly fenced off, again in

Figure 7.3   Light and decorative fencing (ogradi) in front of an apartment building in downtown Sofia, which now houses a trendy first-floor restaurant (hence the waiters in aprons). This type of fencing was typical of "European" Sofia of the early 1900s.

a discreet, decorative fashion, as were many public buildings – galleries, embassies, ministries, museums, etc. Whether these fences erected in fashionable European styles had something to do with the display of status is a matter of debate, but clearly it had little to do with security, since any fit teenager could jump them with ease.

The *ogradi* were not the favorite architectural element of Sofia's socialist planners. As one architectural history project (appropriately titled "In search of the lost fences of Sofia") showed, right after 1945 Sofia's center became subject to intense "de-fencification": first to go were the fences around the Royal Palace, the Botanical Gardens, the Archeological Museum, the Garden of King Boris [the last Bulgarian king], and the National Art Gallery (Dimitrov 1991). (The process was explicitly seen as undoing the spatial legacy of the bourgeois regime and opening Sofia to the proletarian masses; see also Dandolova 2002.) The study's author correctly lamented "de-fencification" as the loss of an important architectural heritage, praised the plastic, sculptural qualities of old Sofia's "small architecture" (as the fences were called), and hoped for their restoration as a spatial element that makes both the public and the private feel at ease. To the author's sorrow, though, there is little evidence that the elegant fences of the early twentieth century are making a comeback in the streets of Sofia; instead, now making a comeback are the massive *duvari* of the more remote past (Figure 7.4).

Figure 7.4 Duvari today.

These *duvari*, which are often erected well before the very building they surround, are often supplemented by a myriad of modern, less visible but more
high-tech security devices. It should be noted, though, that all the new two-
to three-meter-tall *duvari* happen to be illegal. The nation's building code
states that only the bottom 60 centimeters of a fence flanking a main street
may be solid. This part of the code is rarely taken seriously: while comment-
ing on how often the code is violated, one interviewed urban planner called
the *duvari* "the least of our problems."

Answering Anna's Question: Why are
They Building These Walls?

It is impossible to answer Anna's question definitively for all of Sofia,
because there is no comprehensive data on gating and securitization practices throughout the city. However, the survey conducted by the Institute of
Sociology in the "new neighborhoods" located in Sofia's southern periphery
indicates the extent to which the walling trend is spreading, especially among
new suburbanites. The surveyors classified the physical enclosures that surround area homes into three categories: enclosures permitting near-full visibility of the house from the street (e.g., gates that are less than one meter
tall and are made of transparent or semi-transparent materials); enclosures
permitting partial visibility (e.g., fences that are one-to-two meters tall and
have some semi-transparent elements); and enclosures that block nearly all

views except views of the top of the roof (e.g., fences that are more than two meters tall and are made of solid materials; see Table 7.1).[6] According to the data collected, almost all homes in the sample had some type of fencing. Only 5% had none. But there were clear (and statistically significant) differences between the enclosures of long-term residents and those of suburban newcomers. Over half of the homes belonging to post-socialist newcomers had tall gates permitting virtually no visibility from the street (in contrast, the corresponding figure for the homes of people who settled in the area before 1990 was about 9%). And, whereas nearly 40% of the homes of long-term residents had low, permeable fencing, the corresponding figure for the newer residents was less than 10%. Homes belonging to newcomers were also far more likely to be guarded by multiple security devices: guards, guard dogs, video phones, video cameras, panic buttons and alarm systems connected to private security firms (Table 7.1). For instance, whereas only 13% of newcomers had no security devices, almost 40% of long-term residents had none. About 30% of the newcomers had more than one security device, as compared to 3% of the long-term residents.[7]

The questionnaire asked respondents to share briefly, in their own words, the primary reason they live in spaces where outsiders' access is controlled (i.e., in homes whose yards are surrounded by some physical enclosure and/ or in homes that have security devices). Subjects who lived in relatively open-access homes were asked to reflect on the potential motivations of others. Six categories emerged from the open-ended answers: protection from external factors (dust, dirt, noise, smell, etc.), aesthetics, tradition, protection from criminals, protection from "others" (not necessarily only criminals), and demarcation of private territory (Table 7.1). The categories are of course not mutually exclusive. For example, many people started their answers with general allusions to social instability and "strangers in the neighborhood." It may not be possible to fully separate fear of criminals from fear of strangers, but in some cases, even after being probed further, subjects insisted that crime is only part of the problem. Thus the two explanations were coded separately. Fear of crime – the most common motivation for gating and securitization cited in the literature – featured prominently in people's responses. The words "crime" (and "criminals"), "theft" (and "thieves"), "safety," "security" and "protection" were the ones most commonly repeated in the open-ended responses. (As Table 7.1 illustrates, the greatest number of subjects, about 40%, identified protection from crime as their most important reason for gating.) People lived behind gates because "[It is] necessary, makes you feel safer from criminals, more secure" and "They [the gates] are necessary, make you feel safer from criminals, calmer, what else is there to say?" Yet some lamented, "We build it to protect us against theft; it makes me feel a bit safer, although it isn't pretty,"

Table 7.1 Differences in gating and security systems between long-term residents and post-socialist newcomers in the Vitosha Collar (proportions)

	Post-1990 residents	*Pre-1990 residents*	*All*
Type of gate			
None*	.025	.073	.054
Gates with full visibility*	.094	.365	.262
Gates with partial visibility*	.369	.474	.435
Gates with no visibility*	.512	.088	.249

Pearson's chi^2 = 135.120; Pr = 0.000; N valid cases = 534; Cramer's V = .503; gamma = −.710; ASE = .046

Motivation for gating			
Protection from external factors*	.047	.250	.164
Tradition*	.020	.132	.085
Aesthetics	.060	.025	.040
Protection from crime	.375	.402	.391
Protection from strangers*	.181	.093	.130
Demarcation of private territory*	.315	.098	.190

Pearson's chi^2 = 63.874; Pr = 0.000; N valid cases = 353; Cramer's V = .425; gamma = −.559; ASE = .060

Number of security devices			
0*	.137	.393	.299
1	.568	.554	.559
2*	.180	.038	.090
3	.038	.009	.020
4*	.071	.006	.030
5	.006	.000	.002

Pearson's chi^2 = 74.694; Pr = 0.000; N valid cases = 501; Cramer's V = .386; gamma = −.627; ASE = .058

Note: The asterisk (*) denotes statistically significant two-group differences at Pr. ≤ .05.

and "Before [presumably during socialism], people didn't even lock themselves in; now people don't know each other; everyone is afraid these days."

But the interviewees' terms "crime" and "safety" did not provide a simple, straightforward explanation; contradictions were readily apparent, especially when the respondents engaged in a short dialogue with a surveyor. Although many explained that they built gates to reduce the odds of criminal intrusion, they also voluntarily admitted that "All gates can be jumped" and "Even the alarm can't give me peace." And in a peculiar twist, although the tall gates were ostensibly meant to protect residents *from* crime, many interviewees, especially those who lived in non-gated homes, thought of them as protecting crime itself: "Those [people with the gates] are all criminals!"; "They have something to hide"; "They do dirty deals and want nobody to see them"; "It's the mafia guys; they fear their shadows, so they made our neighborhood look like the Bastille!"; "It's an interesting thing. Honestly, I like it quite a bit. One way or another, these guys have to go to jail, right? If we lived in a normal country, they would be in [a state-run] jail, but since we don't, they build their [own] private, and, may I add, fancy jails instead."

The imagined thief seemed to have a particular profile: a gender (male), often an occupation ("The construction workers are everywhere") and even an ethnic origin (Roma): "A gypsy man stole our grill last year. I saw him run with it"; "There are many gypsies and many thefts"; and "There are many gypsies now; they come here to rob." Racial prejudice aside, however, people's fears often seemed to merge with a broader anxiety over social instability. People feel they live in an insecure world – a world better avoided: "There are too many curious people"; "Nobody knows what's coming"; and "Messy times we live in." (As earlier noted, such responses were coded as protection from strangers, rather than protection from criminals; as Table 7.1 shows, 13% of the responses fell into this category.) Thus, some people were not merely afraid of criminals, but also said they had gates because they disliked being seen by all passers-by. They were perpetually concerned about strangers' intentions, which they often identified as outsiders' "curiosity."

A richer, more nuanced picture of what these responses mean emerges from the follow-up interviews I carried out with selected survey subjects. Take Venelin and Kalina, two young professionals who consider each other friends; they live in gated homes in the same neighborhood. I asked them whether there was much of a neighborhood life in the area. Venelin responded, "You can't be very serious. I mean really this was a village, it really still is. Everyone [like Venelin himself, presumably] is here for the mountain and the cleaner air. Otherwise, it's blinds all around." Kalina was a bit more positive: "Well, it could be a nice place to be. But mostly people just get in [their houses] and the garage doors, they shut behind [she claps her hands to show how the doors shut] .... If the outside was nicer and there was something, you know a café, something, maybe people would go out more. But now, mostly we have barbecues in the yard."

I also asked Venelin and Kalina when their gates were built and how necessary they are:

Venelin: [V]ery, very necessary .... When our house was first built [by my parents], we only had bushes. But we built the walls after [renovating the house]. As you know, these [the 1990s] were the big crime-ridden years – not that it's that much better now. So we built them mainly for protection [from theft]; there were thefts here all the time and they have not stopped ....

And then he shifted his explanation from one focused on fear of crime to one stemming from his dislike of all outsiders:

> But also to stop this, what would you call it, curiosity all the time. There always used to be people trying to peek inside – staying right outside the bushes and looking at us. I mean all kinds of people, I don't know them and I don't want to know them, but especially gypsies. And they try to talk to you and tell you some very sad, ah very sad, story. So it was not only more dangerous but also more unpleasant [without gates]. As if we were like on permanent display.

> Kalina: [T]he fence was here to begin with [when the house was bought]. But if I had to choose, I would have built it myself. Everybody needs protection here. It is the times we live in …. And people often stopped and tried to look inside. It is disturbing but also weird, you know! They tried to talk to me and get inside the yard and talk more. They would tell some story and ask me for money. Other times they just came and seemed to begin telling me the most random things about this thing or another, and then I was afraid they were just gauging the house like, like just with spite …. I used to let people in but now normally I don't …. So if you hadn't showed me your business card, I might not have let you in either, although you don't look much like a criminal [*laughs*] ….

And like Venelin she moved from talking about fear criminals to other explanations:

> I didn't like the constant peeking, no. I think it violates my right to feel free when I am home …. Why must I put up with this? … And if I had no gates, I certainly would get more of it [the peeking]. Everybody has them [gates] here …. They are different types but all gates. So if I decide not to have them, I will stand out and even more people will stop to peek, even if it is just out of pure curiosity to see what kind of person is that person who has no gates.

These stories seem to illustrate Lynn Lofland's (1998) point that fear of crime easily dissolves into (and is driven by) a more intangible fear of strangers violating one's private space. For some who live in the most heavily fortified homes, the gates were not at all prison-like; instead, they guaranteed not only privacy but also freedom from the outside. As one interviewee volunteered, "[Before the gates], some people walking by our house would turn their heads so hard that I thought their necks were about to break. I put an end to this," he continued. "What am I? A movie to be watched?" Sometimes, the new lifestyle was viewed as a welcome contrast to collectivist socialist-era living: "Enough is enough," said a middle-aged man, Assen, whom I interviewed in depth. He too disliked the "peeking":

> "No more Big Brother stuff .... Weren't we done with the Big Brother thing years ago, eh? I have always wanted my own house with a yard, where I can do whatever I want to, go naked if I want ... and nobody can watch me .... And I am not going in the cramped panel [socialist] building, in that cramped bus ... it smelled bad."

The appreciation of enclosed private space is certainly fed by some pragmatic considerations. Rather than referring to protection from intrusion, some survey subjects referred to simple things like protection from dust and noise coming from the outside, or protection from stray dogs or speeding cars. These comments reflected the negative (but generally accurate) views of the public streets as dirty and poorly maintained. This rationale was more common among owners of lightly fenced homes, who in turn were more likely to be long-term residents in the area. (As Table 7.1 shows, 15% of all respondents offered this as their primary explanation of why they lived in a home with a fence, but this included 25% of long-term residents as opposed to only 5% of the suburban newcomers.) Arguably, this motivation for gating – much like the one related to crime – adds some fuel to the interpretation of gating as a public-sector failure, a view advanced by Glasze et al. (2006) among others. One middle-aged woman named Bianca put it this way:

> If the municipality would do its job, nobody would have to do that [build tall gates]. But it doesn't .... [U]nless I fence it [my yard] off, my flowers will be all covered in dirt ... pretty soon it will look like a garbage dump. Now only the outside looks like that! [*Laughs.*]

Asked later on in the conversation whether she had ever talked to neighbors about cleaning up the area in front, Bianca decisively shook her head:

> No, this is a real problem here. In Sofia too but here I think worse. People only care about their yards and they are very beautiful inside. But then they leave garbage right in front of the gates ... even in front of the nicest houses here, and that's that. Because it's not theirs. I mean, the municipality is at fault here too, because why don't they clean? I mean I pay my taxes! But also the people, we have become like that, like everybody has given up.

I also asked whether she takes part in any civic or advocacy group. She shook her head again: "No, I don't have that much free time. I did some of that before [she was a member of the Green Party in the early 1990s]. You see where it got us. So nobody does this, really."

Aesthetics and the old Balkan building traditions, often intertwined, also played a role in people's reasons for building gates, even though the percentage of survey respondents who cited these motivations was in the single digits (Table 7.1). The Bulgarian National Revival style, which has come into vogue lately, certainly contributes to the trend, as heavy gates are one of its integral components. One female interviewee, Marina, a successful architect, explained in an in-depth interview:

> I find it [our gates] very beautiful. You see our entire house is in the Bulgarian Revival style and back then, of course, the houses always had such walling, and the front gates were wooden and quite gorgeous really. So we think it fits the whole look of the house.

Marina further presented this return to tradition as a reaction against ascetic socialist style:

> Architects [in Bulgaria] are looking to revive some of these good old traditions, as you know, I am sure. This has been very much a global trend and we [Bulgarians] have been behind, but this is not of course because we didn't have good architects, everyone knows this, but because the communists, they only wanted to spread around this ugly mass construction .... And I think people – not just architects but all people – are looking to have what we may call "an architecture with an address," you know, rooted in our traditions as Bulgarians.

Other, less articulate interviewees, mostly long-term and poorer residents, explained their rationale for having fences as follows: "Everyone has them," "Well, look around!" and "It's a Bulgarian house." Not a single survey respondent or in-depth interviewee mentioned prestige as a reason for erecting gates. Yet some described their gates not only as "beautiful," but also as "sophisticated" and "modern," as conferring "some dignity" and providing "the look it [a house] should have." Such comments may be taken as indirect testimony that gates do sometimes serve as means of elevating prestige. (Because such comments referred to visual appearance, in Table 7.1 they appear in the aesthetics category.) In an in-depth interview, Matei, an architect who spent a few years in the United States, proposed a peculiar theory of how gates enhance the visual integrity of the public street:

> In some cities, in Detroit where I have been, right, as you must know ... they have these streets that have "missing teeth," as they call it. It's very ugly and confusing: a house, a house, a house and then an empty spot – parking or a vacant lot, several of them totally interrupting the whole continuity of the street façade. So it's like the same thing here, but it is the opposite. If you have the whole street framed by tall gates and suddenly one house doesn't have them, it will be like an orphan, all by itself; it ruptures the whole composition.

Aside from fear of criminals and strangers and aside from tradition and aesthetics, another motivation featured prominently. According to the survey,
for about a third of the wealthier post-socialist newcomers – those who
tend to have the massive gates – the primary reason for having a physical
enclosure was to delineate and control private property (in contrast, less
than 10% of the long-term residents mentioned this motivation; Table 7.1).
Of course, this rationale is also difficult to separate from the others: indeed,
one protects private property from crime, from strangers, and from negative
external factors. But there is something more to it, I believe. There is an
intense, deeply emotional attachment to and pride in marking private space
for its own sake by drawing a solid, impermeable border around it. This
"Me against the world!" mentality is well reflected in open-ended answers
such as the following: "As the English say … it's my house and my castle,"
"It marks my place and my property," "This way I know what to take care
of," "So I know what's mine is mine," and "What would it [my house] be
without it? What would set us apart from this 'no man's land' outside?"
Some interviewees even expressed resentment, defiance and anger at the
notion of life without the gates: "This is not Avram's house!" (in Bulgarian,
this means "this is not everybody's house"),[8] "It's my place and I can do
with it whatever I want to … how is this your business?" and "It's my house!
Why are you asking?"

   The gates give a sense of separation from an unstable outside world; they
give residents a feeling of stability. As Setha Low (2003: 89) argues, they
offer a "psychological buffer" against life's turmoil, they are material means
of attaining emotional security. They offer protection not only from crime
but also from intangible, amorphous nets of unpredictable events that may
be happening outside.[9] One young interviewee, Rosa, put it simply: "It [hav-
ing gates] makes me know I am at home, like there's no outside outside."
While gates sometimes usurp public space, they can also become a protest
vote against it. Asked in an in-depth interview why he erected his massive
gates, which clearly encroached on the public sidewalk, a middle-aged man
named Dimitar began answering somewhat half-heartedly, "It's not much of
a sidewalk … everybody does that around here." But then he proceeded in
a firmer, more aggressive tone:

> [N]obody cares; nobody cares for anything here. Look at that sidewalk and
> the road outside! The whole country is like that, falling apart, the whole
> country …. So what am I going to do … everybody is doing it anyway. They
> [presumably corrupt politicians] ate the whole country and she is asking me
> about the sidewalk!

The spread of gated, guarded housing is commonly presented in the literature as the result of public-sector failure: public failure to provide safe

streets, public failure to provide decent services, public failure to provide one thing or another. But in countries like Bulgaria, public failure has occurred across so many facets of life that it has become failure of the public per se. Nobody understands this better than the residents themselves, who, when asked what explains the proliferation of gated housing in Sofia, often begin their answers neither with crime and safety concerns nor with lack of good public spaces. Instead of referring to something tangible and specific, they whisper of mythical, long-ago times of fear and instability: "We live as if the Turks were back." And in a painful display of national nihilism, some start with the most sweeping recognition of systemic public failure: "This is not Sweden!" and "In civilized [Western] countries, people don't have this stuff. I have seen how people live over there [in Germany] ...; their houses sit together like brothers: only grass between. But here, here, this is not a normal country." As one angry interviewee so bluntly put it, "What do you expect? This is Bulgaria!"

Notes

1   Ancient and medieval cities (and certain compounds within them) were of course often walled for military protection and to keep out undesirables. Modernity rendered such walls obsolete, and in many cases they were replaced by spectacular boulevards, most famously in Paris and Vienna. Yet walls never disappeared. Rather, their scale and purpose changed, at least in Europe: instead of surrounding entire towns or royal complexes, they re-emerged to frame the bourgeois enclaves that proliferated during the Industrial Revolution, as I mentioned earlier.

2   See for example Glasze (2006) and Sheinbaum (2008) on places as different as Lebanon and Mexico.

3   For example, see Lang and Danielson (1997) and Blakely and Snyder (1997) on North America; Atkinson and Flint (2004), Blandy (2006) and Raposo (2006) on Europe; Coy and Pohler (2002), Coy (2006), Salcedo and Torres (2004) and Thuillier (2005) on Latin America; Leisch (2002) and Rofe (2006) on Australia and Indonesia; and Grant (2005) on West Africa. These comprise only a small sampling of the literature. I return to some of them in the next chapter.

4   That this architectural tradition has something to do with contemporary gating practices is perhaps most easily proven in Belgrade. The northwestern part of the city – today's district of Zemun – was part of the Austro-Hungarian Empire until 1918, whereas the rest of the city was under Ottoman rule until Serbia's independence in 1815. One can find walled-off residences in southern Belgrade, old and new, much more easily than in Zemun.

5   Here and there some *duvari* remained along Sofia's streets all the way to the socialist 1960s. They were, however, always subjected to ideological and aesthetic scorn as remnants from a backward past (Dichev 2003).

6 This type of coding of course involved some subjective judgment on behalf of the surveyors. This is because no absolute terms could be set of what comprises a "impermeable" versus "semi-impermeable" enclosure. However, subjective judgment is routinely involved in survey questioning (e.g., if respondents are asked to describe themselves as very happy, happy, unhappy or very unhappy, they have to subjectively decide what these categories imply). To reduce the variability in the subjective judgments of the surveyors, the Institute of Sociology held several training seminars in which the gating categories were presented in photographs. The surveyors were then asked to assign a category to each gate in a series of visual exercises. This continued until all surveyors were able to code the fences in a similar fashion.

7 I do not mean to overemphasize the importance of a single binary variable, the year of locating to the suburbs (i.e., before or after the end of socialism) as a predictor of the level of gating and securitization. Other variables, especially household monthly income, also have strong correlations both with the type of enclosure and with the number of security devices. In a multiple regression model which uses the number of security devices as a dependent variable, both the year of settling in the suburbs and the monthly household income have statistically significant coefficients. Since this book uses an ethnographic research approach, I will not discuss the quantitative model here. A journal article using a quantitative model is under development.

8 In Bulgarian: *Tova ne e Avramov dom!*

9 Low refers specifically to the concept of "relational trauma": "Any trauma … violates and ruptures relationships at multiple levels and brings into question basic assumptions about the world as a safe, predictable, and reasonable place. As individuals … [experience] everyday traumas …, they can feel that their home, as well as their self, is threatened. In order to re-create a more secure base to counteract the impact of trauma, they choose homes within what they perceive as protective walls and gates."

8

Iron Curtains II: Gated Complexes

"Residential Park Sofia is a gated residential complex, which implements a vision for a 'city within the city,' where people can live, work, rest, shop and play in the same area. It is created with a holistic concept in mind and with thoughts focused on the family."

Excerpt from the website of the gated complex
Residential Park Sofia, 2010

"I exit the gates and I enter … well, hell."

Excerpt from an interview with a resident of a new gated
community in Sofia, 2009

I recently visited Residential Park Sofia, the largest gated residential complex in the city. When it is completed, it will include over 1300 residences, a supermarket, two pharmacies, a bank branch, a dry cleaner, a beauty salon, two restaurants, two cafés, several swimming pools, a spa and massage center, a fitness center, a sauna, multiple tennis and basketball courts, a kindergarten, several playgrounds, and two underground garages, along with 90,000 square meters of beautifully kept green space (Figure 8.1). The complex is situated on the south edge of Mladost, right across from Business Park Sofia, which I described in Chapter 5. It spreads over 180,000 square meters of land. It is currently in the process of acquiring administrative designation as a separate neighborhood unit in the city. Like Business Park Sofia, the complex was built by the German development group Linder. The project has four controlled access points. In addition, security automobiles are said to "circle all day," and each dwelling is supplied with a video system that allows residents to monitor their dwelling's front door. Entering the complex as a visitor is a

Iron Curtains, First Edition. Sonia A. Hirt.
© 2012 John Wiley & Sons, Ltd. Published 2012 by John Wiley & Sons, Ltd.

Figure 8.1   A view of the row-housing section of Residential Park Sofia.

peculiar experience: not only must one stop at the barrier, talk to the guard and provide an adequate reason for the visit, but one must also submit an ID, of which the guard makes a copy, and obtain an entry permit. The process is not much different from crossing the border between Bulgaria and a neighboring country, except that here, at the gates of Residential Park Sofia, one does not have to go through Customs.

The complex, as its website claims, "implements a vision for a 'city within the city,' where people can live, work, rest, shop and play in the same area" (Residential Park Sofia undated), an idea that, according to one of the realtors advertising it, will prevail as "the city of the future." On the basis of my interviews, the place has a fairly active neighbors' association. It organizes common activities and negotiates issues related to the daily maintenance and functioning of the complex with the development and management firm, which runs the commercial parts, keeps up the green areas and provides the collective security.

According to leading realtors' websites, as of 2010 there are about six dozen "official" gated communities in Sofia, all built over the last five years or so, mostly at the southern rim of the city (see Table 8.1 at the end of this chapter). Of course, this number excludes individually gated homes (described in the previous chapter), residences located in small enclosed compounds, built primarily in the 1990s, which are still advertised as single units rather than as part of a formal gated community with its own name and permanent

Table 8.1   Gated communities in Sofia

Name of complex	District	Units	Amenities in addition to housing	Development firm
Apolona Houses	Pancharevo	10	swimming pool	Bulgarian
Arena Gardens	Vitosha	39	fitness, spa	Bulgarian
Aristocrat	Vitosha	16	swimming pool	Russian
Avalon	Vitosha	125	café, fitness, grocery, spa	Bulgarian
Balnea Hills	Ovcha Kupel	61	dry cleaning, fitness, mini-market, pharmacy, spa, swimming pool	Dutch
Berlin Park Vitosha	Vitosha	102	beauty salon, fitness, restaurant, spa, swimming pool	British
Biala Cherkva I	Pancharevo	12	church	Bulgarian
Biala Cherkva II	Vitosha	9		Bulgarian
Bistrica Gardens	Pancharevo	45	café, grocery	Israeli and Bulgarian
Boutique Apartments	Vitosha	54		Israeli
Boyana Fantasy	Vitosha	n/a	fitness, grocery, restaurant, spa, swimming pool	n/a
Boyana Kinocentura	Vitosha	n/a	beauty salon, fitness, grocery, spa, swimming pool	Bulgarian
Bright Light	Vitosha	n/a		Bulgarian
Buena Vista	Vitosha	117	mini-market	British and Bulgarian
Bulgaria	Krasno Selo	n/a	beauty salon, fitness, spa, swimming pool	n/a
Casa Viva	Izgrev	n/a	fitness, doctor's office, restaurant, swimming pool	Bulgarian
Cherry Gardens	Pancharevo	40	grocery	n/a
Cité Jardin	Vitosha	290	café, fitness, kindergarten, restaurant, spa, swimming pool	Bulgarian
City of Fountains	Mladost	750	doctor's office, grocery, swimming pool	Russian
Crystal Bell	Pancharevo	34	café, doctor's office, fitness, spa, swimming pool	Bulgarian

(*Continued*)

Table 8.1 *(Cont'd)*

Name of complex	District	Units	Amenities in addition to housing	Development firm
Delta Hills	Pancharevo	306	car wash, cocktail bar, grocery, kindergarten, restaurant	n/a
Dragalevtsi Views	Vitosha	n/a	fitness, pharmacy, restaurant	Bulgarian
Embassy Suites	Vitosha	84	bank, beauty salon, café, dry cleaning, fitness, restaurant	British and Bulgarian
Este Home	Izgrev	171	beauty salon, fitness, spa, swimming pool	British and Bulgarian
Flora Bora	Vitosha	57		n/a
Gloria Palace	Ovcha Kupel	78	fitness, spa, swimming pools, tennis courts	n/a
Golden Valley	Vitosha	103	doctor's office, mini-market, pharmacy, swimming pool, tennis courts	Bulgarian
Greenvillage	Pancharevo	24		Israeli and Bulgarian
Hadji Dimitur	Poduyane	n/a	café, doctor's office, kindergarten, pharmacy, restaurant	n/a
Ivaniane	Novi Iskar	n/a		Bulgarian
Komplex Botanika	Vitosha	57	fitness, restaurant, spa	n/a
Koralite	Pancahrevo	n/a		n/a
Krustova Voda	Lozenetz	16		n/a
Kutina Gardens	outside city	n/a	swimming pools	n/a
Lagera Tulip	Krasno Selo	500		Dutch
Lozen Gardens	Pancharevo	120		Israeli and Bulgarian
Magdalena Village	Pancharevo	n/a		Bulgarian
Maxi Green City	Vitosha	200	conference center, fitness, restaurants, spa, swimming pool, tennis courts	n/a
Mercure Sofia	Lozenetz	64	fitness, spa, swimming pool	Israeli
Miramonte	Vitosha	n/a		n/a
Modera	Vitosha	335	kindergarten, mini-market, restaurant	Spanish

Table 8.1 *(Cont'd)*

Name of complex	District	Units	Amenities in addition to housing	Development firm
Mountain View	Vitosha	250	fitness, spa, swimming pools	n/a
Mountain View Vill.	Pancahrevo	30	swimming pool	n/a
Orchid Hills	Studentski	200		British
Palazzo Sofia	Vitosha	23	fitness, spa	n/a
Panorama Life	Vitosha	n/a	fitness, spa, swimming pool	Israeli
Paprat	Vitosha	n/a		Bulgarian
Paradise Vista	Vitosha	46	fitness, spa, swimming pool	n/a
Perlata	Vitosha	n/a		n/a
Perlite	Vitosha	n/a		Bulgarian
Residential Complex Mladost	Mladost	178	restaurant, swimming pool	n/a
Residential Park Sofia	Pancharevo	1300	cafés, fitness, kinder-garten, pharmacy, restaurants, swimming pools	German
Sekvoia	Vitosha	8		Bulgarian
Silver City	Lozenetz	n/a	beauty salon, café, doctor's office, fitness, grocery, spa, swimming pools	Bulgarian
Simeonovo River	Vitosha	207	fitness, mini-market, restaurants, spa, swimming pool, tennis courts	Irish and Bulgarian
Slunchev Dom	Vitosha			Israeli
Sofia Gardens	Pancharevo	73	fitness, spa, swimming pool	Israeli and Bulgarian
Sofia House	Vitosha	n/a	swimming pool	British and Bulgarian
Sofia Ski Resort	Vitosha	n/a	café, dry cleaning, fitness, mini-market, pharmacy, spa, swimming	n/a
Sofia_sky	Vitosha	84		British and German
South Park	Lozenetz	n/a	fitness, spa, swimming pool	Bulgarian
SvetaMagdalena	Vitosha	24		Bulgarian

(Continued)

Table 8.1   (*Cont'd*)

Name of complex	District	Units	Amenities in addition to housing	Development firm
Sveti Georgi	Vitosha	17	church, fitness, spa, swimming pool	Bulgarian
Tsarigradski	Iskar	1300		Bulgarian
Vertu Residence	Vitosha	24	dry cleaning, fitness, spa, swimming pool	n/a
Vishneva Gradina	Studentski	41		n/a
Vista Park	Vitosha	48		Bulgarian
Vitosha Estate	Vitosha	115	fitness, mini-market, spa, swimming pool	Bulgarian
Vitosha Palace	Vitosha	141	fitness, spa, swimming pool	Israeli
Vitosha Tulip	Lozenetz	144	fitness, spa, swimming pool	Dutch
Winslow Gardens	Vitosha	444	fitness, spa, swimming pool	British and Bulgarian
Zornica	Vitosha	39		n/a

Notes: The data was compiled by Christian Smigiel and Sonia Hirt and based on information obtained from the websites of the gated communities, real estate firms, media sources, and personal visits. "n/a" = "not available."

security and property management staff, and countless "regular" multi-family buildings that are locked most hours of the day and employ a security guard. The "official" gated communities still comprise a very small percentage of Sofia's total housing stock. Still, they are a trend so eye-catching as to make foreign visitors remember the city as part of a *Fortress Bulgaria* – a label that has to do entirely with contemporary housing practices, rather than the country's splendid ancient and medieval ruins (Sommerbauer 2007).[1] The gated communities are certainly the residential choice of foreigners working in the country (diplomatic staff, business managers, etc.): an estimated 25% of people living in gated complexes are not Bulgarian citizens – a figure much higher than in any other type of housing (Grozev 2010).

The new gated communities of Sofia are not just quantitatively different from their smaller, 1990s-era predecessors (for example, they cover much greater chunks of land and comprise a much larger number of dwelling units); they are also qualitatively different. We can summarize these differences if we consider the gated community as both a product and a process. As a product, it offers not just a place to live, but a constellation of facilities that allow residents to reduce their dependency on services otherwise offered in the city to a much greater extent than do individual gated homes. As one interviewed realtor noted: "When one buys here, one does not just get some sort of nice dwelling. It is far more than that; it is a whole group of new comforts, a whole new lifestyle." Although few of the gated communities offer Residential Park Sofia's rich variety of services, shared amenities such as swimming pools, beauty salons and fitness centers are becoming standard. Furthermore, the gated complexes offer exactly what most of Sofia is desperately missing: clean and nicely maintained green spaces and a reliable infrastructure. One of Sofia's leading realtors explained this as follows:

> I have said for a long time that this is exactly the market segment to watch. I now see that my prediction is coming true. This makes me exceptionally happy, because this is exactly what our firm specializes in, exactly this type of complexes – gated ones. This is where the future lies: people look for many amenities in one place. These are exactly the advantages of the gated complex: greenery, fitness, spas, tennis courts, restaurants. These are the kinds of things that make people prefer a home in a gated community rather than an individually built house of the older type [the type most commonly built in the 1990s] that is just somewhere. And add this to an improved security situation.[2]

As a result of all the extra amenities, homes in gated communities cost about 30% more per square meter than those of similar quality in non-gated communities (Grozev 2010). The development process and its participants also differ quite markedly from what was the norm in the 1990s. Instead of a fragmented development process, one led by individual actors, the gated community of the post-2000 period is produced (and consumed) in a more organized manner that one could even describe as Fordist. The process is no longer led by individual homeowners and builders but by large-scale investors, both Bulgarian and foreign. It is in fact safe to say that the larger the development, the higher the chances that multi-national capital was involved. Residents of gated complexes tend to exhibit similar social characteristics. According to a recent study conducted by a real estate firm, people living in gated complexes are much more likely to be married with children than are residents of other types of housing.[3] Most household heads residing in gated communities either own a business or are a part of the upper management of a large private firm (Cenova 2008).[4]

This contrasts sharply with the colorful social and spatial mixture that defined Sofia's suburbs in the 1990s. As I discussed in the previous two chapters, these suburbs contained upscale new residences with all sorts of architectural personas located near modest cottages from the socialist period. The new gated communities have introduced a very different type of built fabric, one marked by greater homogeneity. In some of the new projects, economies of scale achieved through standardization have resulted in such a spatial sameness that critics, evoking socialist imagery, call them the "new panels" (*novite panelki*; Kazalarska 2010). In the words of one Bulgarian sociologist, building processes over the last few decades can be described as "moving from collectivism [during socialism] through individualism [during the 1990s] to segmentalism [after 2000]," the latter implying the formation of larger spatial units (segments) produced through single-stroke processes by large development firms and occupied by people of similar social status (Dandolova, interviewed June 6, 2010). In a sense, this residential change parallels changes in the organization of retail spaces in Sofia. Much as the small impromptu shop of the early transition years has been vanishing under pressure from the new hypermarkets, the individually gated home of the 1990s is now overshadowed by the large-scale gated community.

What explains the fast-growing popularity of gated complexes in Sofia? Does Sofia give students of this phenomenon something new to learn? My argument in this chapter is as follows. Although the proliferation of gated communities in Sofia can be attributed largely to processes that have already been presented in the literature on gated communities across the globe, the Bulgarian capital offers a uniquely powerful combination of factors that has made it an exceptionally willing participant in the global trend: (1) In the last couple of decades, the very weak public sector has clearly failed to provide much-needed services and infrastructure, and it has been very eager to outsource them to private hands. (2) The private development sector, with its growing logistical and financial capacity, has built on local traditions by experimenting with various smaller-scale types of gating through the post-socialist years. Private developers have also been exceptionally eager to import trends from abroad. (3) The growing middle- and upper-class population, which has embraced urban spatial secession as a desirable lifestyle goal, has finally been offered a viable, economically efficient and beautifully packaged way of pursuing it. Vesselinov et al. (2007) argues that the essential prerequisite for gated communities to "prosper" in a particular time and place is the development of a "gating machine" – a particular constellation of interests and actions of local governments, the private development industry, and consumers, all of which function in the context of globalizing neo-liberal capitalism. In Sofia, I contend, the gating machine is now in full operation.

Globalization and Gated Communities

As I noted in the previous chapter, the commonly accepted definition of a gated community is a large-scale residential area that is enclosed by walls or other barriers to entry, includes streets and other shared amenities, and involves some sort of private decision-making. (If this is the case, one cannot write a history of the phenomenon in Sofia, as Savage (1987) and Hayden (2004) have done for St. Louis and New York. To my knowledge, no such thing existed in Sofia until recently, although there were numerous early relatives like the Ottoman gated family compound, the socialist-era recreational compound on the Black Sea (intended for the socialist elites), and the post-socialist fenced-off individual home. The question is: why have gated communities proliferated in Sofia exactly at this point in time?

In Chapters 3 and 7, I referred to macro-explanations of the phenomenon nested in theories of globalization. This narrative emphasizes that globalization entails the increased mobility of capital and the marginalization of labor, which in turn exacerbate social disparities, weaken social solidarity, worsen poverty and bolster crime. Thus, globalization creates the very forces propelling urban socio-spatial partitioning (Marcuse and Van Kempen 2000, 2002). Coupled with the failure of a weakened, post-welfare-state public sector to guarantee security and high-quality services, globalization as a structural cause induces demand for living in enclaves that protect the upper and middle classes from all others and provide them with a variety of privatized amenities (Low 2003; Glasze et al. 2006). The building sector, of course, is quick to produce space that generates profit (Logan and Molotch 1987), and under conditions of globalization it can operate at a much larger, multi-national scale. Thus it capitalizes on this demand by developing a corresponding urban form, the gated community, and it uses all available media resources to strengthen this demand.

However, if we take globalization in its broadest sense as the global spread of neo-liberal capitalism, then the collapse of the socialist bloc itself was the result of globalization because the Soviet and East European regimes were unable to survive in an era of global communications and the electronically integrated world economy (Giddens 2006: 57). Yet, despite worsening crime and poverty, weakened solidarity and widened social disparities during the 1990s – all ostensibly induced by globalization – large gated lifestyle communities of the sort defined above did not develop in Bulgaria. Rather, globalization sparked the restoration of a particular *local* tradition – the fortified individual home described in the previous chapter. It took additional offshoots of globalization, including the direct penetration of foreign capital and the further infiltration of foreign cultural ideals and development models after 2000, for the Western-style, large-scale gated community to find a home in Sofia.

Of course, globalization is not some super-process that magically "trickle[s] down from the sky," so the real question is how the "super-process" works on the ground (Keil and Ronneberger 2000: 229); that is, how does the global "gating machine" operate in Sofia? I will attempt to spell this out by discussing the views and actions of the local government and of the producers and residents of gated complexes along the lines proposed by Vesselinov et al. (2007). As in earlier chapters, my focus remains on the residents: on their views, attitudes and lived experiences. Thus I build my case predominantly by citing in-depth interviews. For this chapter, I interviewed twenty-one residents of six gated communities to which I was allowed access. All six communities are located on the southern side of Sofia.[5]

I also use my interviews with urban planners, architects, builders, and real estate agents, as well as the rich advertising materials that have accompanied the spread of the gated complexes in the Bulgarian capital.

The New Gates of Sofia

The development of large-scale gated communities in Sofia cannot be separated from Sofia's suburbanization. The two forms of urban spatial separatism are inescapably intertwined: the overwhelming majority of large-scale gated communities can be located only in outlying areas, where there is sufficient space to build them. In this sense, government support of suburban development (i.e., the privatization of the urban greenbelts, the loosening of building controls, and the new laws giving preferential treatment to large investors such as the German Linder) amounts to indirect support for the growth of gated communities. Certainly, one cannot find government-issued policy and planning documents that embrace the gated complex as explicitly as they endorse suburbanization (i.e., the "dispersed city model" trumpeted in Sofia's newest Master Plan, discussed in Chapter 6). But according to interviews with urban policy-makers, the gated complexes, much like suburban development, are very much perceived as part of a progressive process by which Sofia is becoming a normal, Western-like city. Asked about the new gated communities, interviewed officials expressed views such as the following:

> Well, we can't really have a position as a municipality on this [gated communities]. What I mean is that this is a matter of choice, really a matter of architecture – if people want to live in a complex, which is enclosed by some means, how is it our job to take issue with it, how is this our job? ... Now if you ask me personally, it is a perfectly normal market process, it is a perfectly normal market process in which enclaves of this type are becoming more popular. They have this everywhere, everywhere in cities in the world, you would know better .... You know, our investors travel, they study what other people do, so I do not find this surprising. Plus crime, everybody is concerned about crime ....

> Now, on the other hand, there is something to it .... Look, we are still a poor municipality as far as Europe goes, so we can't solve a lot of problems by ourselves; you see the state of many of the roads and the parks; you understand that. So if the private sector finds ways to solve this even for a small part of Sofia, it is better than not solving it at all.

> My personal opinion here does not matter. I mean personally I would never live in a place like this, all enclosed like I am an animal in a zoo. But as some sort of a public official, it [my view] becomes different. First, there is no legal basis that would stop the construction [of gated complexes] and there would be no obvious

way of justifying it …. But more importantly, it is a trend, I think, that rich people want to live with others like them and as long as this brings growth and new infra-structure, we will have to accept it …. Now, is it pleasant? Maybe not, well, I don't know. But it may be necessary and it can't be stopped.

The extent of local government endorsement is apparent in the fact that the ceremonial opening of the second-largest gated complex in Sofia – Tsarigradski, which has 1300 units – was personally attended by Sofia's Mayor, as well as several other city officials (This Mayor was later elected Bulgaria's Prime Minister). In an on-site media interview, the Mayor declared concisely but enthusiastically, "Undoubtedly, this is beautiful. And it will only get better." In a demonstration of the mutually beneficial relationship between government and business, the municipality promised to extend mass-transit services closer to the gated community, and the development firm declared that all road improvements in the vicinity of the gated complex will become a gift to the municipality (Shumanova 2007).

Who builds the new communities? The short answer is a mixture of local and foreign firms, mostly Israeli, Russian, British, Irish and Dutch (Table 8.1). However, more detailed research into the background of the development firms shows that although many are officially registered as Bulgarian, they do have some foreign participation (e.g., they are local branches of foreign firms). Furthermore, the developments are commonly financed by foreign financial institutions with local representation in Bulgaria, such as the Alianz and Reiffeisen banks, even if the firm building them is in fact Bulgarian. Some firms have clearly attempted to establish gated complexes as their sig-nature contribution to the market: for example, an Israeli-Bulgarian partner-ship (Gardens Group/Perfecto Group) is in the business of building "gardens" around the country (gated gardens, that is). At the time of writing, the firm's website listed the following current and future developments: Sofia Gardens, Bistrica Gardens, Lozen Gardens, Gardens City and Garden Hills. The Dutch AFI Europe has chosen to popularize its home country's symbol, the tulip, in the form of gated complexes: there is now the Lagera Tulip and the Vitosha Tulip; more "tulips" are in a planning phase, although the current recession appears to have slowed them down. From the developers' point of view, gated complexes have thus far succeeded in Sofia because:

> The demand was here … we didn't have to really start it …. People, I mean those people who could, have been trying to find something better than this deteriorating city for some time. But how could they do it? In some home-grown, do-it-yourself way! They hire a builder to make them an elite house in what they hoped was an elite neighborhood like Simeonovo [a neighborhood in the Vitosha Collar]. OK, so they now have their own house with views of the mountain. Whatever. Very nice! But it really isn't that nice because the infra-structure in Simeonovo, and you know this is correct, is not fixed and they have

to go through all sorts of inconveniences day after day ... getting to their house along the terrible roads is the least of their problems .... They have to worry about thieves, they hire their own guard, the guard falls asleep. They have to maintain a garden. You get it. Ah, and their neighbors are there from the old times and watch them weirdly day and night – you know they are all retirees, not much other work to do .... So they have plopped this elite house in the middle of nowhere .... So we had to work to introduce a better alternative – something that is more elegant, modern, so to speak ....

Look, we offer an entire product – not a house but a whole environment, where everything is nice all around them, at least while they are there. We provide the security, the maintenance, the daily conveniences .... Now obviously, we can't help them really solve all the problems – we can't fix all the roads that they drive to get home, nor can we help them when Sofia Water decides to stop services for six straight hours, right? But we certainly have given them an improvement over that house they had .... And none of this is new; I am the first to admit that this kind of a complex is everywhere in the world. From where I am standing, we are simply bringing best practices from around the world.

That the model is heavily promoted as best practices coming from else-where is quite obvious from the names alone. Of the 75 communities in Table 8.1, fewer than 20 have Bulgarian names. English is clearly the language of choice (with occasional forays into French or Italian). The most common words ("hills," "village," "mountain," "estate," "residential," "palace," "view," etc.), all of which could of course easily be translated into Bulgarian, are instead left in English. On billboards and other media outlets, they are sometimes spelled with Latin letters and other times with Cyrillic ones. Promotional materials allude heavily to Western residential lifestyles: "German quality at Bulgarian prices" in the complex of Crystal Bell, or "International Lifestyle" in Sofia_sky. American living is most commonly advertised. The community of Mountain View Village, where the houses with their shingle roofs and vinyl siding really seem to have come from the pattern book of American suburban subdivisions, is an excellent example. In fact, the developer claimed in a newspaper interview that he has built "a small America in Sofia, so that we [Bulgarians] no longer feel like we have to emigrate to America" (cited by Kazalarska 2010). And while gated complexes cannot be credited with curtailing emigration (it has slowed down anyway), the message seems to be working at least to some extent. In the words of some residents, living in a gated community does indeed make them *feel like* a citizen of another, better place: "like a normal person in a normal country," "as if I am not in Bulgaria," and even "like a white man." Once again, much like the residents of individually gated homes, those in gated compounds often subconsciously seem to view their lifestyle choices as a result of gross, systemic public failure – that of the country as a whole.

As I discussed in the previous chapters, the literature offers four main behavioral explanations for the spread of gated communities: security, status, access to amenities, and a homogeneous community. Sofia's case clearly attests to the validity of all four. Twenty-four-hour security assured via multiple means is the very first amenity listed on the websites of most gated communities. Security is heavily touted by developers and real estate agents: "They, the guards are everywhere, so you can really leave all your worries behind," as one realtor put it. It is also something highly valued by interviewed residents: "It's the most important thing," one new homeowner explained. "For us there can be no compromises on this issue, because we have kids." Some residents, though, expressed reservations about the heavy security:

> You sacrifice some of your personal freedom because the cameras, they do not care – they watch you like they watch everyone else …. I couldn't find my cat one night and ran outside to look. I got him [the cat] but then once I crossed the line [i.e., where the gates are], the video projectors were all on me and the guards came running.

> Well, sometimes it is not pleasant to think that you are [guarded] as if you are in a military zone … but what else to do? These, sister, are the times we live in.

Overall, residents accepted this intrusion as the inevitable price of protection from urban crime. The portrait of the imaginary criminal was articulated along the same lines used by the residents of the individually gated homes described in the previous chapter (i.e., male construction workers and "roaming gypsies"). As in the case of gated homes, the desire for protection came not only from fear of criminals, but also from a general anxiety regarding intruding outsiders, as well as intruding homeless dogs and crazy drivers. Protection from other negative aspects of the public space outside, such as dust and dirt, was cited as well. As some residents put it, protection is needed from "a whole package of street unpleasantness, from all the "bad stuff out there that we all know of." One visibly concerned mother explained her view of her gated complex as both an "outside" and "inside" place as follows:

> [B]ut for the kids it's the best. You can let them out, but it is not like you have just let them out there, in the street with all that is happening. They are out but they are also in, within the complex, so that I don't have to be worried. It's a great benefit …. Now as long as they stay inside [the gates], we can provide them with this sense of freedom that I guess I had when I played with kids from the nearby houses [in the small town she is from], back in the day [when it was safer].

A billboard advertising the gated complex of Vista Park offers a particularly imaginative portrait of the threatening "outsider." Playing on what seems to be a common dislike of outsiders (even neighbors) watching one curiously, the billboard shows an enormous, scary owl with wide, bulging eyes (Kazalarksa 2010). The owl is labeled "The Curious Neighbor on Your Left." Vista Park has evidently been built to prevent this neighbor from invading family privacy. (Of course, since it is a complex of forty-eight homes, Vista Park cannot actually prevent the gazes of curious neighbors on either the left or the right, but it certainly blocks the gazes of those who live beyond its gates.)

Few gated complexes, however, are marketed by presenting a grim world outside. In Sofia, this world is there for all to see, so painting a cheerful portrait of the world *inside* the gates is perfectly sufficient. The advertising materials send many recurring messages. Aside from security, the most commonly used themes are the "holistic concept" and the "lifestyle choice" (i.e., the opportunity to access multiple services in a relatively controlled environment), as well as the beautiful greenery and the well-maintained infrastructure (i.e., the kind of public goods that are in short supply in Sofia). As in any advertising, these features are quite often grossly exaggerated. For example, whereas some amenities like the fitness centers and swimming pools are typically accessible to residents alone, only the largest complexes can operate grocery stores that are truly closed to the public. In most cases, the shops are located on the periphery of the complex and serve outside customers as well, thus compromising the advertised rigidity of the community's borders (of course, if the community is far out in the suburbs and can be accessed only by car, the outside clientele is restricted to begin with). The images of picturesque park-like environments in which many of the communities are ostensibly situated are also often misleading: images show exotic flowers that do not thrive in Bulgaria and sparkling lakes that are too blue to be true.[6] In one advertisement, Mount Vitosha, whose tallest point is 2300 m (half that of the Alps), is shown to reach truly monumental heights. The pictures of residents are also highly aesthetized. The most common image seems to be that of the happy couple watching their kids play in a lush park – an image consistent with the message of family lifestyles. Men and women play different roles in these families: men often appear in business suits, and their most common accessory is the expensive car; women, on the other hand, seem to frequent the spas and the swimming pools and are customarily shown armed with shopping bags.

Another, complementary and prevalent, advertising message is that the gated complex is not just a secure home or a convenient new lifestyle, but also a place to vacation away from urban bustle and daily Bulgarian troubles. Depending on the location of the community, its geography is described as "outside the city," "above the city," or "away from the city," as a carefree faraway land where one lives in the kind of peace and comfort that the outside world destroys. (Hence gated communities sport names like Avalon, Bright Light, Paradise Vista and Boyana Fantasy, not to mention names that suggest other countries, like Berlin Park and South Park.) Whether this is necessarily false advertisement is debatable, but many residents sincerely feel as if they have moved into an alternative, better world. One resident put it in strikingly blunt terms: "Here, I feel very comfortable .... I exit the gates and I enter ... well, hell."

"Where is the community in this community?" asked one local cultural anthropologist (Dichev, interviewed June 18, 2009). He asked the question in Bulgarian but used the English word "community." The closest translation of "community" is "*obshtnost*," but nobody uses this Bulgarian word in reference to gated compounds. They are literally called enclosed complexes (*zatvoreni kompleksi*), a term that refers to a physical, built environment rather than one that is human and social. Perhaps hoping to project an image that suggests human interaction, the local arm of Linder, which markets and manages Residential Park Sofia, organized a visit from Santa Claus. The firm then celebrated the children's event as its "first community Christmas." On the website, "first" and "Christmas" are in Bulgarian, but "community" is in English (Residential Park Sofia undated).[7] Clarifying the point of the event and the meaning of "community," the website of Residential Park Sofia says:

> On the eve of the warmest family holiday Christmas, the owners of a secure home in Residential Park Sofia will experience the community spirit of the complex celebrating together the first Community Christmas of Residential Park Sofia .... Because Residential Park Sofia not only unites and brings its residents closer as neighbors, but also links them with common aims, endeavors and high living standards.[8]

It is difficult to assess the extent to which a "community," consisting of individuals with similar interests who actively communicate with each other, does form in the new gated complexes. It is also difficult to determine the extent to which moving into such a community affects one's relationship with the outside. Several interviewees mentioned that they made friends with their new neighbors and that they routinely visit each other for dinner and go together to the complex's restaurants and cafés and, sometimes, to the city theaters. Furthermore, none of the interviewees said that they now visited friends living outside the gated complex less frequently than they used to. According to others, however, few new friendships form in the gated communities, because "except for mothers with children ... people are too busy, so they get in and out of home right away" without "turning their heads to look at anybody." And only three of the twenty-one interviewees claimed that they occasionally participated in civic organizations (these were an architect who had helped a heritage conservation group, a politician who had links to a "save kids from drugs" group, and a homemaker who worked on an anti-AIDS campaign), No one had either joined or left a civic organization during the relatively brief time since they had moved into the gated complex.

Figure 8.2 Not very subtle: the gates of the gated complex Aristocrat.

It can be argued that for many residents, the idea of having a community entails living near individuals with similar socio-economic status. Status and social exclusivity are ubiquitously advertised: "Class in the sky of Sofia" in Sofia_sky; "The right to luxury!" in Arena Gardens & Spa. There is nothing subtle about names such as Aristocrat, The Boutique Apartments, The Golden Valley and Gloria Palace (Figure 8.2). The words "luxurious," "prestigious" and "exclusive" are some of the most commonly used, and the many references to foreign, Western places are undoubtedly intended to convey the feeling of being part of an international highlife.

Advertising aside, for several interviewed residents the concepts of community and exclusivity were irrevocably intertwined. For them, the desire to live among similar people is the primary reason for living in a gated environment. Take, for example, Daniela, an educated young woman who recently moved with her husband and children to a gated community from one of Sofia's central neighborhoods:

> I like it because it is quiet and comfortable here, a good neighborly place …. I personally have no desire to listen again to the really loud TV that my old neighbor watched or be a part of a cooperative in which we were the only ones who regularly paid the building's maintenance fee.

Another interviewed resident was even more explicit:

> I want to live with people like me. I don't want to listen to my neighbor's scandals with her drunken husband or to be near this retiree who couldn't pay her current bills. I do not want to live with the plebeians.[9]

Perhaps most telling was the life story shared by a middle-aged couple, Boris and Elena, who own a chain of local fashion stores. When they were newly married in 1990, they moved to Sofia from their small hometown (which they remember fondly) in order to attend university. They made their first home in one of the socialist housing estates. In the mid-1990s, after opening a successful retail business, they moved to a newly constructed apartment building in one of the "prestigious neighborhoods" in the district of Vitosha. Later, at the end of the 1990s, they purchased a single-family home in the mountain outskirts. Finally, in 2006 they settled in one of Vitosha's new large gated complexes. Their perceptions of the advantages and drawbacks of each setting and their reasons for moving from one to another speak volumes about the deep skepticism toward public space that prevails in Sofia. The couple's first move, from the small town to Sofia's socialist district of Studentski, evokes no fond memories:

> Elena: Awful …. Not nice, not a nice place.
>
> Boris: But that's how it was! We had no other opportunity … we were very young so … no money …. So everybody was doing it – if you wanted to study in Sofia, that's where you lived as students.
>
> Elena: Well, correction! We were young and just married, so we had fun, what did we know?
>
> Boris: But it was difficult. We wanted our boys to learn to ride bicycles when they were little. But the street in front was not well kept …. When it doesn't belong to anybody, nobody maintains it. It was the opposite of what we have now [in the gated community]. So we had to take the kids – I mean they were what, very young kids – and the bicycles and everything … to a park. This took some thirty minutes or more. Now this [the park] was better and the parks were then safer, not like today, but it was a lot of effort!

The move from the socialist-era building to the new one in a better, more "elite" neighborhood was a significant improvement for several practical reasons, including the much larger size of the new dwelling and its higher-quality construction. The quality of the surrounding roads, however, remained a problem. Elena and Boris continued taking their boys to the parks again, although this time they could go by car rather than bus. According to Boris, the developer of their multi-family building had "patched up" the roads in the immediate vicinity, but beyond them, the state of the infrastructure was very poor, so the kids still could not ride their bicycles. Other unpleasant problems remained, as well:

> Boris: There was one thing that the builder really did wrong, I think. Maybe it is natural, maybe now they [builders] have learned better. I am not a specialist

but here is the problem, I think .... So the building had three stories. He [the builder] had put six very small apartments on the first floor, four bigger ones on the second, and the two largest and nicest ones on the top floor [where Boris and Elena lived], right? So you really had very different types of people living there .... I mean on the first floor, you got some older people who probably had sold a larger ... socialist panel-made apartment somewhere; I don't know, maybe it was their [adult] children, who had bought it for them .... So you end up with really very different kinds of people living in that same building and barely speaking to each other.

Elena: Exactly! So every time I came home and brought my groceries or came back from Vitoshka [Sofia's most expensive shopping street] and I unloaded my bags, you see, I felt like these people [from the lower floors] were watching me, I mean watching me with some envy, resentment, or something. I mean, I understand this is perfectly natural and I don't blame them a bit.

Boris: No, no, it's not that they were not nice people. We are not saying that.

Elena: Yes, but here it is: I don't want to feel this way, as if these people wanted me to feel bad every time. Don't get me wrong – that's not exactly why we moved here – we did this because the conditions are better. But I didn't like being watched this way anyway.

Boris: The point is we didn't feel we belonged there, and we didn't have a lot of things in common [with most of the neighbors]. And again, I think the developer made a mistake in building this way.

Boris and Elena's next move was to purchase a single-family home with a large private yard in one of the new neighborhoods of the Vitosha Collar. Their high-quality home offered them more space and more privacy, but some old problems remained; some even got worse. The commute got longer, the electricity would stop more regularly, and the roads were more beat-up. Since their boys (who by that time were pre-teenagers) had no desire to quietly play in the yard, they often had to drive them to the city center. The place was, in Elena's words, a bit boring: "not much to do, always had to drive places." And the issue of neighbors did not get any better: there were various sorts of neighbors, some like Boris and Elena, some not.

The couple's last move was to a lush and green gated complex of over 200 units, which also includes a café, a restaurant, a mini-market, several swimming pools and various additional recreational amenities (some of which are available to outsiders at fairly high prices). This time the move felt right. Boris and Elena appreciated the security of controlled access, as well as the nicely kept greenery and infrastructure – the kind they could not get in any other part of Sofia. They feel very comfortable when their boys, now finishing high school, "hang out" with other kids in the complex: "Of course we can't try to keep them in," says Elena. "They have friends all around, so we still have to do a lot of driving. But when they are here (or at least they call and claim they are!)" – she goes on laughingly – "it's better, they are neither in nor out. I mean they are out of course, but not out there in the street; they are still home." The feeling of hominess is shared by Boris too, as was the idea of the gated complex as a middle space, a space both in and out. They see it as a safe space, familiar enough to be home, yet large and open enough to invite couples for nightly strolls along its groomed alleys – the kind of alleys that did not exist in any of the previous places Boris and Elena lived. "We walk around like the old days, holding hands, like we used walk when we were young, back in the city, and not much else mattered." Asked if it is possible to walk the same way right outside the gates, Boris says that there are no sidewalks and "now there are cars and dogs everywhere." He continues, "Nobody is going to fix this. All I can do is to fix this for myself."

Neighbors are a big part of Boris and Elena's satisfaction with their current residence. Contrasting the gated community with the building where they lived during the 1990s (the one where the apartments were of different sizes), Boris explains: "Here almost all the dwellings are the same size and are [sold] at the same price. So you end up with people with similar interests." Asked what he means by "similar interests," he starts a bit hesitantly:

Well, we all obviously feel, how shall I say, comfortable in the same kind of environment, which is why we all live in the same place, I think, right? So this is one interest .... And, for example, I work from here sometimes. I sit here at the restaurant and drink coffee and check my email. Yeah, but there are ten other people sitting at other tables, drinking coffee and spilling it in on their laptops [laughs] and checking their emails too. So we all look at each other – we are doing the same thing. It's a good feeling, gives you – well, me at least – comfort like I am with my kind of people.

And then he goes on a bit more assuredly:

You see briefcases with laptops on the tables all the time. People are not afraid to leave them and run back home to get something. You could never, never do this thing in those places [where we lived before]. So there was not that sense of security. And this comes not only because the place has controlled access so not everyone can come and just grab your laptop. But it comes from being with people who are not suspicious. I mean who is going to grab your laptop here, really? They all probably have three already (well, I do!). And this is a great advantage!

Maybe Boris and Elena have finally found home, a home behind gates but home nonetheless. What the gated complex offers them is what urban utopians have always sought: a middle space in which two apparent opposites tie the knot. The gated complex offers the marriage of town and country, inside and outside, city and nature, privacy and community; it is a "garden city," an "urban village," a "city in a park," a way of getting the best of both worlds, without any of their sorrows. The complex allows them to escape from the messy collective world outside, yet gives them access to amenities, from alleys to restaurants, which exist only to be consumed collectively. It grants them a border, but a border unlike the one they had around their fancy suburban home. This new border carves out not just an individual territory, but a larger, collective one. It connotes not the rugged, fragmented, "do-it-yourself" privatism of the 1990s, but a more confident, organized privatism that divides "us" and those "like us" from "them"; the "us" being, I suppose, the ones with the three laptops.

Like all utopias, this one has its limits. Boris's cell phone, as further conversation revealed, was stolen from a restaurant table (he thinks a waiter did it and stresses that it was a one-time event). And Elena still believes that some of her neighbors dislike her. Both of them go to Sofia daily for work, shopping and entertainment. It is Elena who says, "I exit the gates and I enter … well, hell." But then she goes on laughingly: "It's not so bad. I exaggerate. It has its problems, but it's Sofia."

Notes

1   Another indication of the growing popularity of gated communities in Sofia is the fact that, since 2008, all major realtors' websites began listing gated communities not merely as a residential sub-category but as a category on their own.

2   The realtor is Ivan Goranov, co-owner of the real-estate consulting company Home for You. He gave an interview to the Bulgarian news agency Focus (Imoti BG 2007).

3   Eighty-four percent of households residing in gated complexes are married couples; 60% are married couples with children.

4   Sixty percent of household heads residing in gated complexes head their own small or medium-size firm; 31% are upper-echelon managers in larger companies.

5   These six communities are: Maxi Green City, Vertu Residence, Residential Park Sofia, Aristocrat, Sveti Georgi, and Sveta Magdalena (Table 8.1). The first two are in urban locations – they are at the edge of parts of Sofia that were built during socialism. Residential Park Sofia is located on the former greenbelt. The last three complexes are extensions of Sofia's socialist-era "villa-zones." Maxi Green City and Vertu Residence include multi-family housing; Residential Park Sofia comprises several types of housing, including individual homes; Aristocrat, Sveti Georgi and Sveta Magdalena have only single-family homes. It is not very easy to reach interviewees in these types of communities. For example, although a few homes in

the large new gated communities were part of the random sample of the survey conducted by the Institute of Sociology, the Institute's surveyors were not allowed in. I obtained access through my contacts with architects, developers and real estate agents, who introduced me to residents they knew, who in turn introduced me to other residents (in Sveta Magdalena I could only interview by phone). This type of interviewee selection does not allow me to claim any statistical representation. Still, having in mind the inherent difficulties with access, this method is commonly used by researchers of gated communities (e.g., Low 2003).

6   The website of the complex Rezidencia Botanika, for example, welcomes with the slogan: Live in flower heaven!

7   That is, the title of the web posting is: *Purvata* community *Koleda v Residential Park Sofia*.

8   This statement is in Bulgarian but the word "community" is, again, in English.

9   Unlike all the other interviews, which I have quoted throughout the book and which I have personally conducted, this excerpt comes from an interview conducted by the Bulgarian sociologist I. Dandolova. The excerpt is also cited in Dandolova (2010).

9

Architecture of Disunity

"I think the new rule [of architecture] is shock your neighbor."
Excerpt from an interview with a Sofia architect, 2005

Ms. Sanborn wished a French chateau built upon their new estate on the Hudson. She wished it to look stately and ancient, as if it had always belonged to the family; of course, she admitted, people would know that it hadn't, but it would appear as if it had.
Ayn Rand, *The Fountainhead* (1971 [1943])

In the previous chapters, we saw how privatism expresses itself in specific housing forms. I will now explore how it manifests itself in the urban aesthetics, in the shape and style of buildings and building ensembles. My observation is simple: urban forms constructed (or remodeled) after socialism tend to turn inwards and have little connection to their surroundings. They are, in this sense, prime examples of architectural disunity, of anti-contextualism or, to use the term from Chapter 3, of stylistic secessionism. They are rich in fractures; i.e., they have a wide variety of discrete, eclectic, unrelated elements – the kind of variety that was to some extent on display in old Sofia but was systematically rooted out during socialism. The eclecticism operates at both the scale of the single building and the scale of the cityscape, leading to an environment that conveys a strong sense of discontinuity, separation and fragmentation. Discontinuity is not only a matter of deliberate stylistic choice; it can be more banal than that. Take, for example, what has become a common practice in the socialist districts. Since there is very little public money for the renovation of the socialist-era panel-made buildings – buildings that happen to be dreadfully energy-inefficient – the

Iron Curtains, First Edition. Sonia A. Hirt.
© 2012 John Wiley & Sons, Ltd. Published 2012 by John Wiley & Sons, Ltd.

owners of individual apartments are hiring private firms that install insulation on the exterior walls of their apartments alone. The visual result is quasi-comic: the otherwise flat and monochromatic façades of the socialist buildings are becoming colorful collages of isolated patches, each one decorated by an advertisement for the firm that installed it. In Bulgaria, the renovation of the socialist housing districts – a challenge taken on by the public sector in more prosperous post-socialist societies like Hungary and the former East Germany – is being tackled privately: one insulation patch, one apartment, one owner at a time. After all, as the popular proverb cited in Chapter 2 goes, in Bulgaria "The act of saving the drowning is an act to be performed by the drowning themselves."

Like all other processes described in the book, this spatial outcome – building and landscape discontinuity – is to a significant extent a function of the political economy. It is the logical product of an economic environment dominated by a fast-growing but cash-poor and fragmented private sector competing for fast, short-term profit. It is also the outcome of the actions (or lack thereof) of weakened public institutions that have neither the funds nor the power to implement comprehensive urban strategies (for example, rehabilitating the socialist housing estates) and often cannot (or do not) enforce the basic planning and building rules. The patches of insulation on the socialist panel-made buildings are not the explicit result of anyone's aesthetic aspirations, but a matter of crude necessity. Similarly, the recent invasion of giant commercial signs – another distinctive characteristic of the city's recent re-styling – is obviously premised on economic grounds (in this case capitalism's eternal need to self-advertise) rather than on anyone's high taste. Still, a cultural motif is a powerful component of the story. The new eclecticism is as much an expression of underlying political economy forces as it is consciously sought after – or at least not resisted – by the current city- builders, users and residents, even if they often complain about it and call it "chaotic" or "zoo-like" in the interviews. People seek difference, even a silly, tasteless difference like a marble eagle on the porch, and they don't care to look around and ask permission. To look around and ask permission would be to conform, and conformity is out. Difference is the new conformity. Every building for itself!

I do not aim to condemn the post-socialist urban fabric. A strong case can be made that the new spatial diversity is a step up from socialist aesthetic monotony. There may be an appeal to this mixed architecture. Indeed, one local architect described the socialist housing district where he lived as follows: "[T]his used to be one of the most boring places on earth. Now look around, you expect the unexpected" (Figure 9.1).

One might also argue that this mixed architecture is a more democratic urban form than the one imposed by a statist regime, that it is a legitimate reaction against old-fashioned top-down rule. Asked whether there

Figure 9.1 A new restaurant in the traditional Bulgarian style in the district of Mladost. The restaurant, the first of many "surprises" erected on the public green spaces of Mladost, is called Piquant – an appropriate name, especially considering the very un-piquant building behind it.

is some overarching rule to the new architecture, another architect responded, "People were so sick of being told how to live that some now take pride in breaking the [building and planning] statutes .... I think the new rule [of architecture] is shock your neighbor." This may be a truly post-modern attitude well suited to creating a new, post-socialist urban fabric (post-modern in the sense that it does away with any semblance of top-down order and discipline). But it is certainly not the post-modernism described by Charles Jencks and others, not post-modernism as a thought-out design vision embraced by professionals and other city-builders who seek to counter modern failures and ultimately build better urban environments. Rather, it is a bottom-up, grassroots post-modernism, a post-modernism of the masses, a post-modernism that entails the "avalanche-like collapse of officialdom" evoked by Kharkhordin (1997), a post-modernism that kills modern sterility but replaces it with colorful disintegration. Perhaps other terms, not post-modernism, would work better and I suggest a few in the next pages. Terms aside, however, it is obvious to anyone who walks the streets of Sofia that, in this disintegration, public space and public interests fade away; they are so passé as to become a mere afterthought, a leftover.

Figure 9.2 Hello Sofia: Hotel Pliska, once considered a fairly good example of modernism in Bulgaria, is now behind a Gap. Its roofline is adorned by bank and insurance company advertisements. At the bottom floor is the blinking logo of one of Sofia's many casinos.

Here are some of the specific and most common problems associated with the fragmentation of the urban environment that I see in today's Sofia:

1 The outright destruction of historic, nineteenth- and early-twentieth-century buildings, or such extensive remodeling that the original structure becomes unrecognizable.[1]
2 The covering of entire façades, often of buildings that are good examples of historic or modern architecture, with advertising signs, logos and billboards (Figure 9.2).
3 The "de-construction" of the downtown fabric through the introduction of extremely awkward shapes and colors in new (or redecorated) buildings. As I mentioned in the introduction, these buildings strive to "out-yell" their neighbors, according to one architectural critic (Cvetkov 2009), or to declare "war" on the public street, according to another (Dandolova 2002). And in some cases, startling new details seem to be introduced in order to declare war not merely on the street, but also on the very building in which the new elements are located.
4 The construction of glitzy commercial buildings – supermarkets, office headquarters and malls – that completely disrespect the street (e.g., by turning blind façades).

Figure 9.3 The Snail House: the black-and-white photo does a disservice to its bold, rainbow-hued exuberance.

5 The growth of suburban residential areas where difference is asserted in peculiar ways: by employing an architectural vocabulary that includes everything from Gothic-like turrets to rococo shell-decorated porticos, from Renaissance palazzos to animal-shaped blobs (Figure 9.3).
6 The ad hoc development of new districts without any attempt to achieve functional coherence (e.g., site layouts with no sidewalks, no alleys and only parking; new buildings blocking all views from the old ones; gas stations between residential buildings).[2]

I cannot describe the city's overall visual effect any better than the Chair of the Department of Cultural Anthropology at the University of Sofia (Kiosev 2005). This is how he angrily depicted Sofia, circa 2000:

> Did somebody eliminate all regulations: building, sanitation, not to mention architectural ones? What is going on? The visual geography of Sofia has "globalized" in its own, local way: around the national parliament, there are striptease bars; in the place of the demolished mausoleum – a giant whisky bottle; in the socialist districts – Arizona malls and Chinese pagodas. The [façade] of the Academy of Sciences is overtaken by a Nestle billboard; by the landmarks of early modernism one finds money-laundering casinos and bingo-halls, and in the "prestigious" neighborhoods – the heavy gates, the turrets and the colonnades of our local, turn-of-the-century Baroque fans.[3]

This startling sign-saturated symphony (or cacophony) is possible because the planning standards have become extremely relaxed since the end of socialism (for example, requirements for green and other public space have been reduced, the coefficients for development density have been increased, virtually all land-use combinations have been permitted, and site plans are approved in piecemeal fashion). And even these standards are, as I keep repeating, routinely ignored. Design guidelines – perhaps because of their association with socialist-era state intervention in the arts – are non-existent, except when it comes to buildings that are nationally designated as historic landmarks (note that the guidelines apply only to the buildings themselves, not to their surroundings). This is not likely to change in the near future. Applying any design criteria before granting building permits, even in the very heart of Sofia, is "simply not feasible," as top officials in the municipal office for architecture and planning explained:

> At one time [during socialism], there used to be a commission that would look at the building designs; some Commission on Synthesis of the Arts, or Aesthetics maybe, I think officially .... So it had, you know, the regular "court" artists, not just architects, but sculptors, painters and [others] like that. So the official artistic elite, big names, you know. But how can you do this today? You would have to ... have them elected in some way, but this would be silly because how do you elect an art commission? But if they are appointed, it will look like a throwback. People will be sensitive; who will decide, who will agree to this scheme? You will read in the press: ah, censorship! So this would be seen as totally impossible, unacceptable.
>
> Not that I really like what I see every day. I mean it is another kind of extremism, you know, there is a lot of pollution, architectural garbage on the street – everyone can see. But what to do? This is the situation. We can't control like before [during socialism] and we should not. It will get better ... but it may take longer for things to calm down.

To simply declare that the new built fabric is chaotic or eclectic, however, is to avoid the difficulty of categorizing and evaluating it. Is there an architectural "language" to post-socialism, to paraphrase Jencks (1984); is there a visual logic to it, to paraphrase Jameson (1984)? Certain styles and certain elements have clearly taken precedence over others. What are they, and how can we make sense of their appeal? I will attempt to decipher the new visual logic using both my own subjective judgment of styles and buildings and what I have learned from my interviewees. But before delving into the "language" of post-socialist architecture, let me offer a brief note on Sofia's architectural evolution since national independence in 1878.

Precursors: The Styles of Old Sofia

From the moment Sofia was declared capital of Bulgaria, it became the site of fervid building experimentation. As I explained in Chapter 5, the civilizational identity of both the city and the entire nation was at stake. What would that identity be? Backward or modern? "Oriental" or Western? Then, like now, the urban fabric was changing quickly and chaotically; old (i.e., Ottoman) things were on their way out, while Europeanness became increasingly visible. Foreign observers routinely commented on the colorful street life of the young Bulgarian capital, where men and women in the highest European fashions mixed with others wearing traditional peasant clothes, and where buildings came in all sizes and colors. In 1879, Konstantin Jire ek, a Czech historian who spent most of his distinguished career in post-Ottoman Bulgaria and served as Minister of Education, lamented the noise and clutter resulting from the destruction of Turkish monuments, many in good condition and decorated with marvelous Arabic letters (Jeleva-Martins 1999). The new government and the aspiring bourgeoisie hired architects (not all of them first-rate) from virtually every corner of Western Europe to design what Bulgarians then saw as "fashionable houses," as well as some peculiar "box-like houses" and houses that copied "some sort of Secession and other styles" mixed with "our [Bulgarian] national and local motifs" (cited by Faitondjieva 2008). In 1907, the Austrian professor Gurlit, traveling through Sofia to Istanbul, noted: "Here I saw a lot of Baroque … and many architectonic show-offs and hotshots" (cited by Faitondjieva 2008). In 1902, a local observer critiqued the frivolous references to the Renaissance and the Baroque that were rampant in the bourgeois parts of Sofia:

> Today we have an endless variety of motifs … in which capricious choices depend on nothing else but on the architect's fantasy and the client's inklings and it has all become just a fashion. This mix of motifs, which were invented for a purpose entirely different, for a time and place where they probably did belong, are now spread around all over, under the cornices and under the windows, to the ground and to the sky. All these decorations, which have no use, lack any sort of meaning, meaning that should characterize any decoration. (Cited by Faitondjieva 2008)

Of course, there was some very good architecture created by both foreign and Bulgarian designers. The city center exhibits many lovely examples, including Sofia's boutique Russian Church (architect Preobrajenski, 1905–12), the slightly pompous but otherwise well-proportioned National Theater (architects Helner and Felner, 1906), the Central Military Club (architects Kolar and Lazarov, 1895–1907) and the University of Sofia (architects Breason, Lazarov, Nenov and Milanov, 1907–20). The last three, in their relative, neo-classical simplicity, stood in contrast to the otherwise hectic and colorful landscape of downtown Sofia. The Viennese Secession made an early-twentieth-century entrance in a number of residential buildings and, as national confidence grew, it incorporated various allusions to local, national and regional aesthetics from Byzantine palaces to Bulgarian medieval and Ottoman-era monasteries. Known as neo-Byzantism or National-Romantic Secession, this colorful composite style became very popular by about 1910–20 and is on display in landmark buildings such as the Central Mineral Baths (currently the Museum of Sofia, architects Momchilov and Grunanger, 1905–10), the Central Halls (architect Torbov, 1902–5), and the spectacular and highly ornate Synagogue of Sofia (architect Grunanger, 1909), the third largest synagogue in Europe, which has fascinating Spanish-Moorish as well as Byzantine architectural elements.

Rationalism entered the landscape about a decade later. The trend began in residential structures, especially in the so-called cooperatives (multi-family buildings, funded by capital raised jointly by their future owners) that became very popular in the 1920s and 1930s. By the dawn of World War II, rationalism had established itself as the dominant style in office buildings, hotels, hospitals and factories. By that time, the large majority of representative buildings were designed by Bulgarian architects, most of them returning from the universities of Western Europe. Some good examples include the Workers' Hospital (architect Ovcharov, 1935), Hotel Bulgaria (architects Belkovski and Danchov, 1936) and the Macedonian Institute of Culture (architects Ovcharov and Jordanov, 1939), all of which exhibit the flat roofs, light color schemes and clean horizontal belts of windows that are typical of modernism.

The Socialist Style

In the aftermath of communist victory in 1945, modernism was no longer tolerated. In 1948, the Bulgarian Communist Party, quite obviously following Stalin's political directives, issued at its Fifth Congress a statement calling for the systematic elimination of modernism, rationalism and all other Western "bourgeois" influences in the arts. Whereas the Russo-Soviet world was from then on to be the only proper source for aesthetic learning, eliminating Western influence turned out to be a hard task, since Soviet "socialist realism" was based on the Russian imperial classicist tradition, which itself was the product of Western influences through the eighteenth and nineteenth centuries. The official formula for socialist realism in architecture (that is, architecture that must be "national in form and socialist in content") was first officially spelled out in Bulgaria in 1950 at a high-profile international conference held at the Bulgarian Academy of Sciences (Ivanova 2008). By then, however, the style had already penetrated the landscape of Sofia's downtown in the form of prominent new buildings such as the National Library (architects Vasiliov and Tsolov, 1948) and the Telephone Central (architect Belkovski, 1949), both notable for their explicit reliance on the classical orders, arcades and colonnades. "National in content" meant occasional references to the neo-Byzantine and National-Romantic Secessionist styles of the 1920s, to convey the message that Bulgaria, like other East European countries, would be permitted some cultural autonomy in the Soviet world after all.

The culmination of socialist realism in Bulgaria was Sofia's Largo – the monumental civic complex including several extraordinarily large (at least for Sofia) limestone structures, as mentioned in Chapter 5 (Figure 5.1). The project was initiated following a 1951 government decree stating that Sofia's center must be converted into a "unitary ensemble that expresses the glory of the epoch." The most grandiose of these buildings was, naturally, the House of the Communist Party, whose initial design was prepared by architects Tsolov and Blochin (a Bulgaro-Soviet team), with later modifications by architects Vasiliov and Belkovski. The building's design made references to Soviet supremacy in two key ways: its trapezoid layout alluded to the Kremlin (much as Joltovski's unbuilt House of the Soviets had twenty years earlier), and its front façade was dominated by a strong vertical axis – a tall, stepwise tower that hints at Moscow State University (even though it is much smaller and not nearly as Gothic). The style is positively neo-classical (the tower sits somewhat awkwardly on top of a colonnade). The other buildings, such as the State Council and the Councils of Ministers, were also classicist but included some local, neo-Byzantine details (the House of the Communist Party has no such details). Their subdued horizontal volumes, however, convey the dominance of the House of the Communist Party quite clearly, thus settling once and for all the proper hierarchical relationship: first Soviet, then national (Ivanova 2008).

The dominance of Soviet imperial classicism was of course short-lived. The farewell to Stalin meant a farewell to his architecture as well. From the 1950s, modernism re-entered the scene, initially in a fairly gracious shape: residential buildings, a few stories high, that were often positioned away from the street yet formed human-scale pedestrian areas. The gargantuan scale and the soulless composition of mass housing did not define fast-growing Sofia until the mid-1960s, when industrialized building methods were used for the first time. From then until the early 1980s, architecture generally moved in one direction: it became bigger and more boring. Of course, there were exceptions here and there: the most representative public buildings (e.g., concert halls and sports palaces) and the residential buildings erected for the party elites. In these buildings, modernism showed that it could be elegant and even complex, and architects did not necessarily shun elements of Sofia's traditional architecture. From about 1980 on, imagination and human scale in architecture were slowly and timidly allowed back. For instance, the last of the panel-made buildings in the socialist district of Mladost were only four stories high and had sloped red roofs, generous balconies, and even semi-private interior yards. Even the Largo area livened up. Its amorphous north–south axis was framed by a new national bank building, which not only alluded subtly to the architecture of medieval Bulgarian castles, but also dared to incorporate a very large and splendid "post-modern" arched window as a central vertical accent.

The Good, the Bad and the Ugly: Styles after Socialism

The most notable feature of architecture immediately following socialism is simply that there was less of it. Because of the severe economic crisis, the number of building permits issued per year dropped dramatically. Architecture became a semi-endangered profession, and some of its practitioners turned to cab-driving, home-style retail, and whatever else was available. Enrollment in university architecture classes declined. The sheer size of structures and developments decreased significantly as well.[4] This trend was largely a function of the changing economic context. The gigantic state-owned corporations that had for years constructed the large socialist civic projects and the panel-made housing districts were quickly dismantled, and there was nobody left to erect projects of similar magnitude.

More importantly, perhaps, the very shape of buildings altered. Texture replaced flatness. Buildings acquired peculiar extensions, lively roof-lines and never-before-seen ornaments including "Hundertwasser-esque slopes and angles, Gothic pointed arches, romantic mansards, round and hexagonal turrets (that looked as if they were used by medieval alchemists), and some penthouse additions so bizarre as to be worthy of Hitchcock's imagination" (Kiosev, cited by Kazalarska 2010). Some of these details were added onto existing buildings, with or without an architect's plan; most adorned brand-new structures. Along with flatness departed grayness. If a casual visitor to the streets of Sofia circa 1995 knew nothing about what was built before versus after socialism, she or he could apply a simple litmus test to determine the age of a building: What color is it? Socialist taste gravitated toward grey, dirty white, brown and a particularly unattractive mustard hue of ochre; post-socialist taste, on the other hand, tends toward bright pink, sparkling white, sky blue, sunny yellow and the full Miami-Beach spectrum of pastels. In the words of one sociologist, it is as if color meant freedom (Dandolova 2002).

In the next few pages, I offer a typology of post-socialist styles (most of which I have already alluded to). I distinguish six styles. Although they have co-existed throughout the last twenty years, they follow a rough chronology:

as we move into this millennium's second decade, we see less of the first few
and more of the last few. I then briefly describe each style's characteristics,
point to its sources, and reflect on the message it conveys (or is intended to
convey), drawing on information from the interviews and my own subjective
judgment. I also give some examples.

Anarchitecture

Anarchitecture (my shorthand for "anarchy in architecture") is the
architecture of the 1990s. It may describe Sofia better than "post-
modernism." Another possibility would be adhocism, a term coined several decades ago by Charles Jencks and Nathan Silver (1972). Perhaps
anarchitecture is not technically an architectural "style," if style means a
well-thought-out set of forms, techniques and materials used by builders
during a particular historic period. Anarchitecture involves informal
methods of creation and is typically practiced by users of urban spaces
rather than architects and other expert builders (thus, if we take a
benign view, we can call it "participatory architecture"). This method
uses readily available materials to solve immediate needs. As it lacks
official "leaders," it is not associated with any lofty architectural credo.
In Sofia, it developed intensely in the early 1990s, when formal architectural commissions became a rarity, and citizens, whether seeking profit
or survival, decorated the city with their kaleidoscopic self-styled creations.
This approach has produced a wide variety of informal commercial places –
self-built retail stands, kiosks, and bazaars, as well as various shops located in
converted garages, entryways and basements (hence the popular, semi-jok-
ing term "garage architecture" or perhaps "bazaarchitecture"; Figures 5.10
and 5.11). In residential architecture, examples of adhocism or anarchitecture include the various extensions put on existing buildings (e.g., roof
additions including the "round and hexagonal turrets" mentioned earlier,
and enclosed balconies used for living space), which became very widespread in the 1990s. The patches of insulation adorning the panel-made
socialist buildings can be considered examples of the same "style" as well.
Anarchitecture is characterized by small and very colorful forms. It is very
utilitarian in the sense that it fulfills specific needs without "wasting" funds
and efforts on decorative details aside from bright paint and surprising but
very functional extensions. In retail, signs and logos are typically the only
decorations; they serve the specific and much-needed function of advertisement. Anarchitecture was certainly not welcome during socialism, because
its very presence would have attested to the regime's failure to control. Some
informal construction and remodeling occurred, of course, but generally in
small towns, in villages and on the periphery of big cities. Photographs of
older, pre-socialist Sofia also reveal much anarchitecture in the city fabric,

especially right after the end of Ottoman rule. Then as now, anarchitecture was not well loved by architects and other elites. Today, adhocist forms are perceived as making Sofia "ugly" or "zoo-like" – both terms volunteered by some of the architects I interviewed. This view is not necessarily shared by most citizens, but it is perpetually advanced in the media. Perhaps the worst sin of anarchitecture is that, in the words of a top municipal official, it "gives us a bad image," specifically, "that oriental look." Much to the official's surprise, a colleague visiting from Denmark once expressed the opposite view – that Sofia's kiosks, bazaars and turrets were charming in their own way. Nonetheless, anarchitecture is now definitely on the decline. Authorities have started to issue fines for building extensions erected without permits and have finally managed to root out many of the informal retail places of the 1990s. Western-style malls and supermarkets are doing the rest.

Bulgarian Revival

Bulgarian Revival is the only style that appears to be universally appreciated in Sofia (and in Bulgaria as a whole). Its point of reference is the traditional Bulgarian house of the eighteenth and nineteenth centuries, which became popular in the wealthier Bulgarian towns of the Ottoman Empire. These homes were characterized by red-clay roofs and white-stucco façades decorated with bright and exquisite paintings and splendid dark-wood porches, balconies and rafters. These elements are also found in Bulgarian monasteries (the only characteristically Bulgarian public buildings to flourish during Ottoman rule). The houses were, as noted earlier, typically surrounded by massive stone walls and heavy wooden gates. Because of the style's decorative qualities, as well as its association with the period called Bulgarian Renaissance (during which multiple anti-Ottoman riots led to independence), it is commonly called Bulgarian Renaissance or Bulgarian Baroque. It has always been portrayed as the nation's most significant and genuine contribution to world architecture. The media and the architectural academy have consistently promoted its virtues.

Thus, although Sofia's bourgeoisie of the early twentieth century leaned toward the European fashions of the day (e.g., Viennese Secession) for their urban residences, many of its members maintained secondary, "typically Bulgarian" homes in towns and villages around the country. Even socialist elites, despite their fascination first with neo-classicism and then with modernism, had a "soft spot" for the Bulgarian style. The regime made a concerted effort to demonstrate its patriotism by heavily investing in the preservation of Bulgaria's traditional folk arts and music. Party elites often owned Bulgarian-style villas, while also maintaining an urban flat. Today, the style's influence is limited mostly to single-family homes. However, restaurants, pubs, hotels and resort villages that try to capitalize on "cultural tourism" have incorporated some of its elements as well (Figure 9.1 shows one perhaps not-so-good example of such a restaurant, which provides a striking contrast with the socialist panel-made building behind it). The style is spreading in Sofia's suburban areas as well (even a couple of new gated communities use it; in another allusion to Bulgarian tradition, these communities are usually named after various Christian saints). There are some excellent examples of new Bulgarian-style homes, most of which are actually the homes of architects. These homes, however, are being increasingly over-shadowed by their more fashionable and certainly more eccentric neighbors erected in various Western styles, past and present. Furthermore, some houses exhibit rather uneasy, "glocalized" (Robertson 1992) combinations with other styles (e.g., the first floor is in the Bulgarian style, but the second floor is decorated with Tudor rafters; façades are covered with "American" vinyl siding but decorated with dark-wood balconies and topped by bright shingled roofs).

Historical eclecticism, Balkan version

The frivolous importation of Western styles – Gothic, classical, Baroque, and their post-modern semi-serious interpretations – is one of the most obvious ways in which post-socialist Sofia has been redecorating itself. The trend is of course reminiscent of an older, early-twentieth-century Sofia, but this time around the borrowing seems to be much freer – one might even characterize it as promiscuous. The Gothic, for example, rarely showed up in old Sofia. Yet one of the largest and fanciest new hotels erected at the very beginning of the transition was the Castle Hotel. The name derives from its obvious but rather poorly executed attempt to crown itself with Gothic-like towers. (This hotel is now closed; according to unconfirmed rumors, its owner is in prison for money-laundering.) It must be said, how-ever, that Sofia has hardly any examples of prominent large new build-ings erected in purely Western styles (though such styles are common in hotels along the Black Sea coast). Rather, elements of Western styles are sprinkled throughout the city landscape on buildings new and old. For example, there are plain new buildings housing gyms, and internet cafés with white marble balustrades; there are older downtown buildings in the early functionalist style whose first floors now operate as casinos and whose once simple rectangular windows have been replaced by Romanesque or Palladian arched ones. Casino architecture deserves a special mention here, as it represents one of the most obvious means that introduce visual shock in Sofia's fabric. In the absence of any design standards, the streetscapes of some of Sofia's most elegant, if somewhat plain, early-twentieth-century boulevards are now "adorned" with low-quality sculptures encompassing the entire Greek Pantheon – excellent examples of how a new detail can declare war on the very building in which it is located. In addition to the Greek Pantheon, we can see Caesar, Cleopatra, anonymous Roman soldiers, Arabian genies and Egyptian pharaohs. It is difficult to say whether the visual chaos is greater when these novel "decorations" appear downtown or in the socialist districts (Figures 9.4, 9.5 and 9.6).

Figure 9.4   Casino Caesar; Roman soldiers guard this 1930s rationalist building on Boulevard Macedonia in downtown Sofia.

Figure 9.5   War on the street: This shiny bright blue genie, which helps create the ambiance of Casino Sesame, frames the entrance of a 1930s building on Boulevard Skobelev in the center of the city.

Figure 9.6 Jackpot in the socialist mass housing districts. Photo by Svetla Kazalarska.

The triumph of the Balkan version of Western-like historicism comes in the homes of the new bourgeoisie, mostly in the growing suburban areas but, here and there, in the older parts of town as well. (This seems also the case in other Balkan capitals.) Among the many faces of historical eclecticism, though, one style is surely king: the neo-classical (Figure 9.7). The first homes to display the neo-classical belonged to the "cigarette tsars" (i.e., people whose fast-accumulated wealth was ostensibly linked to the drugs, alcohol and cigarettes trade, which prospered during the years of the Yugoslav embargo); thus the style is sometimes referred to as Mafia Baroque (in Bulgarian, *mutrenski barok*; Hirt 2008a). Since then, however, it has spread to the homes of the legitimate professional class. It is hard to discern the underlying reasons for the nouveau riche's love of the Greek column and its many later reincarnations. Interviews offer a few clues. Asked why they chose this style, homeowners give answers such as, "Well, I like it. It is the most beautiful; it always has been." Some mentioned that the style gives their home "dignity," "real class" and a "sense of good tradition." The style also seems to express a quasi-heroic (if quasi-comic) spirit of anti-socialist resistance – it is seen as a way to defy sameness, boredom and conformity. In admiring his bright pink house, heavily adorned with Ionic columns, one interviewee remarked, "Well, what? I am not going to go all gray again, like the old times." One architect, who had designed several "palazzos" (despite apparently hating them), speculated that his clients preferred the style since it was the traditional symbol of "state power" (i.e., Stalinist socialist realism); thus, in his view, the newly rich liked to appropriate it in order to show "who holds the power now." Whether or not this thought actually passes through the minds of the new elites may be impossible to determine. But

Figure 9.7   A fairly tasteful example of the neo-classic in Sofia's suburbs.

the association of classical splendor with tradition, legitimacy and authority is hard to deny. Perhaps when the timeless visual symbols of public grandeur are adopted to glorify recently found private wealth, they endow it with the elusive legitimacy that it craves. Indeed, what else does a newly built house say, with its marvelous Baroque gates, but "It's not what you think. I am not new. The wealth of the family that owns me goes back centuries" (Figure 9.8)? Perhaps Ayn Rand said it best in *The Fountainhead*. Rand's Ms. Sanborn, a wealthy parvenu, "wished a French chateau built upon their new estate on the Hudson. She wished it to look stately and ancient, as if it had always belonged to the family; of course, she admitted, people would know that it hadn't, but it would *appear* as if it had."

The fortress look

The fortress look first appeared at the beginning of the transition, but it has evolved significantly since then. One of its earliest and most obvious manifestations was, of course, the tall stone walls surrounding new suburban houses discussed in the previous chapters. This rather crude, old-fashioned version of residential enclosure, however, has increasingly given way to a slicker, more modern alternative. Here and there in Sofia's suburbs, one now sees more "elegant," thinner enclosures made of thin, semi-perforated

Figure 9.8   The new Baroque: a spectacular example, this time from Belgrade. On the left side is the kiosk of the armed security guard.

metal and dark-shaded glass panels. If the nominal transparency of the panels compromises a sense of separation from public space, this "loss" is presumably offset by the latest in security technology. Behind the panels, there are homes whose entire front façades are covered by dark-glass "skins" wrapped in nets of metal beams in various cross-diagonal or crystal-like shapes – a very high-tech look. This way, no passer-by can guess much about the house's interior (normally, one can at least tell where the living room or bedrooms are by the location of familiar elements such as windows or balconies). This look has become increasingly popular in commercial structures: those in Business Park Sofia are a good example. Other landmark examples include the glossy office building called (of all things) Bench Mark, which is wrapped in a metal framework providing a sense of full autonomy from its surroundings, and the equally fancy Crete office building, which has three blind concrete mega-walls. Crete's front façade, located along one of Sofia's busiest streets, has a tall, impermeable-looking indented first floor crowned by a flat and even more impermeable-looking dark-glass multi-story body. One cannot help but wonder, "Where is the door?" It does not take much imagination to classify all two dozen of Sofia's malls and hyper-markets as fortress architecture, as well. True, their front doors are quite visible, thanks to their giant "Metro," "Billa," "Hit" and "Carrefour" logos. But aside from this, all they give the city are more blank façades.

American suburban

This style is a clear copycat of the post-World War II American single-family home, and it has no pre-socialist precursors in Bulgaria. Homes built in this style are located mostly in the wealthy southern suburbs of Sofia. They include homes in several of the new gated communities such as Mountain View Village, whose designers have managed to "enliven" the otherwise plain style with marble lions and balustrades. Homes of this type have shingle hip roofs, vinyl siding, windows with shutters, sliding glass doors opening to the back yards, and relatively flat two-story bodies with attached garages. Here and there, one also finds single-story ranches and split-levels – structures that are extremely unusual for the Bulgarian landscape and stand in sharp contrast to traditional Balkan architecture with its red roofs and white-stucco two-story façades that are more plastic and decorative. In the early 1990s, the first propagandists of this type of architecture were real estate firms with peculiar names such as NATO Properties. It took a few years for the style to penetrate the residential market, and initially its influence was limited to individual elements inserted into traditional Bulgarian houses and, occasionally, neo-classical ones. By around 2000, however, fully executed American-style homes were relatively common. Even some hotels and restaurants now show traces of the style. Real estate and home décor magazines are full of advertisements for American-style homes. According to the interviews, however, there is a growing concern among architectural professionals and others that the style is one of the least appropriate recent architectural imports.

Capitalist realism

The term capitalist realism has been used for quite some time to denote any type of commodity-based art (e.g., big business- and market-friendly architecture) that serves as a counterpoint to its socialist "cousin" (that is, whereas socialist realism projected the state's supremacy, capitalist realism projects corporate control). In the post-Soviet Russian context, Goldhoorn and Meuser (2006) proposed an alternative way to highlight the contrast: whereas socialist realism was Stalin's attempt to build "palaces for the proletariat" (while expressing via spatial means his regime's absolute power over the proletariat), capitalist realism is the contemporary elites' effort to build palaces for themselves. I view capitalist realism a bit differently. To me, the term connotes the strong recent trend in Sofia (and, as far as I can tell, in all of post-socialist Southeast Europe) to insert, with the state's blessing, some corporate-style (i.e., Fordist-capitalist) discipline into the urban fabric, to get away from the whimsical Balkan anarchitecture of the 1990s and endow the urban landscape with a shinier and more orderly, business-like (more realist?) West European look. The stylistic transition is premised on changes in both aesthetic preferences and the political economy. In terms of aesthetics, there appears to be a growing reaction among architectural professionals against what was built in the first post-socialist decade – an age the interviewed architects referred to as that of "total architectural confusion," when "architecture in Bulgaria died" (also Kazalarska 2010). Also part of this trend were incoming Western retailers and other businesses, which brought their slicker, more standardized architecture in the form of hyper-markets, Hiltons and Holiday Inns. With their detached, self-absorbed forms that make no attempt to connect with their surroundings, many of them are examples of both the new "capitalist realism" and "fortress architecture" (in fact, the two styles could potentially be merged into one). The direction of change has been toward larger, cleaner and more futuristic (rather than historicist) glass and metal shapes that are in line with West European neo-modernism. Some examples include the office buildings of Bulgaria 2000, Bellissimo and Nike. The trend has clearly been endorsed by the highest levels of the municipal bureaucracy, which has used its slightly strengthened power to control the urban landscape and outlaw what were perceived as the worst manifestations of post-socialist chaos – the self-styled kiosks and bazaars.

The most concerted municipal effort to endow Sofia with a Western-like image was the much-talked-about competition to design a monumental secondary City Center, held in 2008 and 2009. The media debated for some time whether Sofia really needed a secondary center that would include several fancy new multi-million-dollar government buildings as well as Dubai-style hotels, located between the southern border of downtown and the socialist housing district of Mladost. Should there really be a new, larger, post-socialist Largo? Municipal wisdom prevailed, though, and the competition attracted some of the world's greatest architects: Norman Foster, Massimiliano Fuksas, Zaha Hadid, and Dominique Perrault. The entries certainly had some remarkable qualities (for example, all presented some version of green, ecologically certifiable buildings and landscapes). Still, their glittering "star-architecture," consisting of various skyscrapers, each several times larger than any of the nearest existing structures, produced serious confusion and even resentment among citizens and local architects alike. Thus, despite their sincerest admiration for their famous international colleagues, some local members of the jury characterized the proposals as "extra-terrestrial" (Kovachev 2009). It was the French architect Dominique Perrault who finally won the competition with a set of super-spectacular pyramidal structures in Christo-like wrappings. (Rumor had it that Perrault won because he was the only "star architect" who bothered to fly to Sofia and personally present his project to the jury.) Because of the recession-era budget crunch, however, the municipality was forced to place his contract on hold for the time being. Stay tuned for updates on Sofia's twenty-first-century Largo.

In twenty years, Sofia's built fabric has been transformed from bland to brassy, from conformist to rebellious, from openly emphasizing public space to openly emphasizing private space, from reflecting a single, state-led vision to one accommodating a multiplicity of private choices, tastes and strategies. The six styles outlined above attempt to capture the new diversity. In the sense that they are the temporal successors of socialist-type architectural modernism, they could be referred to as "post." And they do seem to incorporate some of post-modernism's paradigmatic characteristics, such as pluralism, frivolousness and texture, as well as its allegiance to decorating highly privatized spaces. But the term has acquired a specific meaning in the Western world, associated with the deliberate attempt to combine fancy historicist references with advanced, super-modern structural elements – a strategy more popular among Western architectural elites in the 1980s and 1990s than today. Defined in this narrow way, post-modernism describes Sofia's post-socialist architectural transformation only to an extent. Perhaps anarchitecture, even as it has started to fade away lately, really sums it all much better.

Notes

1 The Citizen Committee for Preserving Cultural Landmarks at Risk in Bulgaria publishes a Red Book. The book lists hundreds of historic buildings which have been "devoured by the transition."

2 Let me give an example that illustrates the last point. In the 1980s, along a busy boulevard called Alexander Malinov in the socialist district of Mladost, all one could find were rows of boring collectivist buildings separated from the street (and each other) by large chunks of green space. By about 2000, the green space filled up with a lively mixture of new structures, big and small. A sparkling yellow supermarket with a large red logo now acts as a focal point of the composition. It is located amidst an oversized parking lot, which is partially fenced off. Two sides of the parking lot are framed by a colorful mosaic of kiosks and semi-covered bazaar stalls situated in a peculiarly meandering way. The composition is framed on its south side by a new office building which flaunts a glassy but very dark façade (the other three façades, all blind, are made of exposed concrete). Nearby is a tall, multi-story flat-roofed and ultra-modern restaurant in an intense purple hue. It is so located that it blocks all views from the residences behind it. A new residential building, much smaller than its socialist-era neighbors, is surrounded by a tall semi-transparent fence. This building has a bright shingled roof and a large arched (post-modern) window. Across the street is another restaurant, a low-level traditional one, dressed in white stucco with a tiled red roof. Along one of its sides is a row of small and exceptionally dull gray warehouses. Walking across this landscape is a true urban adventure. No logical

system of pathways can be detected and there is no clear view from one building to another. The situation remained bearable for some years since one large piece of green space was left untouched and, if one were to stand there, she or he could get some sense of orientation. But one summer, a very large new structure came, all covered in a cheerful blue-and-white striped tent. Its blinking logo said it all: "Balkan Circus."

3   Kisiov shared these remarks at a seminar on the future of Sofia's architecture. The seminar was held at the University of Sofia. The remarks were published in a revised form (Kiosev 2005), in which the author called for an expansion of Lefebvre's idea of "the right to the city" to include "the right to taste [in the city]".

4   For instance, the number of dwelling units produced annually during the first post-socialist decade in Sofia was only one-third of the number of units produced annually during the last socialist decade. The average number of units per residential building produced during the first post-socialist decade in Sofia was half of the corresponding number during the last socialist decade. In socialist housing districts such as Mladost, the number decreased to a third. Predictably, the height and size of residential buildings decreased notably as well (Hirt 2006).

10

Possibilities

"Something there is that doesn't love a wall".

Robert Frost

Ask any *Sofianetz* (citizen of Sofia) where the Russian Church is. Everyone knows. The church is a small, decorative structure: white with a green roof and several little onion-shaped golden domes, nothing like the monumental Alexander Nevsky Cathedral that often appears on postcards of Sofia. Some may not know the church's official name (the Church of Saint Nikolas the Miracle-maker), but everyone knows where it is: in the middle of town. The church was built right after national independence as a testimony to Russo-Bulgarian friendship. Now "Russianness" has not always been in vogue in Bulgaria (especially during the late 1800s, the 1930s and the 1990s); nor has religion. Yet the church's image was never tarnished by changes in the political climate. It has always been what it is today: a small architectural jewel, a symbol of Sofia, as Bulgarian as the capital city itself. On the south side of the church is a small garden. In the spring it comes to life with bright red and yellow flowers. The garden is a lovers' place: it has bushes and benches and a modest monument to Alexander Pushkin, perhaps the most romantic of all of Russia's great poets. Once upon a time there were a couple of buildings in the garden. There was a Russian Center, but it was destroyed by bombs in World War II. And there was another, less decorative building: the Writers' Club, a favorite place of Pushkin's colleagues in Sofia, where many cigarettes must have been smoked and many coffees drunk. This club, which partially blocked the view to Saint Nikolas, was taken down sometime in the 1970s because Sofia's planners saw it – perhaps correctly – as a bit dingy and unfit for its central position. From

Iron Curtains, First Edition. Sonia A. Hirt.
© 2012 John Wiley & Sons, Ltd. Published 2012 by John Wiley & Sons, Ltd.

then on, the little golden domes glittered so that all could see. The garden was and still is one of the very few open green spaces in Sofia's dense center and thus, from a real estate point of view, one of the most valuable.

In 1994, it came to light that the former site of the Writers' Club (a civic building), as well as some of the surrounding land, had once been private property. An old bourgeois family had documents to show. Sofia's authorities, in contrast, could find nothing in their archives to show that the garden had ever been zoned as public green space. They could muster no proof that the garden was in fact a garden. Part of the garden was thus restituted to its pre-war owners and then purchased by the Israeli firm Ashtrom, part of Abrotea International. Ashtrom soon unveiled plans for an office building with 16 stories, not counting the multi-level underground garages. The proposal was later scaled back to "only" 13 stories. The building, whether 13 or 16 stories, would not only have taken over most of the garden, but would also have blocked views to the little golden domes behind. Over the next fifteen years, the fate of the Russian Church garden was one of hottest topics in Sofia. Three warring parties faced off, primarily in the courts but also in the media and sometimes in the street: the company, the municipality, and some very agitated members of Sofia's citizenry. The latter wrote petitions, letters to newspaper editors and letters to the Mayor. They slept in the garden and threatened to block bulldozers with human chains. Surprisingly, a fourth party entered the war a few years later: Moscow's powerful Mayor J. Luzhkov declared his city's intention to build a House of Moscow on what was once, before the bombs, the Russian Center (the land under the center was apparently the property of Russia). Like all good stories this one had many twists, and many victories – all temporary – were declared along the way. In 1999, the municipality, having once again been defeated in court, issued a building permit for a four-story building (again, not counting the garages). In 2000, several small citizen groups formed a grand coalition to save the garden. The coalition was named, somewhat provocatively, Salvation 2000 (despite the name's religious connotations, the coalition, which was led by area residents, architects and ecological activists, had little interest in religion and chose the name only for its dramatic effect). After collecting 15,000 signatures in record time, the coalition threatened to wreak such havoc that it prevented Ashrom's first serious attempt to cement its control over the garden by erecting – remember, this is Sofia – what else but a *fence*? In 2010, Salvation 2000 claimed what one hopes is the final victory. By then, Sofia's new Master Plan had at last recognized the garden as what it was: a public green space. The municipality voted to revoke the building permit it had issued earlier. According to interviews and media reports, it is currently working out a compensation deal with the private developer. At the time of writing, the intentions of Moscow's new Mayor remain unclear.

I tell this story because I see it as one of the first and most powerful cracks in the culture of privatism in Sofia. Cultural privatism (and the potential beginning of its decline) is of course not the only analytical frame by which to understand this story. The conflict over the Russian Church and its garden can be analyzed in the way similar urban land conflicts have been analyzed in capitalist contexts all over the world. Power shifts have occurred, political parties have gone up and down, new interest groups and alliances have been formed, grass-root movements have strengthened, the media has started to expose corruption and other abuses undermining the public interest more aggressively, privatization laws have been clarified after two decades of debate. Still, the story is, as I see it, a story of a declining privatism, of a citizenry that is replacing indifference with energy, activism and faith that collective spaces matter and can be defended. For the record, I have yet to find any citizen group in Sofia opposed explicitly to some of the other spatial privatization trends described in the book, e.g., suburbanization or gated complexes per se. But there are dozens of such groups that focus on preserving the city's architectural heritage and protecting parks and green space (including the northern slopes of Mount Vitosha, where most new gated suburban complexes are located). Each of Sofia's twenty-four administrative districts has at least one group of each kind. There are citywide preservation councils, and most of the district-based groups are parts of national environmental and cultural preservation organizations. These groups have been fighting to save some of the collective spaces in the city – collective not only in terms of ownership but also, as in the case of the Russian Church's garden, in terms of public use, image and memory. They fight for one city block, playground or historic building at a time. Their recent successes include saving parts of the South Park and King Boris's Garden; in both of these cases, the municipality and the developers caved in under public pressure. This pressure doesn't always work, but sometimes it does, and this "sometimes" is definitely a beginning. Furthermore, the municipality, which after all is not some monolithic body imported from Mars but rather a group of Sofia citizens voted into office by their fellow Sofia citizens, seems to be listening at least on occasion. Sofia's Mayor and Chief Architect, who issued the permit to build over the Russian Church's garden, have long since been voted out of office; both are still entangled in various corruption-related legal battles. The current Mayor (who happens to be Sofia's first female top executive) and the current Chief Architect have never dared to say publicly anything that could be construed as challenging the space's continued existence as a public garden.

Perhaps this is the time to reiterate the definition of privatism. In the first chapter, I called it the widespread disbelief in a benevolent public realm and the widespread sense that appropriating the public may be the best way to thrive in private. In Sofia, as I have argued throughout this book, privatism has existed in an especially powerful form; its impact on space has thus been exceptionally destructive. This outcome has occurred for a number of reasons. Sofia's citizens, who lived through grand public failures during both socialism and its aftermath, and lacked the opportunity to build a strong civic society, have only now begun to mobilize and more actively resist the private usurpations of public space. The post-socialist public sector – a successor of the failed communist institutions – has for some twenty years nearly abandoned its responsibility to protect public space, in both its material and non-material connotations. And the private sector, in an exceptionally aggressive manner, has asserted itself in the vacuum created by the failure of both official institutions and civil society. If we put it this way, we see that privatism is not a monolithic term. Rather, there are at least three complementary privatisms: that of the private sector (which in its efforts to maximize private gain has worked relentlessly to confiscate public space); that of the formal public sector (which has allowed and sometimes even encouraged the confiscation partially because some of its members had their own businesses on the side which profited from the privatization); and that of the citizenry at large (which had for the most part seceded from the public conversation, did not resist the actions of the other two, and often embraced largely private concerns – a tendency that is part of what Bodnar (2001) calls the "turning inwards" of people's lives after socialism). The lines between the three types of privatism are of course blurry. For example, those who are building the walled mansions that usurp public space in the suburbs are simultaneously members of the profit-driven private sector *and* members of the citizenry at large, who in their disappointment in private aggression and public inaction are themselves protesting against it all by seceding from the city. If change is to happen, however, I believe citizen organizations hold the key to unlocking it. The case of the Russian Church's garden gives us a potential model.

Privatism, as I proposed in the Introduction, expresses itself in space much as it expresses itself in social practices. This is because, like institutions, spaces vary, to paraphrase Plato, in accordance with the dispositions of those who make them (cited by Putnam 1993: 11). These dispositions affect spaces both directly (by shaping what people like to build and ultimately what they do build) and indirectly (by affecting all of society's institutions, economic and political, which in turn shape city-building itself). There are many examples of how this occurs: arguably, all sorts of cultural preferences and identities (having to do with nationality, race, ethnicity, gender, religion, government ideology, etc.) do somehow end up imprinted in space. Alternative stories of Sofia's new spaces can be told from any of these perspectives. After all, as Michael Conzen once said, few social norms and values are so abstract that they are *not* manifested in spatial form (cited by Kostof 1991: 25). Still, I believe that the story of the new walls that stand between expanding private and shrinking public realms offers insight into one of the most visible and telling material "signs of the times" in the post-socialist city.

In Germany, people still talk of the "wall in the mind." It means something different there: Germans use the term to highlight persistent economic and cultural rifts between the two sides of what is now a united country. But I like the metaphor; it would have made a good book title. So let me use it to rephrase my thesis: there would not have been so many walls in Sofia if it were not for the "wall(s) in the mind(s)." By the former I mean not only physical walls, but also vanquished public spaces, grossly individualistic buildings, and all other outright secessions from the urban collective. By "wall(s) in the mind(s)" I mean the walls of fear, disbelief and disillusionment. The material walls exist in space – they have been built, tolerated and even encouraged – partially because they first existed in the mind. In saying this, I do not aspire to resolve the eternal Weberian-Marxist debate on the hierarchical relationship between mind and matter, between culture and the economy. Rather, I mean only to say that without the "walls in the mind," the material walls would have had real difficulty in popping up so ubiquitously. Furthermore, the walls in the mind may prove to be the longer-lasting (example: Germany).

I do not find it particularly surprising that developers in post-socialist Sofia build gated complexes, exclusive malls and distant business parks, or that Sofia's Mayor (Bulgaria's Prime Minister at the time of writing) would cut ribbons at their openings. What did we all think would happen, back in 1989? Did we not know that capitalism exists to turn a profit? And can we, today, expect different behavior from the leaders of a city that has long been voraciously hungry to "catch up with the West," both in economic growth and in image? Of all the stories I heard, I found one the most telling (if not the most surprising). I will repeat it here. It is the story of the man I called Victor. (Perhaps I chose this name because I subconsciously wanted him to be the winner his pseudonym suggests – and yet he was so far from it.) Victor was the man who watched from his terrace as the bulldozers destroyed the little playground near his home, to make room for a pay-for-parking lot. Shrugging his shoulders, he said: "I am no longer surprised. Honestly, it barely bothers me … so I move on, take care of my business." I don't know whether Victor, a grandfather of three in his sixties, will find the energy to do more than simply move on and tend to his own business. But I think his grandchildren may. Although the playground is now long gone, Victor's granddaughter Maya, a girl of eighteen who had recently started her university studies, was one of the young people collecting petition signatures in the campaign to save the small garden by the Russian Church.

It has been over twenty years since socialism, "the movement which represents the ultimate elevation of the public over the private[,] was toppled in its own home" (Wolfe 1997: 200). Will it take another twenty before today's type of development, which may well represent the ultimate elevation of the private over the public, is toppled as well (peacefully, one hopes)? If modernity – the movement that sought to discipline humankind's energies in the name of collective utopias – imploded in Eastern Europe, as I argued in Chapter 4, will post-modernity – the movement that challenged these collective utopias and replaced them with others, focused on private, individual advancement – implode there as well?

On the twentieth anniversary of the fall of the Wall, the Slovenian philosopher Slavoj Žižek wrote a brief piece called "Post-Wall" in the *London Review of Books* (2009). He did not write about cities but, like me, wondered why the post-wall world was so busy building walls. And why were people asking themselves, "If capitalism is so much better than socialism, why are our lives still miserable?" Žižek went on to argue:

> When people protested against Communist regimes in Eastern Europe, most of them weren't asking for capitalism. They wanted solidarity and a rough kind of justice; they wanted the freedom to live their own lives outside state control, to come together and talk as they pleased; they wanted to be liberated from primitive ideological indoctrination and hypocrisy. In effect they aspired to something that could best be described as "socialism with a human face". Perhaps this sentiment deserves a second chance.

I would venture to say that despite all the nostalgia for the past, which is plainly evident in survey after survey, few people *really* want socialism back – perhaps because none of its regimes ever showed a truly "human face." An entire generation today does not even know socialism, except through the stories they hear from their elders. These stories, like all nostalgic tales, are stories of imaginary pasts. I am not sure whether people were really "not asking for capitalism." Perhaps what they were asking for was what Samuel Brittan (1996), among others, has called "capitalism with a human face," a capitalism in which some measure of equal opportunity exists, in which public interests are not routinely trumped by private ones, in which the public is not so subservient as to take only the spaces that the private does not want, in which the walls are just a bit more porous. In other words, a type of capitalism in which privatism is not as overwhelming.

How can we make the walls more porous? Can privatism save itself from itself? How can extreme privatism be resisted? What's wrong with the idea of the private anyway, if it is not elevated to an impossibly high pedestal? Private homes, private bodies, private dreams. Who would want to live without them? Does privatism have a softer, gentler side? The private once stood in opposition to totalitarian regimes. Can it stand in opposition to their successors? It would have to take a different form – a private that does not see itself as opposed to the public, a private that does not draw a line and then retreat from it (or, worse, swallow the public altogether). It would be a privatism that cares less where public ends and private starts, a privatism that does not seek to devour the public but rather sees it as home, as part of itself.

So I asked Maya, Victor's granddaughter (who was sitting in the living room when I was re-interviewing her grandfather a few years after his neighborhood playground was gone), why she fought to save the garden – a place far away from where she lives. She responded, "But please, how is it far? It's not that far, really! Isn't this our city? There are many students like me ... we like to hang out there. It's one of the best places, so we want to keep it like it's ours."

Here's to a different privatism. And to Maya.

References

Adorno, M. and Horkheimer, T. 2002 [1947]. *The dialectic of the Enlightenment*. Stanford, CA: Stanford University Press.

Allmendigner, P. 2001. *Planning in post-modern times*. London and New York: Routledge.

Aman, A. 1992. *Architecture and ideology in Eastern Europe during the Stalin Era: an aspect of Cold War history*. Cambridge, MA: MIT Press.

Amin, A. (ed.) 1994. *Post-Fordism: a reader*. Oxford: Blackwell.

Anderson, P. 1984. Modernity and revolution. *New Left Review*, 114: 96–113.

Anderson, P. 1998. *The origins of postmodernity*. New York: Verso.

Andrusz, G. 1984. *Housing and urban development in the USSR*. Albany: State University of New York Press.

Andrusz, G. 1996. Structural change and boundary instability. In G. Andrusz, M. Harloe and I. Szelényi (eds.), *Cities after socialism: urban and regional change and conflict in post-socialist societies*. Oxford: Blackwell.

Andrusz, G. 2006. Wall and mall: a metaphor for metamorphosis. In S. Tsenkova and Z. Nedovi -Budi (eds.), *The urban mosaic of post-socialist Europe: space, institutions and policy*. Heidelberg: Springer Physica.

Andrusz, G., Harloe, M. and Szelényi, I. (eds.) 1996. *Cities after socialism: urban and regional change and conflict in post-socialist societies*. Malden, MA, and Oxford: Blackwell.

Arendt, H. 1958. *The human condition*. Chicago: University of Chicago Press.

Atkins, P. 1993. How the West End was won: the struggle to remove street barriers in Victorian London. *Journal of Historical Geography*, 19(3): 265–77.

Atkinson, R. and Flint, J. 2004. Fortress UK? Gated communities, the spatial revolt of the elites and time-space trajectories of segregation. *Housing Studies*, 19(6): 875–92.

Axenov, K., Brade, I. and Bondarchuk, E. 2006. *The transformation of urban space in post-Soviet Russia*. New York: Routledge.

Iron Curtains, First Edition. Sonia A. Hirt.

© 2012 John Wiley & Sons, Ltd. Published 2012 by John Wiley & Sons, Ltd.

Badjeva, M. 2002. Bulgarkata ne e feministka, no bulgarskata bednost e feminizirana [Bulgarian women are not feminists, but Bulgarian poverty is feminized]. *Karavan* [Caravan], November 7: 23–4 [in Bulgarian].

Bailey, J. 2000. Some meanings of "the private" in sociological thought. *Sociology: The Journal of the British Sociological Association*, 34: 381–401.

Bailey, J. 2002. From public to private: the development of the concept of the "private." *Social Research*, 69: 15–31.

Banerjee, T. 2004. *Beijing, Berlin, and Bucharest: legacies of socialist modernity at the end of history*. Paper presented at the Biannual Conference of the International Planning History Society, Barcelona.

Barr, A. and Serra, D. 2006. Culture and corruption. GPRG-WPS-040. Global Poverty Research Group. http://digitallibrary.unicreditanduniversities.org/3/1/culture_corruption.pdf. Accessed October 29, 2010.

Bauman, Z. 1991. Living without an alternative. *Political Quarterly*, 62: 35–44.

Bauman, Z. 1992. *Intimations of post-modernity*. London and New York: Routledge.

Bauman, Z. 1993. *Modernity and ambivalence*. Malden, MA, and Oxford: Blackwell.

Bauman, Z. 1995. Searching for a center that holds. In M. Featherstone, S. Lash and R. Robertson (eds.), *Global modernities*. Thousand Oaks, CA: Sage.

Bauman, Z. 2000. *Liquid modernity*. Malden, MA, and Oxford: Blackwell.

Beauregard, R. 1989. Between modernity and post-modernity: the ambiguous position of US planning. *Environment and Planning D: Society and Space*, 7(4): 381–95.

Beecher, C. 2006 [1865]. How to redeem woman's profession from dishonor (excerpts). Reprinted as "Catharine Beecher outlines the proper role for women 1865" in B. Nicolaides and A. Wiese (eds.), *The suburb reader*. New York, and Abingdon, Oxon: Routledge.

Benn, S. and Gaus, G. 1983. The public and private: concepts and action. In G. Benn and G. Gaus (eds.), *Public and private in social life*. New York: St. Martin's Press.

Bennet, R. 1990. *Decentralization, local governments and markets: towards a post-welfare agenda*. Oxford: Clarendon Press.

Berman, M. 1983. *All that is solid melts into air: the experience of modernity*. New York: Penguin Press.

Bernhardt, C. 2005. Planning urbanization and urban growth in the socialist period: the case of East German towns. *Journal of Urban History*, 32(1): 104–19.

Bertaud, A. 2004. The spatial structure of Central and East European Cities: more European than socialist. Paper presented at the conference "Winds of Societal Change: Remaking Post-socialist Cities," June 18–19, University of Illinois, Urbana-Champaign.

Bertaud, A. and Renaud, B. 1995. Cities without markets: location and land use in the socialist city. Policy Research Working Paper WPS 1477. Washington, DC: World Bank.

Bittman, M., England, P., Sayer, L., Folbe, N. and Matheson, G. 2003. When does gender trump money? Bargaining and time in household work. *American Journal of Sociology*, 109(1): 186–214.

Blakely, E. and Snyder, M. 1997. *Fortress America: gated communities in the United States*. Washington, DC: Brookings Institution Press, and Cambridge, MA: Lincoln Institute of Land Policy.

Blandy, S. 2006. Gated communities in England: historic perspectives and current developments. *GeoJournal*, 66: 15–26.

Blau, E. and Rupnik, I. 2007. *Project Zagreb: transition as condition, strategy, practice.* Barcelona: Actar, and New York: Harvard University Graduate School of Design.

Blinnikov, M., Shannin, A., Sobolev, N. and Volkova, L. 2006. Gated communities in the Moscow greenbelt: newly segregated landscapes and the suburban Russian environment. *GeoJournal*, 66(1–2): 65–81.

Blumen, O. 1994. Gender differences in the journey to work. *Urban Geography*, 15(3): 223–45.

Bodnar, J. 2001. *Fin de millénaire Budapest: metamorphoses of urban life.* Minneapolis: University of Minnesota Press.

Boentje, J. and Blinnikov, M. 2007. Post-Soviet forest fragmentation and loss of the Green Belt around Moscow, Russia (1991–2001): a remote sensing perspective. *Landscape and Urban Planning*, 82(4): 208–21.

Boggs, C. 1997. The great retreat: decline of the public sphere in late twentieth-century America. *Theory and Society*, 26: 741–80.

Boym, S. 2001a. *The future of nostalgia.* New York: Basic Books.

Boym, S. 2001b. Nostalgia, Moscow style. *Harvard Design Magazine*, 13: 1–8.

Bozoki, A. 2003. Theoretical interpretations of elite change in East Central Europe. *Comparative Sociology*, 2(1): 215–47.

Brade, I., Herfert, G. and Wiest, K. 2009. Lull before the storm? Recent trends and future prospects of socio-spatial differentiation in urban regions of Central and Eastern Europe. *Cities*, 26(5): 233–44.

Brainerd, E. 2000. Women in transition: changes in gender wage differentials in Eastern Europe and the former Soviet Union. *Industrial and Labor Relations Review*, 54(1): 138–62.

Brenner, N. 2003. Metropolitan institutional reform and the rescaling of state space in contemporary Western Europe. *European Urban and Regional Studies*, 10: 297–324.

Brenner, N. 2004a. *New state spaces: urban governance and the rescaling of statehood.* Oxford: Oxford University Press.

Brenner, N. 2004b. Urban governance and the production of new state spaces in Western Europe, 1960–2000. *Review of International Political Economy*, 11: 447–88.

Brenner, N., Jessop, B., Jones, M. and Macleod, G. (eds.) 2003. *State/space: a reader.* Oxford: Blackwell.

Brian, D. 1997. From public housing to private communities: the discipline of design and the materialization of the public and private distinction in the built environment. In J. Weintraub and K. Kumar (eds.), *Public and private in theory and practice: perspectives on a grand dichotomy.* Chicago: University of Chicago Press.

Brittan, S. 1996. *Capitalism with a human face.* Cambridge, MA: Harvard University Press.

Buckley, R. and Tsenkova, S. 2001. *Strategia za razvitie na grad Sofia: predvaritelna ocenka* [Development strategy for the City of Sofia: a preliminary assessment]. Sofia: Stolichna Obshtina. [In Bulgarian.]

Buckwalter, D. 1995. Spatial inequality, foreign investment and economic transition in Bulgaria. *Professional Geographer*, 47(3): 288–97.

Burawoy, M. and Verdery, K. 1999. *Uncertain transition: ethnographies of change in the postsocialist world.* Lanham, MD, and Oxford: Rowman & Littlefield.

Business Park Sofia undated. *Business Park Sofia.* www.businesspark-sofia.com/. Accessed February 19, 2010.

Caldeira, T. 2000. *City of walls: crime, segregation, and citizenship in São Paulo.* Berkeley: University of California Press.

Carter, F. 1979, Prague and Sofia: an analysis of their changing internal structure. In R. A. French and R. I. Hamilton (eds.), *The socialist city: spatial structure and urban policy.* Chichester and New York: Wiley.

Carvajal, D. and Castle, S. 2008. Mob muscles its way into politics in Bulgaria. *New York Times,* October 15.

Castells, M. 1989. *The informational city: information technology, economic restructuring, and the urban regional process.* Oxford, and Malden, MA: Blackwell.

Castells, M. 1998. *The information age: economy, society and culture. Volume III: End of millennium.* Malden, MA, and Oxford: Blackwell.

Cenova, K. 2008. Kupuvachut v zatvoreni kompleksi: semeen s chasten business [The property buyer in gated complexes: a family man with a private business]. *24 Chasa* [24 hours], June 26 [in Bulgarian].

Chipova, I. and Feuer, K. 2007. *Moscow: architecture and design.* Kempen, Germany: TeNeues.

CIAM (International Congress of Modern Architecture) 1973 [1934]. *Athens charter.* New York: Grossman Publishers.

Clapham, D., Hegedüs, J., Kintrea, K., Tosics, I. and Kay, H. (eds.) 1996. *Housing privatization in Eastern Europe.* Westport, CT: Greenwood Press.

Clarke S., Varshavskaya, L., Alasheev, S. and Karelina, M. 2000. The myth of the urban peasant. *Work, Employment and Society,* 14: 481–99.

Colliers International Bulgaria 2004a. *Office real estate market: 1st half 2004 report.* www.colliers.com/Content/Repositories/Base/Markets/Bulgaria/English/Market_Report/PDFs/OfficeFirstHalf2004.pdf. Accessed February 15, 2005.

Colliers International Bulgaria 2004b. *Office real estate market: 2nd half 2004 report.* www.colliers.com/Content/Repositories/Base/Markets/Bulgaria/English/Market_Report/PDFs/OfficeFirstHalf2004.pdf. Accessed February 15, 2005.

Corrin, C. (ed.) 1992. *Superwomen and the double burden: women's experience in Central and Eastern Europe and the former Soviet Union.* Toronto: Second Story.

Coy, M. 2006. Gated communities and urban fragmentation in Latin America: the Brazilian experience. *Urban Geography,* 66: 121–32.

Coy, M. and Pohler, M. 2002. Gated communities in Latin American megacities: case studies in Brazil and Argentina. *Environment and Planning B: Planning and Design,* 29(3): 355–70.

Crane, R. 2007. Is there a quiet revolution in women's travel? Revisiting the gender gap in commuting. *Journal of the American Planning Association,* 73(3): 298–316.

Cristaldi, F. 2005. Commuting and gender in Italy: a methodological issue. *Professional Geographer,* 57(2): 268–84.

Crook, S., Pulaski, J. and Waters, M. 1994. *Post-modernization: change in advanced societies.* London and New York: Routledge.

Crowley. D. 2002. Warsaw interiors. In D. Crowley and S. Reid (eds.), *Socialist spaces: sites of everyday life in the Eastern Bloc.* Oxford: Berg.

Crowley, D. and Reid, S. 2002. *Socialist spaces: sites of everyday life in the Eastern Bloc.* Oxford: Berg.

Cséfalvay, Z. 2009. The demystification of gating. *Debate February 2009, European Journal of Spatial Development*. www.nordregio.se/EJSD/Debate/debate200902.pdf. Accessed February 2, 2009.

Cvetkov, E. 2009. Esteticheski kriterii za ocenka na arhitekturata [Aesthetic criteria for evaluating architecture]. *Arhitektura [Architecture]*, 1: 55–9 [in Bulgarian].

Czaplicka, J., Gelazis, N. and Ruble, B. 2008. *Cities after the fall of communism: reshaping cultural landscapes and European identity.* Baltimore: Johns Hopkins University Press, and Washington, DC: Woodrow Wilson Center Press.

Czepczynski, M. 2008. *Cultural landscapes of post-socialist cities: representation of powers and needs.* Burlington, VT: Ashgate.

Dandolova, I. 2002. Ot kolektivism kum individualism: novi znaci i simvoli v jilishtnata arhitektura na 90-te godini v bulgariskia grad [From collectivism toward individualism: new signs and symbols in residential architecture in the Bulgarian city during the 1990s]. In S. Hristova (ed.), *Gradut: simvoli, obrazi, identichnosti [The city: symbols, images, identities]*. Sofia: Lik. [In Bulgarian.]

Dandolova, I. 2010. *Socialnite neravenstva v jilishtnata sreda* [Social inequalities in the housing environment]. Unpublished paper made available to the author.

Daskalova, K. 2005. *Bulgarian women's history and socialist myths*. www.cwsp.bg/upload/docs/history_and_myths_en.pdf. Accessed December 5, 2011.

Davis, M. 1990. *City of quartz: excavating the future in Los Angeles.* New York: Verso.

Davis, M. 1992. Fortress LA: the militarization of urban space. In M. Sorkin (ed.), *Variations on a theme park: the new American city and the end of public space.* New York: Hill and Wang.

Dear, M. 2000. *The post-modern urban condition.* Oxford: Blackwell.

Dear, M. and Dahmann, N. 2008. Urban politics and the Los Angeles school of urbanism. *Urban Affairs Review*, 44(2): 266–79.

Dear, M. and Flusty, S. 1997. The iron lotus: Los Angeles and post-modern urbanism. *Annals of the American academy of political and social science*, 551(1): 151–63.

Dear, M. and Flusty, S. 1998. Post-modern urbanism. *Annals of the American Association of Geographers*, 88(1): 50–72.

Delijska, A. 2008. Vlastta da ne se pravi na oshtipana za stroitelnia terrorism [Authorities should no longer ignore the construction terrorism]. *Novinar [Newsmaker]*, June 17: 12–13 [in Bulgarian].

Dichev, I. 2003. Usiadaneto na nomadskia komunism: socialisticheskata urbanizacia i krugovete na grajdanstvoto [Nomadic communism settles down: socialist urbanization and the circles of citizenship]. *Sociologicheski Problemi [Sociological issues]*, 35(3–4): 33–63 [in Bulgarian].

Dikov, P. 2009. Zashto? Zashto bulgarinut gazi pravilata u nas i striktno gi spazva v chujbina [Why? Why Bulgarian break rules at home but abide by them abroad], *24 Chasa [24 hours]*, June 27 [in Bulgarian].

Dimitrov, L. 1991. V tursene na izcheznalite ogradi na Sofia [In search of the lost fences of Sofia]. *Arhitektura [Architecture]*, 3–4: 34–6.

Dimitrovska-Andrews, K., Miheli , B. and Stani , I. 2007. The post-socialist urban restructuring of Ljubljana: strengthening identity. In K. Stanilov (ed.), *The post-socialist city: urban form and space transformations in Central and Eastern Europe after socialism.* New York: Springer.

Dingsdale, A. 1999. Budapest's built environment in transition. *GeoJournal*, 49: 63–78.

Dingsdale, A. 2001. *Mapping modernities: geographies of Central and Eastern Europe*. London and New York: Routledge.

Dobrinsky, R., Hesse, D. and Traeger, R. 2006. Understanding the long-term growth performance of the East European and CIS Economies. UNECE (United Nations Economic Commission for Europe) Discussion Paper Series, 2006-1, March. www.unece.org/fileadmin/DAM/ead/misc/Dobrinsky_Hesse_Traeger. pdf. Accessed December 5, 2011.

Droste, M. 2006. *The Bauhaus 1919–1933: reform and avant-garde*. Cologne: Taschen.

Eade, J. and Mele, C. 2003. *Understanding the city: contemporary and future perspectives*. Malden, MA, and Oxford: Blackwell.

EAUE (European Academy of the Urban Environment) 2000. *A future for large housing estates: European strategies for prefabricated housing estates in Central and Eastern Europe*. Berlin: European Academy of the Urban Environment with the Institute for Regional Development and Structural Planning, Erkner, Germany.

EAUE (European Academy of the Urban Environment) 2003. *Twelve candidate countries overview report on sustainable urban management, sustainable urban transport, sustainable urban design and sustainable construction*. Berlin: European Academy of the Urban Environment.

EEA 2006a. *Urban sprawl in Europe: the ignored challenge*. Copenhagen: European Environment Agency.

EEA 2006b. *Land accounts in Europe, 1990–2000: towards integrated land and ecosystem accounting*. Copenhagen: European Environment Agency.

Ellin, N. 1996. *Postmodern urbanism*. Cambridge, MA: Blackwell.

Ellin, N. 1997. *Architecture of fear*. Princeton: Princeton Architectural Press.

Emerson, R., Fretz, R. and Shaw, L. 1995. *Writing ethnographic fieldnotes*. Chicago: University of Chicago Press.

Enyedi, G. 1992. *Social transition and urban restructuring in Central Europe*. Budapest: European Science Foundation.

Enyedi, G. 1998. Transformation in Central East European post-socialist cities. Discussion papers of the Centre for Regional Studies of the Hungarian Academy of Sciences, 21.

European Social Watch Report. 2010. Time for action: responding to poverty, social exclusion and inequality in Europe and beyond. www.socialwatch.eu/wcm/ Bulgaria.html. Accessed December 1, 2011.

EUROSTAT undated. In cooperation with the Directorate-General for Regional Policy at the European Commission. *Urban audit*. www.urbanaudit.org. Accessed July 16, 2009. Also data queries through http://epp.eurostat.ec. europa.eu.

Fainstein, S., Gordon, I. and Harloe, M. (eds.) 1992. *Divided cities: New York and London in the contemporary world*. Malden, MA, and Oxford: Blackwell.

Faitondjieva, I. 2008. Problemut za stila na stranicite na arhitekturnia pechat u nas v purvite desetiletia na XX v [The problem of style in the pages of Bulgarian architectural journals during the first decades of the twentieth century]. In *Prostranstvo i arhitektura* [Space and architecture]. Sofia: Marin Drinov. [In Bulgarian.]

Fehér, F., Heller, A. and Marcus, G. 1984. *Dictatorship over needs: an analysis of Soviet societies*. Malden, MA, and London: Blackwell.

Fielding, A. 1982. Migration and urbanization in Western Europe since 1950. *Geographical Journal*, 155(1): 60–9.

Fishman, R. 1987. *Bourgeois utopias: the rise and fall of suburbia*. New York: Basic Books.

Flint, A. 2009. *Wrestling with Moses: how Jane Jacobs took on New York's master builder and transformed the American city*. New York: Random House.

Flusty, S. 1997. Building paranoia. In N. Ellin (ed.), *Architecture of fear*. Princeton: Princeton Architectural Press.

French, R. and Hamilton, F. 1979. *The socialist city: spatial structure and urban policy*. Chichester and New York: Wiley.

Frost, R., Poirier, R. and Richardson, M., 1995. *Robert Frost: collected poems, prose and plays*. New York: Penguin Putnam.

Gandy, M. 2002. *Concrete and clay: reworking nature in New York City*. Cambridge, MA: MIT Press.

Ganev, V. 2007. *Preying on the state: the transformation of Bulgaria after 1989*. Ithaca, NY: Cornell University Press.

Garcelon, M. 1997. In the shadow of the Leviathan: public and private in socialist and post-socialist society. In J. Weintraub and K. Kumar (eds.), *Public and private in theory and practice: perspectives on a grand dichotomy*. Chicago: University of Chicago Press.

Garreau, J. 1991. *Edge city: life on the new frontier*. New York: Anchor Books.

Genis, S. 2007. Producing elite localities: the rise of gated communities in Istanbul. *Urban Studies*, 44(4): 771–98.

Genova, B. 2000. Jilishtnata sreda v Sofia: sustojanie i perspektivi. In *Godishnik na Universiteta po Arhitektura, Stroitelstvo i Geodezia Tom XL, Svituk I, Arhitektura: Istoria, Tipologia, Obrazovanie*, pp. 146-127-144. Sofia: Universitet po *Arhitektura, Stroitelstvo i Geodezia*. [In Bulgarian.]

Gerasimov, G. 1999. Past and new cleavages in post-socialist Bulgaria. In K. Lawson, A. Rommelle and G. Karasimeonov (eds.), *Cleavages, parties, and voters: studies from Bulgaria, the Czech Republic, Hungary, Poland, and Romania*. Santa Barbara, CA: Praeger.

Gerasimova, K. 2002. Public privacy in the Soviet communal apartment. In D. Crowley and S. Reid (eds.), *Socialist spaces: sites of everyday life in the Eastern Bloc*. Oxford: Berg.

Ghodsee, K. and Henry, L. 2010. Redefining the common good after communism: beyond ideology. *Newsnet: News of the Association of Slavic, East European and Eurasian Studies*, 50(4): 1–7.

Giddens, A. 2000. *The third way: the renewal of social democracy*. Cambridge, and Malden, MA: Polity Press.

Giddens, A. 2006. *Sociology*. 5th edn. Cambridge, and Malden, MA: Polity.

Glasze, G. 2006. The spread of private guarded neighborhoods in Lebanon and the significance of historically and geographically specific governmentality. In G. Glasze, C. Webster and K. Frantz (eds.), *Private cities: global and local perspectives*. London and New York: Routledge.

Glasze, G., Webster, C. and Frantz, K. (eds.) 2006. *Private cities: global and local perspectives*. London and New York: Routledge.

Goffman, E. 1959. *The presentation of self in everyday life*. Garden City, NY: Doubleday.

Goldhoorn, B. and Meuser, P. 2006. *Capitalist realism: new architecture in Russia.* Berlin: DOM Publishers.

Goscilo, H. and Norris, S. (eds.) 2008. *Preserving Petersburg: history, memory, nostalgia.* Bloomington: Indiana University Press.

Grabher, G. 1997. Adaptation at the cost of adaptability? Restructuring the East German economy. In G. Grabher and D. Stark (eds.), *Restructuring networks in post-socialism: legacies, linkages, and localities.* Oxford: Oxford University Press.

Grant, R. 2005. The emergence of gated communities in a West African context: evidence from greater Accra, Ghana. *Urban Geography,* 26(8): 661–83.

Grozev, B. 2010. Moiat kompleks e moiata krepost [My complex is my fortress]. *Tema* [Theme]. www.temanews.com/index.php?p=tema&iid=180aid=4726. Accessed July 7, 2010. [In Bulgarian.]

Gutkind, E. 1972. *Urban development in Eastern Europe: Bulgaria, Romania, and the USSR.* New York: Free Press.

Habermas, J. 1989. *The structural transformation of the public sphere: an inquiry into a category of bourgeois society.* Cambridge, MA: MIT Press.

Habermas, J. 1990. What does socialism mean today? The rectifying revolution and the need for new thinking on the left. *New Left Review,* 183: 3–22.

Habermas, J. 1994. *The past as future.* Cambridge: Polity Press.

Hamilton, F. 1999. Transformation and space in Central and Eastern Europe. *Geographical Journal,* 165(2): 135–44.

Hamilton, F., Andrews, K. and Pichler-Milanovic, N. 2005. *Transformation of cities in Central and Eastern Europe: towards globalization.* New York: United Nations University Press.

Hanson, S. and Johnson, I. 1985. Gender differences in work-length trip explanations and implications. *Urban Geography,* 6(3): 193–219.

Hanson, S. and Pratt, G. 1995. *Gender, work and space.* London: Routledge.

Harloe, M. 1996. Cities in the transition. In G. Andrusz, M. Harloe and I. Szelényi (eds.), *Cities after socialism: urban and regional change and conflict in post-socialist societies.* Malden, MA, and Oxford: Blackwell.

Harris, R. 2011. Meaningful types in a world of suburbs. *Research in Urban Sociology,* 10: 15–47.

Harvey, D. 1989a. *The condition of post-modernity: an enquiry into the origins of cultural change.* Malden, MA, and Oxford: Blackwell.

Harvey, D. 1989b. *The Urban Experience.* Oxford: Blackwell.

Hassan, I. 1985. The culture of post-modernism. *Theory, Culture and Society,* 2(3): 119–32.

Häussermann, H. 1996. From the socialist to the capitalist city: experiences from Germany. In G. Andrusz, M. Harloe and I. Szelényi (eds.), *Cities after socialism: urban and regional change and conflict in post-socialist societies.* Malden, MA, and Oxford: Blackwell.

Häussermann, H. and Kapplan, A. 2005. Berlin: from divided to fragmented city. In F. Hamilton, K. Andrews and N. Pichler-Milanovic (eds.), *Transformation of cities in Central and Eastern Europe: towards globalization.* New York: United Nations University Press.

Havel, V. 1992a. *Summer meditations.* Trans. P. Wilson. New York: Alfred Knopf.

Havel, V. 1992b. The end of the modern era. *New York Times,* March 1.

Havel, V. 1994. Search for something of value: man as observer increasingly alienated from himself as being. *Buffalo News*, July 10.

Hayden, D. 2004. *Building suburbia: green fields and urban growth, 1820–2000*. New York: Vintage Books.

Hirt, S. 2005a. Planning the post-communist city: experiences from Sofia. *International Planning Studies*, 10: 219–40.

Hirt, S. 2005b. Toward post-modern urbanism: evolution of planning in Cleveland, Ohio. *Journal of Planning Education and Research*, 25(1): 27–42.

Hirt, S. 2006. Post-socialist urban forms: notes from Sofia. *Urban Geography*, 27: 464–88.

Hirt, S. 2007a. The compact vs. the dispersed city: history of planning debates on Sofia's urban form. *Journal of Planning History*, 6: 138–65.

Hirt, S. 2007b. Suburbanizing Sofia: characteristics of post-socialist peri-urban change. *Urban Geography*, 28(8): 755–80.

Hirt, S. 2008a. Landscapes of post-modernity: changes in the built fabric of Belgrade and Sofia since the end of socialism. *Urban Geography*, 29: 785–809.

Hirt, S. 2008b. Stuck in the suburbs? Gendered perspectives of living at the edge of the post-socialist city. *Cities*, 25(6): 340–54.

Hirt, S. 2009a. City profile: Belgrade. *Cities*, 26(5): 293–303.

Hirt, S. 2009b. Pre-modern, modern, post-modern? Placing New Urbanism into a historical perspective. *Journal of Planning History*, 8(3): 248–73.

Hirt, S. 2011. Integrating city and nature: urban planning debates in Sofia, Bulgaria. In D. Brantz and S. Dumpelmann (eds.), *Greening the city: urban landscapes in twentieth-century history*. Charlottesville: University of Virginia Press.

Hirt, S. and Kovachev, A. 2006. The changing spatial structure of post-socialist Sofia. In S. Tsenkova and Z. Nedovi|-Budic (eds.), *The urban mosaic of post-socialist Europe: space, institutions and policy*. Heidelberg and New York: Springer-Physica.

Hirt, S. and Petrović, M. 2010. The gates of Belgrade: housing, security and neighborhood conditions in the post-communist city. *Problems of Post-communism*, 57(5): 3–19.

Hirt, S. and Petrović, M. 2011. The Belgrade wall: the proliferation of gated housing in the Serbian capital after socialism. *International Journal of Urban and Regional Research*, 35(4): 753–77.

Hirt, S. and Stanilov, K. 2007. The perils of post-socialist transformation: residential development in Sofia. In K. Stanilov, *The post-socialist city: urban form and space transformations in Central and Eastern Europe after Socialism*. Dordrecht: Springer.

Hirt, S. and Stanilov, K. 2009. *Twenty years of transition: the evolution of urban planning in Eastern Europe and the former Soviet Union, 1989–2009*. Nairobi: UN-HABITAT.

Holmes, L. 1997. *Post-communism: an introduction*. Cambridge: Polity Press.

Holston, J. 1987. *The modernist city: an anthropological critique of Brasília*. Chicago: University of Chicago Press.

Holston, J. and Appadurai, A. 2003. Cities and citizenship. In N. Brenner, B. Jessop, M. Jones and G. MacLeod (eds.), *State/space: a reader*. Malden, MA, and Oxford: Blackwell.

Howard, E. 1946 [1898] *Garden cities of tomorrow: a peaceful path to reform*. London: Faber and Faber.

Hristić, N. 2005. Aspects of gated neighborhoods in transitional society. Paper presented at the 33rd World Congress on Housing, Pretoria, September 27–30.

Humphrey, C. 2002. *The unmaking of Soviet life: everyday economies after socialism*. Ithaca, NY: Cornell University Press.

IIDEA 2002. *Voter turnout since 1945: a global report*. Stockholm: International Institute for Democracy and Electoral Assistance.

IMF 2009. *International Monetary Fund: World economic outlook database 2009*. www.imf. org/external/pubs/ft/weo/2009/01/weodata/index.aspx. Accessed August 28, 2009.

Imoti BG 2007. [Real estate Bulgaria.] Pazarut na nedvijimite imoti se nasochva kum kompleksite ot zatvoren tip [The real estate market is turning to gated communities]. www.imotibg.com. Accessed July 4, 2010.

Inglehart, R. 1997. *Modernization and post-modernization: cultural, economic, and political change in 43 societies*. Princeton: Princeton University Press.

Inglehart, R. and Catterberg, G. 2002. Trends in political action: the developmental trend and the post-honeymoon decline. *International Journal of Comparative Sociology*, 43: 300–16.

Ioffe, G. and Nefedova, T. 1999. *The environs of Russian cities*. Lewiston, NY: Edwin Mellen Press.

Ivanov, I. 1938, Rech na stolichnia kmet ingener Ivan Ivanov po gradoustroistvenia plan na Sofia izraboten ot professor Musman proiznesena pred Stolichnia Obshtinski Suvet na 18 mai 1938g [Speech by the Mayor of Sofia, Engineer Ivan Ivanov, on the subject of Sofia's Master Plan prepared by Professor Muessman at the meeting of the Municipal Council of Sofia on May 18, 1938]. In *Izgrajdaneto na budeshta goliama Sofia: kakvo predvijda Musmanovia plan* [Building future Greater Sofia: what the Muessman plan envisions]. Sofia: Stolichna Goliama Obshtina. [In Bulgarian.]

Ivanova, E. 2008. Imperski sintez na universalnoto i lokalnoto: arhitekturata na Stalinizma, 30-te-50-te godini [Imperial synthesis of the universal and the local: the architecture of Stalinism, 1930s–1950s]. *Prostranstvo i arhitektura* [Space and architecture]. Sofia: Marin Drinov. [In Bulgarian.]

Iyer, S. 2003. The urban context for adjustments to the planning process in post-Soviet Russia: responses from local planners in Siberia. *International Planning Studies*, 8: 201–23.

Jackson, K. 1985. *Crabgrass frontier: the suburbanization of the United States*. Oxford: Oxford University Press.

Jacobs, J. 1961. *The death and life of great American cities*. New York: Random House.

Jameson, F. 1984. Postmodernism, or the cultural logic of late capitalism. *New Left Review*, 146: 53–92.

Jameson, F. 1991. *Postmodernism, or, The Cultural Logic of Late Capitalism*. Durham, NC: Duke University Press.

Jeleva-Martins, D. 1991. Horizontalna organizacia na grada: sinhronichen analiz [Horizontal organization of the city: synchronic analysis]. *Arhitekura* [Architecture], 3: 22–5 [in Bulgarian].

Jeleva-Martins, D. 1998. Dokrinata na modernizma: edna interpretacia na Musmanovia plan, 1938 [The modernist doctrine: an interpretation of Muessman's plan from 1938]. *Arhitekura* [Architecture], 5: 36–9 [in Bulgarian].

Jeleva-Martins, D. 1999. Izbrani fakti i komentar za purvia regulacionen plan na stolicata [Selected facts and commentary on the first regulatory plan of the state capital]. *Arhitekura* [Architecture], 2: 38–40 and 3: 38–40 [in Bulgarian].

Jeleva-Martins, D. 2000. Suvremenennto bulgarsko gradoustristvo kato presechna tochka na Iztochnia i Zapadnia avantgard [Contemporary Bulgarian urban design as cross-roads of the Eastern and Western avant-garde]. *Arhitekura* [Architecture], 2: 21–4 [in Bulgarian].

Jencks, C. 1984. *The language of post-modern architecture*. New York: Rizzoli.

Jencks, C. 1993. *Heteropolis Los Angeles: the riots and strange beauty of hetero-architecture*. New York: St. Martin's Press.

Jencks, C. and Silver, N. 1972. *Adhocism: the case of improvisation*. New York: Doubleday.

Jowitt, K. 1992. *New world disorder: the Leninist extinction*. Berkeley: University of California Press.

Kasabova, K. 2008. *Street without a name*. London: Portobello Books.

Kazalarska, S. 2010. Obrazi na novata bulgarska mechta: Ot grada na mechtite do grada na fontanite [Images of the new Bulgarian dream: from the city of dreams to the city of fountains]. Unpublished paper made available to the author.

Keil, R. and Ronneberger, K. 2000. The globalization of Frankfurt am Main: core, periphery and social conflict. In P. Marcuse and R. van Kempen (eds.), *Globalizing cities: a new spatial order*. Oxford, and Malden, MA: Blackwell.

Kelleher, M. 2004. *Social problems in a free society: myths, absurdities and realities*. Lanham, MD: University Press of America.

Kenworthy, J., Laube, F., Newman, P., Barter, P., Raad, T. and Poboon, C. 1999. *An international sourcebook of automobile dependence in cities, 1960–1990*. Boulder: University of Colorado Press.

Keynes, J. 1933. National self-sufficiency. *Yale Review*, 22(4): 755–69. Reprinted in *The collected writings of John Maynard Keynes*, vol. 11, ed. D. Moggridge (1982). London: Macmillan, and New York: Cambridge University Press, pp. 233–46.

Kharkhordin, O. 1995. The Soviet individual: genealogy of a dissimulating animal. In M. Featherstone, S. Lash and R. Robertson (eds.), *Global modernities*. Thousand Oaks, CA: Sage.

Kharkhordin, O. 1997. Reveal and dissimulate: a genealogy of private life in Russia. In J. Weintraub and K. Kumar (eds.), *Public and private in theory and practice: perspectives on a grand dichotomy*. Chicago: University of Chicago Press.

Kiosev, A. 2005. Mishelovkata [The mousetrap]. *Kritika i humanism* [Critique and humanism], 20(1): 53–73 [in Bulgarian].

Kiss, E. 2007. The evolution of industrial areas in Budapest after 1989. In K. Stanilov (ed.), *The post-socialist city: urban form and space transformations in Central and Eastern Europe after socialism*. New York: Springer.

Klassanov, M. 1992. Totalitarisum, democrciya, arhitectura [Totalitarianism, democracy, architecture]. *Arhitektura* [Architecture], 6: 26–31 [in Bulgarian].

Knox, P. and McCarthy, L. 2005. *Urbanization: an introduction to urban geography*. Upper Saddle River, NJ: Prentice Hall.

Koeva, S. and Bould, S. 2007. Women as workers and as carers under communism and after: the case of Bulgaria. *International Review of Sociology*, 17(2): 303–18.

Kok, H. and Kovacs, Z. 1999. The process of suburbanization in the agglomeration of Budapest. *Netherlands Journal of Housing and the Built Environment*, 14(2): 119–41.

Kolev, K., Piseva, V., Petkov, E., Devetakova, L. and Grigorova, M. 2007. *Socialnata straficacia v Bulgaria* [Social stratification in Bulgaria]. Unpublished report made available to the author by Agencia Meridina [Meridiana Agency], Sofia. [In Bulgarian.]

Kornai, J. 1997. Editorial: reforming the welfare state in post-socialist societies. *World Development*, 25: 1183–6.

Kostof, S. 1991. *The city shaped: urban patterns and meanings through history*. Boston: Bulfinch.

Kovachev, A. 2001. *Zelenata sistema na Sofia: urbanistichni aspekti* [Sofia's green system: urban planning aspects]. Sofia: Pensoft. [In Bulgarian.]

Kovachev, A. 2009. Mejdunaroden konkurs za mnogofuncionalen centur [International competition for multifunctional center]. *Arhitektura* [Architecture], 4: 28–31.

Kovacs, Z. 1994. A city at the crossroads: social and economic transformation in Budapest. *Urban Studies*, 31: 1081–96.

Kovacs, Z. 1998. Ghettoization or gentrification? Post-socialist scenarios for Budapest. *Netherlands Journal of Housing and the Built Environment*, 13(1): 63–81.

Krier, L. 1981. Forward, comrades, we must go back! *Oppositions*, 24: 26–37.

Kumar, K. 1995. *From post-industrial to post-modern society*. Oxford, and Malden, MA: Blackwell.

Kumar, K. 1997. Home: The promise and predicament of private life at the end of the twentieth century. In J. Weintraub and K. Kumar (eds.), *Public and private in theory and practice: perspectives on a grand dichotomy*. Chicago: University of Chicago Press.

Kumar, K. and Makarova, E. 2008. The portable home: the domestication of public space. *Sociological Theory*, 26(4): 324–43.

Kurkovsky, D. 2009. Post-Soviet pre/post-modern: style, architecture and national identity in contemporary Moscow. Paper presented at the Annual Meeting of the American Association for the Advancement of Slavic Studies, Boston.

Labov, G. 1979. *Arhitekturata na Sofia* [The Architecture of Sofia]. Sofia: Tehnika. [In Bulgarian.]

Ladányi, J. 1995. Market, state and informal networks in the growth of private housing in Hungary. In R. Forrest and A. Murie (eds.), *Housing and Family Wealth*. London and New York: Routledge.

Ladányi, J. and Szelényi, I. 1998. Class, ethnicity and urban restructuring in postcommunist Hungary. In G. Enyedi (ed.), *Social change and urban restructuring in Central Europe*. Budapest: Akademiai Klado.

Lampe, J. 1984. Inter-war Sofia versus the Nazi-style Garden City: the struggle over the Muessman plan. *Journal of Urban History*, 11(1): 39–62.

Lang, R. and Danielson, K. 1997. Gated communities in America: walling out the world. *Housing Policy Debate* 8(4): 867–99.

Latour, B. 2001. *We were never modern*. Cambridge, MA: Harvard University Press.

Leach, N. 1998. The dark side of the domus. *Journal of Architecture*, 3(1): 31–42.

Le Corbusier 1987 [1929]. *The city of tomorrow and its planning*. New York: Dover.

Lee, D. 1973. Requiem for large-scale models. *Journal of the American Planning Association*, 39(3): 163–78.

Lefebvre, H. 1991 [1974]. *The production of space*. Trans. D. Nicholson-Smith. Oxford: Blackwell.

LeFont, S. 2001. One step forward, two steps back: women in the post-communist states. *Communist and Post-communist Studies*, 34(2): 203–20.

Le Gallès, P. 2000. Private-sector interests and urban governance. In A. Bagnasco and P. Le Gallès (eds.), *Cities in contemporary Europe* (Cambridge: Cambridge University Press.

Leisch, H. 2002. Gated communities in Indonesia. *Cities*, 19(5): 341–50.

Leontidou, L. 1993. Post-modernism and the city. *Urban Studies*, 30(6): 949–65.

Lewis, M. 2003. All sail, no anchor: architecture after modernism. *New Criterion*, 22(4): 4–16.

Libertun De Duren, N. 2006. Planning à la carte: the location patterns of gated communities around Buenos Aires in a decentralized planning context. *International Journal of Urban and Regional Research*, 30(2): 308–27.

Lizon, P. 1996. East Central Europe: the unhappy heritage of socialist mass housing. *Journal of Architectural Education*, 50: 104–14.

Local Development Initiative 2004. *Suhraniavane na parkovete i zelenite ploshti v Sofia; pravno izsledvane* [Park and green-space preservation in Sofia: legal analysis]. Unpublished document made available to the author by Local Development Initiative, Sofia.

Lofland, L. 1991. The urban milieu: locales, public sociability, and moral concern. In D. Maines (ed.), *Social organization and social process: essays in honor of Anselm Strauss*. Hawthorne, NY: Aldine de Gruyter.

Lofland, L. 1998. *The public realm*. Hawthorne, NY: Aldine de Gruyter

Logan, J. and Molotch, H. 1987. *Urban fortunes: the political economy of space*. Berkeley: University of California Press.

Loukaitou-Sideris, A. and Banerjee, T. 1998. *Urban design downtown: poetics and politics of form*. Berkeley: University of Califorrnia Press.

Lovenduski, J., and Woodall, J. 1987. *Politics and society in Eastern Europe*. Bloomington: Indiana University Press.

Low, S. 2001. The edge and the center: gated communities and the discourse of urban fear. *American Anthropologist*, 103(1): 45–58.

Low, S. 2003, *Behind the gates: Life, security and the pursuit of happiness in fortress America*. London and New York: Routledge.

Lynch, K. 1984. *Good city form*. Cambridge, MA: MIT Press.

Lyon, D. 1999. *Post-modernity*. Minneapolis: University of Minnesota Press.

Lyotard, J.-F., 1984. *The post-modern condition: a report on knowledge*. Trans. G. Bennington and B. Massumi. Minneapolis: University of Minnesota Press.

Maier, K. 1994. Planning and an education in planning in the Czech Republic. *Journal of Planning Education and Research*, 13: 263–9.

Maier, K. 1998. Czech planning in transition: assets and deficiencies. *International Planning Studies*, 3(3): 351–65.

Makarova, E. 2006. The new urbanism in Moscow: the redefinition of public and private space. Paper presented at the Annual Meeting of the American Sociological Association, Montreal.

Makarova, E. 2009. Gentrification and the transformation of urban space in contemporary Moscow. Paper presented at the Annual Meeting of the American Association for the Advancement of Slavic Studies, Boston.

Manzi, T. and Smith-Bowers, B. 2005. Gated communities as club goods: segregation or social cohesion? *Housing Studies*, 20(2): 345–59.

Marcuse, P. 1996. Privatization and its discontents: property rights in land and housing in the transition in Eastern Europe. In G. Andrusz, M. Harloe and I. Szelényi (eds.), *Cities after socialism: urban and regional change and conflict in post-socialist societies*. Oxford: Blackwell.

Marcuse, P. 1997. Walls of fear and walls of support. In N. Ellin (ed.), *Architecture of fear*. Princeton: Princeton Architectural Press.

Marcuse, P. 2006. Space in the globalizing city. In N. Brenner and R. Keil (eds.), *The global cities reader*. London and New York: Routledge.

Marcuse, P. 2002. The partitioned city in history. In P. Marcuse and R. van Kempen (eds.), *Of states and cities: the partitioning of urban space*. Oxford: Oxford University Press.

Marcuse, P. and van Kempen, R. 2000. *Globalizing cities: a new spatial order*. Malden, MA, and Oxford: Blackwell.

Marcuse, P. and van Kempen, R. (eds.) 2002. *Of state and cities: the partitioning of urban space*. Oxford: Oxford University Press.

Marx, K. and Engels, F. 1975. *Karl Marx, Frederick Engels: collected works*. London: Lawrence and Wishart.

Matei, S. 2004. The emergent Romanian post-socialist ethos: from nationalism to privatism. *Problems of Post-communism*, 51: 40–7.

Mayer, K., Diewald, M. and Solga, H. 1999. Transitions to post-communism in East Germany: worklife mobility of men and women between 1989 and 1993. *Acta sociologica*, 42(1): 35–53.

Metcalfe, B. and Afanassieva, M. 2005. Gender work and equal opportunities in Central and Eastern Europe. *Women in Management Review*, 20(6): 397–416.

Miao, P. 2003. Deserted streets in a jammed town: the gated community in Chinese cities and its solution. *Journal of Urban Design*, 8(1): 45–66.

Muller, P. 1981. *Contemporary suburban America*. Englewood Cliffs, NJ: Prentice-Hall.

Mumford, L. 1938. *The culture of cities*. New York: Harcourt Brace.

Murray, R. 1992. Fordism and post-Fordism. In C. Jencks (ed.), *The post-modern reader*. London: Academy Editions.

Mushev, D. 1992. Za stolicata i neinite proektanti [About the capital city and its planners]. *Arhitektura [Architecture]*, 7–8: 21–3.

Nacionalen Centur za Regionalno Razvitie i Jilishtna Politika [National Center for Regional Development and Housing Policy] 1999. Plan za regionalnoto razvitie na Oblast Sofia [Regional Development Plan for the Development of Sofia]. Unpublished document made available to the author by the National Center for Regional Development and Housing Policy, Sofia. [In Bulgarian.]

Nacionalen Statisticheski Institut [National Statistical Institute] undated. Jilishta po etajnost na sgradata v kojato se namirat v Sofia po oblasti, obshtini i naseleni mesta [Dwellings by the number of floors of the building within which they are located in Sofia by municipality and settlement]. Unpublished data made available to the author. [In Bulgarian.]

Nacionalen Statisticheski Institut [National Statistical Institute] 1993. *Statisticheski Sbornik – Sofia* [Statistical compilation of Sofia]. Nacionalen Statisticheski Institut, Stolichno Teritorialno Bjuro, Sofia. [In Bulgarian.]

Nacionalen Statisticheski Institut [National Statistical Institute] 2003. *Sofia v Chisla* [Sofia in figures]. Nacionalen Statisticheski Institut, Stolichno Teritorialno Bjuro, Sofia. [In Bulgarian.]

Neikov, L. and Samodumov, B. 1952. *Uchebnik po gradoustrojstvo* [Urban planning textbook]. Sofia: Narodna Prosveta. [In Bulgarian.]

Newman, O. 1996 [1972] *Creating defensible space.* Washington, DC: US Department of Housing and Urban Development.

Newman, P. and Thornley, A. 1996. *Urban planning in Europe: international competition, national systems and planning projects.* London and New York: Routledge.

Nientied, P. 1998. The question of town and regional planning in Albania. *Habitat International,* 22(1): 41–7.

Novak, J. and Sýkora, L. 2007. City in motion: time-space activity and mobility patterns of suburban inhabitants and the structuration of the spatial organization of the Prague metropolitan area. *Geografiska annaler,* 89(B): 147–67.

Nuissl, H. and Rink, D. 2005. The "production" of urban sprawl in eastern Germany as a phenomenon of post-socialist transformation. *Cities,* 22(2): 123–34.

Oberhauser, A. 2000. Feminism and economic geography: gendering work and working gender. In E. Sheppard and T. Barnes (eds.), *A Companion to Economic Geography.* Oxford: Oxford University Press.

Ohmae, K. 1990. *Borderless world: Power and strategy in the interlinked economy.* New York: Harper.

Ost, D. 1990. *Solidarity and the politics of anti-politics: opposition and reform in Poland since 1968.* Philadelphia: Temple University Press.

Pagonis, T. and Thornley, A. 2000. Urban development projects in Moscow: Market/state relations in the new Russia. *European Planning Studies,* 8(6): 751–66.

Pateman, C. 1983. Feminist critiques of the public/private dichotomy. In S. Benn and G. Gaus (eds.), *Public and private in social life.* New York: St. Martin's Press.

Petrunov, G. 2006. Organized crime and social transformation in Bulgaria. *European Journal of Sociology,* 47: 297–325.

Pickles, J. and Smith, A. 1998. *Theorising transition: the political economy of post-communist transformations.* New York: Routledge.

Pickvance, C. 1996. Environmental and housing movements in cities after socialism. In G. Andrusz, M. Harloe and I. Szelényi (eds.), *Cities after socialism: urban and regional change and conflict in post-socialist societies.* Malden, MA, and Oxford: Blackwell.

Pickvance, C. 2003. State socialism, post-socialism and their urban patterns: theorizing the Central and Eastern European experience. In J. Eade and C. Mele (eds.), *Understanding the city: contemporary and future perspectives.* Malden, MA, and Oxford: Blackwell.

Pickvance, K. 1997. Social movements in Hungary and Russia: the case of environmental movements. *European Sociological Review,* 13: 35–54.

Polanyi, K. 1967 [1944]. *The great transformation: the political and economic origins of our time.* Boston: Beacon Press.

Putnam, R. 1993. *Making democracy work: civic traditions in modern Italy.* Princeton: Princeton University Press.

Putnam, R. 2000. *Bowling alone: the collapse and revival of American community.* New York: Simon & Schuster.

Raban, J. 1974, *Soft city.* London: Harvill Press.

Radoslavova, J. 2008. Zelenata sistema v gradoustroistvenoto planirane na Sofia [The green system in the planning of Sofia]. In *Prostranstvo – arhitektura II* [Space architecture II]. Sofia: Publishing house of the Bulgarian Academy of Sciences. [In Bulgarian.]

Rajchev, A., Kolev, K., Boundjoulov, A. and Dimova, L. 2000. *Social stratification in Bulgaria*. Sofia: Social Democratic Institute.

Rand, A. 1971 [1943]. *The Fountainhead*. Bergefield, NJ: New American Library.

Raposo, R. 2006. Gated communities, commodification and aesthetization: the case of the Lisbon metropolitan area. *GeoJournal*, 66: 43–56.

Ray, L. 1995. The rectifying revolutions? Organizational features in the new Eastern Europe. *Organization*, 2(3–4): 441–65.

Ray, L. 1996. *Social theory and the crisis of state socialism*. Aldershot: Edward Elgar.

Ray, L. 1997. Post-communism: postmodernity or modernity revisited. *British Journal of Sociology*, 48(4): 543–60.

Raymond, A. 1989. Islamic city, Arab city: oriental myths and recent views. *British Journal of Middle Eastern Studies*, 21: 3–18.

Relph, E. C. 1987. *The modern urban landscape*. Baltimore: Johns Hopkins University Press.

Residential Park Sofia undated. www.residentialpark-sofia.com. Accessed July 4, 2010.

Roberts, P. and LaFollette, K. 1990. *Meltdown: inside the Soviet economy*. Washington, DC: Cato Institute.

Robertson, R. 1992. *Globalization: social theory and global culture*. London: Sage.

Robinson, J. 2006. *Ordinary cities: questioning modernity and development*. Abingdon, Oxon, and New York: Routledge.

Rofe, M. 2006. New landscapes of gated communities: Australia's Sovereign Islands. *Landscape Research*, 31(3): 309–17.

Rose-Ackerman, S. 1996. The political economy of corruption: causes and consequences. World Bank note 74. http://rru.worldbank.org/documents/publicpolicyjournal/074ackerm.pdf. Accessed October 29, 2010.

Rowe, P. 1997. *Civic realism*. Cambridge, MA: MIT Press.

Ruble, B. 1990. *Leningrad: shaping a Soviet city*. Berkeley: University of California Press.

Ruble, B. 1995. *Money sings: the changing politics of urban space in post-Soviet Yaroslav*. Washington, DC: Woodrow Wilson Center Press, and Cambridge: University of Cambridge Press.

Ruble, B., Koehn, J. and Popson, N. 2001. *Fragmented space in the Russian Federation*. Washington, DC: Woodrow Wilson Center Press, and Baltimore: Johns Hopkins University Press.

Rudd, E. 2006. Gendering unemployment in post-socialist Germany: "What I do is work, even if it's not paid." *Ethnos*, 71(2): 191–212.

Rudolph, R. and Brade, I. 2005. Moscow: processes of restructuring in the post-Soviet metropolitan periphery. *Cities*, 22(2): 135–50.

Ruoppila, S. 1998. The changing urban landscape of Tallinn. *Finnish Journal of Urban Studies*, 35(3): 36–43.

Ruoppila, S. 2005. Housing policy and residential differentiation in post-socialist Tallinn. *European Journal of Housing Policy*, 5(3): 279–300.

Ruoppila, S. and Kährik, A. 2003. Socio-economic residential differentiation in post-socialist Tallinn. *Netherlands Journal of Housing and the Built Environment*, 18(1): 49–73.

Salcedo, R. and Torres, A. 2004. Gated communities in Santiago: wall or frontier? *International Journal of Urban and Regional Research*, 28(1): 27–44.

Sármány-Parsons, I. 1998. Aesthetic aspects of change in urban space in Prague and Budapest during the transition. In G. Enyedi (ed), *Social change and urban restructuring in Central Europe*. Budapest: Akademiai Klado.

Savage, C. 1987. *Architecture of the private streets of St. Louis: the architects and the houses they designed*. Columbia: University of Missouri Press.

Schwanen, T. (2007) Gender differences in chauffeuring children among dual-earner families. *Professional Geographer*, 59(4): 447–67.

Scott, J. C. 1998. *Seeing like a state: how certain schemes to improve the human conditions have failed*. New Haven, CT: Yale University Press.

Scott, J. W. 2009. *De-coding new regionalism: shifting socio-political contexts in Central Europe and Latin America*. Aldershot: Ashgate.

Scruton, R. 1984. Public space and the classical vernacular. *Public Interest*, 74: 5–16.

Seeth, H., Chachnov, S., Surikov, A. and von Braun, J. 1998. Russian poverty: muddling through economic transition with garden plots. *World Development*, 26(9): 1611–23.

Seligman, A. 1992. *The idea of civil society*. New York: Free Press, and Oxford: Maxwell Macmillan International.

Sennett, R. 1977. *The fall of the public man*. New York: Knopf.

Sheinbaum, D. 2008. Gated communities in Mexico City: a historical perspective. *Urban Design International*, 13: 241–52.

Sheppard, E. 2000. Socialist cities? *Urban Geography*, 21: 758–63.

Shlapentokh, V. 1989. *Public and private life of the Soviet people: changing values in post-Stalin Russia*. New York: Oxford University Press.

Shumanova, D. 2007. *Kompleks Tsarigradski posreshna novodomcite si* [Tsarigradski Complex welcomes its first residents]. http:money.ibox.bg/news/id_1079229069. Accessed July 7, 2010. [In Bulgarian.]

Silverman, D. 1993. *Interpreting qualitative data: methods for analyzing talk, text and interaction*. Thousand Oaks, CA: Sage.

Simmel, G. and Wolff, K. 1964. *The sociology of Georg Simmel*. New York: Free Press.

Slavova, P. 2003. Metamorfozi na stroitelnia process v sledosvobojdenska Sofia (1878–1912) [Metamorphoses of the building process in Sofia after independence, 1878–1912]. *Sociologicheski problemi* [Sociological issues], 35(3–4): 206–24. [In Bulgarian.]

Smith, A. 2000. Employment restructuring and household survival in postcommunist transition: rethinking economic practices in Eastern Europe. *Environment and Planning A*, 32(10): 1759–80.

Smith, A. and Stenning, A. 2006. Beyond household economies: articulations and spaces of economic practice in post-socialism. *Progress in Human Geography*, 30(2): 190–213.

Soja, E. 1989. *Post-modern geographies: the reassertion of space in critical social theory*. New York: Verso.

Sommerbauer, J. 2007. Fortress Bulgaria: gated communities. *CafeBabel.com, the European magazine*. www.cafebabel.co.uk/article/19593/fortress-bulgaria-gated-communties.html. Accessed July 4, 2010.

Sorkin, M. 1992. *Variations on a theme park: the new American city and the end of public space.* New York: Hill and Wang.

Spain, D. 1992. *Gendered spaces.* Chapel Hill: University of North Carolina Press.

Spretnak, C. 1999. *The resurgence of the real: body, nature and place in a hypermodern world.* London and New York: Routledge.

Staddon, C. and Mollov, B. 2000. City profile: Sofia, Bulgaria. *Cities*, 17(5): 379–87.

Stanilov, K. 2007. *The post-socialist city: urban form and space transformations in Central and Eastern Europe after socialism.* New York: Springer.

Stanilov, K. 2009. *Sofia's thorny road to Europe.* www.capital.bg/weekly/06-09/12-09. htm. Accessed February 25, 2010.

Stanilov, K. and Hirt, S. forthcoming 2012. Suburban growth in post-socialist Sofia. In K. Stanilov and L. Sýkora (eds.), *Confronting suburbanization: patterns, processes, and management of urban decentralization in post-socialist Central and Eastern Europe.* Oxford: Wiley-Blackwell.

Stanilov, K. and Sýkora, L. (eds.) forthcoming 2012. *Confronting suburbanization: Patterns, processes, and management of urban decentralization in post-socialist Central and Eastern Europe.* Oxford: Wiley-Blackwell.

Stark, D. 1992. Path dependence and privatization strategies in East Central Europe. *East European Politics and Societies*, 6: 17–54.

Stark, D. 1996. Recombinant property in East European capitalism. *American Journal of Sociology*, 101(4): 993–1027.

Starr, F. 1983. *Red and hot: the fate of jazz in the Soviet Union.* New York: Oxford University Press.

Stevens, G. 1990. *The reasoning architect: mathematics and science in design.* New York: McGraw-Hill.

Stimpson, C., Dixler, E., Nelson, M. and Yatrauis, K (eds.) 1981. *Women and the American city.* Chicago: University of Chicago Press.

Stoilova, R. 2006. Neraventstra mejdu polovete: Sravnitelni socialni politiki za izeavnyarance na shansovete [Gender inequality: comparative social policies for equal opportunity]. In K. Petkov (ed.), *Sravnitelna socialna politika: Sociologicheski analizi* [Comparative social policy: sociological analyses]. Sofia: Institute for Sociology. [In Bulgarian.]

Stolichna Obshtina [Municipality of Sofia] 2003. *Obsht ustroistven plan na Sofia i Stolichnata Obshtina: Sukraten predaritelen doklad* [General development plan of the City of Sofia and the Municipality of the Capital City: abbreviated preliminary report]. Sofia: Stolichna Obshtina. [In Bulgarian.]

Stolichna Obshtina [Municipality of Sofia] 1928. *Jubilejna kniga na grad Sofia* [Commemorative book of the city of Sofia]. Sofia: Knipegraph. [In Bulgarian.]

Stoyanov, A. 2008. Administrative and political corruption in Bulgaria: status and dynamics (1998–2006). *Romanian Journal of Political Science*, 8: 5–23.

Stoyanov, P. and Glaze, G. 2006. Gated communities in Bulgaria: interpreting a new trend in post-communist urban development. *GeoJournal*, 66(1–2): 57–63.

Sudjic, D. 1993. *The 100 mile city.* London: Flamingo.

Swidler, A. 1986. Culture in action: symbols and strategies. *American Sociological Review*, 51(2): 273–86.

Sýkora, L. 1994. Local urban restructuring as a mirror of globalization processes: Prague in the 1990s. *Urban Studies*, 31(7): 1149–66.

Sýkora, L. 1998. Commercial property development in Budapest, Prague and Warsaw. *Social Change and Urban Restructuring in Central Europe*. Budapest: Akademiai Klado.

Sýkora, L. 1999a. Changes in the internal structure of post-socialist Prague. *GeoJournal*, 49: 79–89.

Sýkora, L. 1999b. Processes of socio-spatial differentiation in post-socialist Prague. *Housing Studies*, 14(5): 679–701.

Syrett, S. 1995. *Local development: restructuring, locality, and economic initiative in Portugal*. Aldershot: Avebury.

Szelényi, I. 1983. *Urban inequalities under state socialism*. Oxford: Oxford University Press.

Szelényi, I. 1996. Cities under socialism – and after. In G. Andrusz, M. Harloe and I. Szelényi (eds.), *Cities after socialism: urban and regional change and conflict in post-socialist societies*. Malden, MA, and Oxford: Blackwell.

Sztompka. P. 1991. The intangibles and the imponderables of the transition to democracy. *Studies in Comparative Communism*, 24(3): 295–311.

Tammaru, T. 2001. Suburban growth and suburbanization under central planning: the case of Soviet Estonia. *Urban Studies*, 38(8): 1341–57.

Tammaru, T., Kulu, H. and Kask, I. 2007. Urbanization, suburbanization, and counter-urbanization in Estonia. *Eurasian Geography and Economics*, 45(3): 212–29.

Tangurov, J. 2000. Modernata arhitektura 1944–1990 [Modern architecture 1944–1990], *Arhitektura* [Architecture], 2: 46–8. [In Bulgarian.]

Tasan-Kok, T. 2004. *Budapest, Istanbul and Warsaw: institutional and spatial change*. Delft: Eburon.

Tashev, P. 1972. Sofia: *Arhitekturno gradoustrojstveno razvitie – Etapi, postijenia, problemi* [Sofia: Architectural and urban development – stages, achievements and issues]. Sofia: Tehnika. [In Bulgarian.]

Taylor, C. 2004. *Modern social imaginaries*. Durham, NC: Duke University Press.

Therborn, G. 1995. *European modernity and beyond: the trajectory of European societies 1945–2000*. London: Sage.

Thuillier, G. 2005. Gated communities in the Metropolitan Area of Buenos Aires, Argentina: a challenge for town planning. *Housing Studies*, 20(2): 255–71.

Till, K. 2005. *The new Berlin: memory, politics, place*. Minneapolis: University of Minnesota Press.

Timar, J. and Varadi, M. 2001. The uneven development of suburbanization during the transition in Hungary. *European Urban and Regional Studies*, 8(4): 349–60.

Tonev, L. 1987 [1945]. Golemite greshki na Musmanovia plan [The grave errors of Muessman's plan]. In *Po putya na bulgarskoto gradoustroistvo* [Following the path of Bulgarian urban planning]. Sofia: Bulgarian Academy of Sciences. [In Bulgarian.]

Tosics, I. 2005. City development in Central and Eastern Europe since 1990: the impact of the internal forces. In F. Hamilton, K. Andrews and N. Pichler-Milanovic (eds.), *Transformation of cities in Central and Eastern Europe: towards globalization*. Tokyo and New York: United Nations University Press.

Tsenkova, S. and Z. Nedovi -Budi 2006. *The urban mosaic of post-socialist Europe: space, institutions and policy.* Heidelberg: Springer Physica.

Tulu, H. 2003. Housing differences in the late Soviet city. *International Journal of Urban and Regional Research,* 27: 897–911.

Tworzecki, H. 2008. A disaffected new democracy? Identities, institutions and civic engagement in post-communist Poland. *Communist and Post-communist Studies,* 41(1): 1–16.

UNDP (United Nations Development Program) 2008. *2007/2008 human development report: Fighting climate change: human solidarity in a divided world.* http://hdr.undp.org/en/reports/global/hdr2007-8/. Accessed December 5, 2011.

UNECE (United Nations Economic Commission for Europe) 2006. *Trends in Europe and North America 2005.* www.unece.org/stats/trends2005/map_c.htm. Accessed August 28, 2009.

UN-HABITAT (United Nations Human Settlements Programme) 2005. *Poverty, crime and migration are acute issues as Eastern European cities continue to grow.* Excerpts at www.citymayors.com/society/easteurope_cities.html. Accessed August 14, 2009.

United Nations Office on Drugs and Crime. 2004. *International homicide statistics, 2004,* www.unodc.org/documents/data-and-analysis/IHS-rates-05012009.pdf. Accessed December 5, 2011.

US CIA (United States Central Intelligence Agency) 2009. *The world factbook.* https://www.cia.gov/library/publications/the-world-factbook/region/region_eur.html. Accessed August 28, 2009.

US CIA (United States Central Intelligence Agency) undated. *The world factbook: Bulgaria,* https://www.cia.gov/library/publications/the-world-factbook/geos/bu.html. Accessed February 18, 2010.

Valkanov, Y. 2006. Suburbanization in Sofia: changing spatial structure of post-socialist city. In F. Eckardt (ed.), *The European city in transition.* Frankfurt: Peter Lang.

Van den Berg, L. 1987. *Urban systems in a dynamic society.* Aldershot: Gower.

Van den Berg, L. Drewett, R., Klaassen, L., Rossi, A. and Vijverberg, K. 1982. *Urban Europe: a study of growth and decline.* Oxford: Pergamon Press.

Van Kempen, R. 2002. The academic formulations: explanations for the partitioned city. In P. Marcuse and R. van Kempen (eds.), *Of states and cities: the partitioning of urban space.* Oxford: Oxford University Press.

Van Kempen, R. and Özüekren, A. 1998. Ethnic segregation in cities: new forms and explanations in a dynamic world. *Urban Studies,* 35: 1631–56.

Vartianen, P. 1989. Counterurbanization: a challenge for socio-theoretical geography. *Journal of Rural Studies,* 5: 123–36.

Venturi, R., Brown, D. and Izenour, S. 1977. *Learning from Las Vegas: the forgotten symbolism of architectural form.* Cambridge, MA: MIT Press.

Verdery, K. and Humphrey, C. 2004. *Property in question: value transformation in the global economy.* Oxford: Berg.

Verhoeven, W. 2007. Stratification in post-communist societies. http://igitur-archive.library.uu.nl/dissertations/2007-0312-083351/c1.pdf. Accessed July 11, 2009.

Vesselinov, E., Cazessus, M. and Falk, W. 2007. Gated communities and spatial inequality. *Journal of Urban Affairs,* 29(2): 109–27.

Vesselinov, E. and Logan, J. 2005. Mixed success: economic stability and urban inequality in Sofia. In F. Hamilton, K. Andrews and N. Pichler-Milanovic (eds.), *Transformation of cities in Central and Eastern Europe: towards globalization*. New York: United Nations University Press.

Volgyi, B. 2007. Ethno-nationalism during democratic transition in Bulgaria: political pluralism as an effective remedy for ethnic conflict. YCISS Post-socialist Studies Programme Research Paper Series, 3. www.yorku.ca/yciss/activities/documents/PCSPPaper003.pdf. Accessed March 3, 2010.

von Beyme, K. 1996. A new movement on an ideological vacuum: nationalism in Eastern Europe. In G. Andrusz, M. Harloe and I. Szelényi (eds.), *Cities after socialism: urban and regional change and conflict in post-socialist societies*. Oxford: Blackwell.

Vujović, S. and Petrović, M. 2007. Belgrade's post-socialist urban evolution. In K. Stanilov (ed.), *The post-socialist city: urban form and space transformations in Central and Eastern Europe after socialism*. Dordrecht: Springer.

Wacquant, L. 2009. *Punishing the poor: the neoliberal government of social insecurity*. Durham: University of North Carolina Press.

Wagner, O. 1986 [1895]. *Modern architecture*. Oxford: Oxford University Press.

Walicki, A. 1983. Marx and freedom. *New York Review of Books*, 30: 50–5.

Watson, P. 1993. The rise of masculinism in Eastern Europe. *New Left Review*, 198: 71–82.

Watson, S. 2002. The public city. In J. Eade and C. Mele (eds.), *Understanding the city: contemporary and future perspectives*. Malden, MA, and Oxford: Blackwell.

Webster, C. and Glasze, G. 2006. Dynamic urban order and the rise of residential clubs. In G. Glasze, C. Webster and K. Frantz (eds.), *Private cities: global and local perspectives*.

Webster, C., Glasze, G. and Frantz, K. 2002. The global spread of gated communities. *Environment and planning B: Planning and design*, 29(3): 315–20.

W cławowicz, G. 2002. From egalitarian cities in theory to non-egalitarian cities in practice: changing socio-spatial patterns in Polish cities. In P. Marcuse and R. van Kempen (eds.), *Of states and cities: the partitioning of urban space*. Oxford: Oxford University Press.

Weintraub, J. 1997. The theory and politics of the public/private distinction. In J. Weintraub and K. Kumar (eds.), *Public and private in theory and practice: perspectives on a grand dichotomy*. Chicago: University of Chicago Press.

Weiss, S. 2006. *Turbo architecture*. Stuttgart: Schloss Akademie.

White, P. 1984. *The West European city*. London and New York: Longman.

Wolfe, A. 1997. Public and private in theory and practice: some implications of an uncertain boundary. In iJ. Weintraub and K. Kumar (eds.), *Public and private in theory and practice: perspectives on a grand dichotomy*. Chicago: University of Chicago Press.

World Values Survey undated. Data queries through www.worldvaluessurvey.org. Accessed March 24, 2010.

Wu, F. 2003. Transitional cities (commentary). *Environment and Planning A*, 35(8): 1331–8.

Wyly, E. 1998. Containment and mismatch: gender differences in commuting in metropolitan labor markets. *Urban Geography*, 19(5): 395–430.

Yin, R. 1984. *Case study research: design and methods.* Beverly Hills, CA: Sage.

Yoveva, A., Dimitrov, A. and Dimitrova, R. 2003. Housing policy: the stepchild of the transition. In M. Lux (ed.), *Housing policy: an end or a new beginning?* Budapest: Open Society Institute.

Žižek, S. 2009. Post-Wall. *London Review of Books*, 31(2): 10.

Zukin, S. 1995. *The cultures of cities.* Malden, MA, and Oxford: Blackwell.

Index

Iron Curtains, First Edition. Sonia A. Hirt.
© 2012 John Wiley & Sons, Ltd. Published 2012 by John Wiley & Sons, Ltd.

Printed and bound by CPI Group (UK) Ltd, Croydon, CR0 4YY

09/06/2025

14685991-0001